HOWARD MUMFORD JONES
AN AUTOBIOGRAPHY

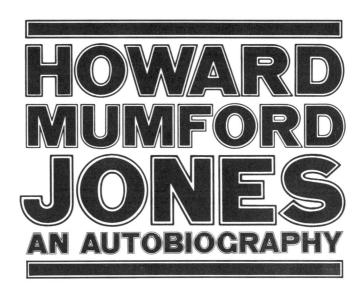

HOWARD
MUMFORD
JONES
AN AUTOBIOGRAPHY

The University of Wisconsin Press

Published 1979

The University of Wisconsin Press
114 North Murray Street
Madison, Wisconsin 53715

The University of Wisconsin Press, Ltd.
1 Gower Street
London WC1E 6HA, England

First printing

Printed in the United States of America

For LC CIP information see the colophon

ISBN 0-299-07770-5

This book is dedicated to

RICHARD M. LUDWIG

as a token of affection and support

that has run for so many years

I know not when it began.

Well, I have had my day, been loved and hated,
Heard the first Roosevelt bellow, the second croon,
Played Romeo beneath a waning moon,
Polonius in the daylight; I have debated
Futilities in Pullmans, have lied, have waited
Convenient deaths politely, have been too soon
Arrogant of a morning, tired of an afternoon,
Outlived a war or two—I should be sated.

But the head grown balder and the eyesight failing,
And the imperceptible shortening of the breath
Quench not the old regrets, the aches that smolder
And sting again in the blood as one grows older,
And dry rot eats the heart, and the soul is ailing
With faint, miasmic prophecies of death.

—from *They Say the Forties*

Contents

Contents

Preface

THE LONG CURVE of this book begins with my birth as the only child of my parents, each of New England ancestry, and ends with my eighty-fifth year, a professor emeritus at Harvard. The tale concerns a lonely childhood, a confused groping during adolescence and youth for what my ancestors would have dubbed a "calling," a decision, half-unconscious, to become a scholar rather than a writer or a journalist. One large fraction of the material concerns my extraordinary plunge into the educational frontiers of the Southwest and the West. For this I was entirely unprepared, and my slow backward trek to the Upper South, to Michigan (my native state), and to Harvard ends with the achievement, if it be one, of a philosophy of scholarship as this involves literature, history, culture, and the present predicament of the world. Inevitably, the tone of the book changes as I advance. This is deliberate. I want to break down the still popular concept of the humanist as an impractical dreamer living in an ivory tower. I have touched life on too many sides to believe that the university world is remote from the "real" world of business, politics, and women's clubs.

Such is the general structure of my story. Its triple import will, I trust, gradually dawn upon the reader. I am trying to tell not only my personal adventures and mistakes, but also the slow shaping of my interpretation of American culture and my theory of what we vaguely call the humanities. To the explication of certain parts of my story as a university professor I have devoted some pages that read more like history than like confession. This is of my intent. Few persons nowadays are remotely aware of the picturesque, comic, yet profoundly disturbing story of "Fergusonianism" in Texas or of the struggle between corporate wealth and the plain citizenry of Montana for the control of higher education in that mountain state. I was new in both these institutions and therefore played no role in these amazing histories, but I could observe, and observe I did; and if I set down my observations here and occasionally elsewhere in the manner of a historian rather than that of the autobiographer, I ask my readers to understand this necessary change of tone. I can plead in extenuation the great example of Henry Adams, who did not want his book known as an autobiography but as a study in twentieth-century multiplicity. I am not Henry Adams, but three-quarters of the twentieth century have elapsed, and multiplicity grows no simpler. Given the present violent state of the world and of the United States, I hold that intelligently managed higher education is quintessential to that more perfect union the Founding Fathers dreamed of.

Universities have honored me with a variety of honorary degrees, medals, citations, and the like, and if I mention only one or two, it is not because I am ungrateful to the others but because I cannot name them all. I have never kept a diary, preserve no letters, and depend upon memory, buttressed now and again by consulting printed or written documents.

This volume would never have been completed had it not been for the constant encouragement of Richard M. Ludwig of Princeton, to whom I have dedicated my book. Equally I owe gratitude to "my Bessie," more formally my wife, to whom I have dedicated other books. I owe thanks to hundreds of persons, among whom I must name Arthur Hepner of Cambridge, Marc Friedlaender of the Adams Papers, Mrs. C. J. Otjen of Milwaukee, with whom I went through high school, normal school, and the university, Herschel and Barbara Baker and Jerome H. and Elizabeth Buckley of Harvard, the late Russell R. Potter, once of Chapel Hill, then of Columbia, Charlotte Bowman of the ACLS, and four persons in La Crosse, Wisconsin, friends by correspondence—James J. Holland, Richard Boudreau, Larry L. Dittman, and Chancellor Kenneth E. Lindner of the University of Wisconsin—La Crosse. My lasting gratitude goes out to the late Thomas J. Wilson, former director of Harvard University Press, and to my faithful former student, colleague and friend, Walter B. Rideout of the University of Wisconsin and Jean, his wife. I must express my profound thanks to my fellow Wisconsinite for all he has done in the final shaping of this book.

As for some scores of friends and helpers in the Harvard faculty, living or dead, at the University of Michigan, the University of Wisconsin, the University of North Carolina, the Weil Institute of Cincinnati, the Modern Language Association of America, the Society of American Historians, the American Academy of Arts and Sciences in Boston, the American Philosophical Society, the American Council of Learned Societies, the world of publishing, the literary community, and the universe of philosophy (for example, Maurice Mandelbaum, just retired from The Johns Hopkins University), the Center for Advanced Study in the Behavioral Sciences near Stanford, and the St. Botolph Club of Boston—what can I do other than write this ineffectual word of thanks and appreciation? Nor should I forget the staff of the Widener Library.

Howard Mumford Jones

Cambridge, Massachusetts
April 16, 1977

BOOK ONE

CHILDHOOD
AND YOUTH

Chapter I

Beginnings
in Saginaw

AS I HAVE NO DESIRE to imitate Tristram Shandy and postpone my beginnings by several chapters, I must set about the fateful act of getting myself born. This was accomplished on April 16, 1892, in the city of Saginaw, Michigan, or so I am led to believe by the historical evidence of a birth certificate and by the opinions of my parents, who of all people ought to know. The fact that I do not remember anything about the episode is not meant as a wisecrack. It seems that most people do not, and only the learned researches of certain types of depth psychologists have persuaded the twentieth century, or part of it, that everybody undergoes something dreadful known as a birth trauma. The latest fad, as I write, is to deliver babies in rooms kept as dark as possible in order that the delicate little angels may be deluded as long as may be into the belief that they are still enjoying the comforts of the womb. The theory is that the womb is simultaneously Plato's cave turned inside out, and the dark night of the racial unconscious, and that is why, on first experiencing sunlight (or its hospital equivalent) and breathing air independently (or its hygienic surrogate), the infant utters a cry of anguish. Some old-fashioned doctors, including the one who birthed me, incline to the simple view that the baby has to take in a lungful of air, a novel experience. Old-line obstetrical nurses like to be assured, it appears, that the little darling is alive. Considering the fact that myriads of babies have been born before 1977 in what I may call the normal way, I wonder how the human race has managed to survive. In the wilderness of articles on psychology, most of them badly written, there are doubtless case reports on infants brought into the world by a Caesarean operation who ought, if the new theory be correct, to exhibit fearful psychic wounds. It is a curious commentary that Shakespeare, who is supposed to have held a mirror up to nature, makes Macduff, who was from his mother's womb untimely ripped, quite a decent fellow, whereas the unspeakable Macbeth, normally born, is among Shakespeare's more lurid creations. But I had better get back to Saginaw, Michigan.

In 1892 Saginaw was a lumber town on both sides of the Saginaw River some fifteen miles south of Bay City, which lies at the foot of Saginaw Bay, that curious indentation of Lake Huron which makes lower Michigan look on the map like a gigantic mitten with a thumb on the right-hand side. The settlements on the two sides of the river were originally separate entities, but in 1889 they were consolidated into a single city. In May, 1893, a fire broke out in an abandoned sawmill owned by a company named Sample & Camp. The wind blew a gale, burning embers were carried half a mile, the important Standard Lumber Company caught on fire and so did St. Vincent's Orphan Home. The heat was so great it drove the firefighters off Washington Street. The gale continued and new fires caught in dozens of places, nor was the con-flagration brought under something like control until evening. Even then, at six o'clock another fire started in a planing mill a mile from the origin of the blaze. Twenty-three square blocks were destroyed, 257 buildings went down, and many families were rendered homeless. We were, I was later told, among those who were burned out.

My memories of Saginaw are vague. I recall a noble river, what seemed to my infant eyes a noble bridge spanning the river, and on one side of the river near its bank a majestic hostelry called, I think, the Saginaw House, built of wood (these were the splendid twilight days of Michigan as a lumber state), the amplitude of whose rocking-chair porch used to frighten me, and the grandeur of whose regal lobby (were there palm trees in tubs?) was clearly out of a fairy tale. I attended the World's Columbian Exposition of 1893 in a baby carriage (we had relatives in Chicago); and as, when we got back to Saginaw, we lived in a "new" house with shiny varnished floors and an even shinier and more slippery staircase and "landing," we must have occupied something built just after the fire. I commonly crawled up these steps like the baby in the print, once popular, entitled "On the Dark Stairs Where a Bear is So Liable to Follow One," but only after an invariable evening ritual: "D'ink water. Go to bed."

The streets in our part of town were dirt and the sidewalks wood, and the roadways were roughly graded so that, across from our house, a drainage ditch about three and a half feet deep yawned dreadfully. My instructions were to stay on my side of the street. Cater-corner from our house was a rather imposing mansion of heavily Victorian vintage lived in by an elderly lady and her daughter, whom we did not "know." The drainage ditch was on their side of the street and was crossed by a small, neat wooden bridge with a guard rail. One winter at a very early age I had received a pair of red rubber boots with tassels, which gave me infinite satisfaction. In pursuit of adventure and thus masculinely equipped, I crossed the street one afternoon and paused on the little bridge over the drainage ditch which held, I suppose, about two feet of water. The guard rail had been put there for adults, not urchins, and though I held on with one hand while I bent over to inspect the horrid mysteries below, my hold slipped and I plunged headforemost into the water, my little red boots waving feebly in the air. Fortunately the chatelaine of the Victorian castle happened to be looking out a front window, saw what had happened, rushed out, pulled me up by my boots, and bore me homewards, where I was put to bed and dosed with that most satisfying of home remedies, the syrup obtained by slicing a big Bermuda onion, laying the slices in a larger saucer, sprinkling each slice with sugar, and pouring boiling water over the whole. When the heat had subsided to a comfortable warmth, the syrup could be skimmed off and administered, spoonful by spoonful, to the small patient. The only other liquid half as ambrosial was spoonfuls of Dr. Fletcher's Castoria, a patent medicine that seemed like candy and had, I am sure, its expected effect upon my small bowels.

I remember one or two other incidents from my babyhood. One concerned my maternal grandmother, who had come to live with us, I suppose after the death of her husband. My mother, returning from a shopping expedition "downtown" (my father owned a partnership in a firm known as Jones & McCall, which did printing and binding and sold stationery), entered the house to find my grandmother almost hysterical with laughter as she rocked back and forth in her chair and continued her knitting, while I, sitting on the varnished landing in a pool of tears, howled to high heaven with rage. "What in the world's the matter?" asked my mother, who was easily outraged. My grandmother could not speak, but I managed to say, between sobs: "Mamma, she called me a ho-ax." I had no notion what a ho-ax might be, and my grandmother, in refusing a request for a cookie (I had said I was hungry), had thought to amuse by mispronouncing the word *hoax*. I was not amused.

A second incident concerns my earliest introduction to sex. There was a little girl of my age who lived on the street behind us and whose parents had not merely a coach house but several superfluous and dusty carriages. Into one of these it was the delight of my small female

5

playmate and me to crawl. One day she proposed that we feel each other. I was by no means certain what she meant, since I had felt her a good many times and she seemed to me normal flesh and blood. She explained that we were not built the same, and plunging a small hand into my pants, she managed to get hold of my penis. By way of recompense she invited me to do the same with her. I groped around her panties, but I could find nothing at all. I asked her what the matter was, but still clutching my penis, she merely pressed my hand between her small thighs. I do not know that she got any satisfaction out of the performance, which I think we never repeated, but I felt cheated, and was then and there confirmed in the belief that all the things said about girls being untrustworthy were true.

I was the only child of Frank Alexander Jones and Josephine Whitman Miles Jones, each born in Port Huron, Michigan, and each the product of a long line of New England ancestry that stretches back to the seventeenth century. I have no magpie interests, keep no diary, and do not even retain copies of my own letters unless they are of special business importance. But in rummaging around some ancient bits of baggage that have wandered with me or mine around half the United States, I discovered various envelopes stuffed with manuscripts, old newspapers, family trees, and several yards of mortuary verses which, unless they comforted the feelings of those who wept, have no virtue whatsoever. I also ran across several solemn Moral Essays of the most improving sort, the penmanship being so fine and firm I cannot to this day make out whether it is that of a man or a woman.

A Jones family tree is an awesome thing to imagine, and I am tempted to exclaim with the poet Matt Prior:

> The son of Adam and of Eve:
> Can Bourbon or Nassau claim higher?

But one Mrs. Amelia D. Stearns, filled with an enthusiasm for genealogy, apparently began constructing one the year of my birth; at any rate, among the fragments that time has left me, I find a crowded letterhead from the office of Raymond's Vacation Excursions under date of August 6, 1892, closely written on both sides of the sheet (they made better paper in those days), which not only gives a vast deal of miscellaneous information about the Jones clan, and all its related septs, tribes, and families, but which includes a prim, neat note at the top of the letter: "My daughter is engaged in the office of this firm." The combination of commercialism and elegance in this brief sentence has charmed me ever since I discovered it. Mrs. Stearns says frankly that she has spent considerable money in procuring records and intimates that

6

she will have to spend a great deal more "Before we get to our book."
Apparently the offer was refused, for I don't find the book was completed. Enclosed in the letter are two family trees, accompanied by what
I can only describe as minor saplings; and in the same brown envelope
some early specimens of typing (the daughter's?) simplify what I may
call my own line. I am glad I have the typed material, for the family
trees look as if an insane geometric bug had started an infinite series of
short wanderings, leaving behind him a kind of coconut grove of proper
names along the branches, including such sound biblical appellations as
Caleb, Sarah, Abner, Ezra, Samuel, Abigail, Ezekiel, and Benajah. It is a
relief from this monotony to find Mindwell, Experience, and Charity,
and—of all names!—Rozanna roosting on one or another twig of the tree.
I find an extraordinary number of military titles, earned or not, in these
faded documents. I have tried to crawl from one of the obscurer
branches back to the main trunk. I find I am descended from a Captain
Samuel Jones who settled in Saybrook, Connecticut, born, say these
veracious documents, in the early years of "1600." He married Mary
Bushnell January 1, 1663 (I suppose this is time counted before the
reformed calendar upset all datings), and died in Saybrook in 1704. His
offspring were numerous, including one Ensign Samuel Jones, whose
title seems to have been won fighting the French and the Indians. His
wife was Mindwell Beach, who lived to be 88, whereas the ensign died at
60, but not before fathering ten children. One of these was Ezekiel, who
in turn produced ten children, the eldest of whom, named Samuel, married a woman named Huldah Pepoon, a name that not even a Victorian
caricaturist could have invented, but whom, alack! I cannot claim as a
direct ancestor. I omit a generation or two to get to my great-
grandfather, Elisha Jones, who left Hebron, Connecticut, for Port
Huron, marrying one Sally Meacham in 1802 and dying in Michigan in
1855. He had a son named Asa Selden Jones, who was born in Hinsdale,
Massachusetts, in 1817 (why Hinsdale? I don't know) and who married
Abigail Alexander at St. Clair, Michigan, on July 11, 1844. Unfortunately for history, Mrs. Stearns's papers and genealogical information
now give out altogether; and though I know I had several aunts and
uncles, I can be confident only of my father, Frank Alexander Jones,
whose middle name obviously came from the family name of his mother.
The papers include a number of letters from Aba (as she was known) to
Selden (he dropped the Asa), and these frequently mention "the children," but as they name no particular child, they leave the autobiographer in the dark.

My mother compensated, I think, for the many misfortunes of her life
by joining the DAR, which requires proof of lineage; and I find a faded

typewritten sheet tracing her (and my) descent. One John Carleton of London and Surrey was the great-grandfather of an Edward Carleton, who settled at Rowley, Massachusetts, and apparently fathered a "Lieutenant" John Carleton, who in turn had four sons. One of these sons was named Edward; and Edward, marrying (but whom?), fathered another Edward born October 28, 1639, who was the first white child born in Rowley, Massachusetts. A Carleton girl in 1828 married a man named Whitman, and these were my mother's grandparents. My mother's mother married one Cyrus W. Miles, born in St. Lawrence County, New York, on April 13, 1828. He came to Port Huron about 1852, where with one W. T. Mitchell he set up a law practice. This he soon abandoned for the banking business, establishing with a man named John Miller the First National Bank of Port Huron. But Mr. Miller and he dissolved whatever partnership there was, and my grandfather Miles went back to law—and politics. He was twice mayor of Port Huron, he was a member of the legislature in 1869, and his obituary notice in the Port Huron *Daily Times* for March 4, 1877, calls him "a social and genial companion, a kind husband, an indulgent father" mourned by "a true and loving wife and three affectionate daughters." I am in no position to doubt this, but as Dr. Johnson once said, "The writer of an epitaph should not be considered as saying nothing but what is strictly true. Allowance must be made for some degree of exaggerated praise. In lapidary inscriptions a man is not upon oath."

Lapidary or typographical, this inscription omits the fact that my grandfather could be on occasion an irascible personage. I think, though I do not know, that he was a Copperhead Democrat during the Civil War. A family legend runs that when he retired from office as mayor, a committee of his fellow Democrats resolved to present Cyrus with a silver-headed cane as a token of esteem. The chairman, having regard for the portentous presence of my grandfather, prepared, memorized, and rehearsed an appropriate speech. But when the committee filed into the mayor's office and my grandfather impressively inquired what he could do for them, every word of the oration fled from the chairman's mind. He thrust the cane at my grandfather, saying, "Here, take this," to which my grandfather responded: "Damn it, I will," and did.

In fairness to my father's clan I add that Selden A. Jones, as my paternal grandfather came to call himself, was appointed Deputy Collector in and for the District of Huron in the State of Michigan under date of August 23, 1876, by a document with the American eagle at the top and the seal of the United States of America in the lower left-hand corner.

It is evident that the Joneses, the Carletons, and the rest of these true-blue Yankees participated in that amazing migration of New Englanders from eastern Massachusetts through Connecticut to Albany; thence continued by way of the Erie Canal to the Great Lakes region, notably including northern Ohio and southern Michigan; and stopped only at the Pacific, if then. I have driven my automobile along the line they took, and it is fascinating to observe the continuance of New England courthouses and New England domestic architecture along the way until they seem to crumble somewhere in Nebraska. My migrating ancestors set up colonies en route. One, for example, was at Canandaigua, New York, where a cousin by the name of Charlie Sackett built a large frame house not far from the lake and occupied his leisure hours by attending sessions of the state legislature at Albany. When we visited the Sacketts we always had, I remember, delicious creamed potatoes for breakfast, whatever else was served—and breakfasts in western New York at the opening of this century were hearty. There was a small steamboat on the lake, on which it was a pleasure to glide rather than ride, for if there were waves on Lake Canandaigua, they were, in my memory, infinitesimal. I also remember an Aunt May who married a man by the amazing name of Xenophon Xerxes Crumm and went to live in Troy or Watervliet.

I had an aunt and uncle living in Bay City, which was not, I now suspect, much of a city. This uncle was the proprietor or part-owner of a lumberyard and also, unless I am confusing him with another male relative, the owner or manager of a small fleet of tugboats mainly designed to get lumber rafts out of the lake and up the Saginaw River. My uncle's house, ample and made of wood, stood on a hill overlooking his own lumber mill. The mill of a Saturday afternoon was always quiet, deserted by its working force except for a watchman who, so far as I could discover, spent his time sleeping comfortably in a chair by a gate overlooking the water. Now any lumber mill worth its salt is built on two levels: a ground floor containing the machinery and piles of logs and timber, and a second floor which is mainly a set of trestles running in a series of right angles among the piles of boards and logs. A simple derrick and grapple can lift logs and lumber off the piles and load the cargo on a sturdy pushcart, or handcar, that runs on rails laid on the trestles; the car can then be pushed to an appropriate spot elsewhere in the mill so that the cargo can be sawed or loaded on wagons for distribution and sale.

Although I have a feeling that my parents frequently sent me to my aunt when they were off on a trip somewhere else, I apparently did not acquire any playmates there. It didn't really matter, since I was perfectly happy on any weekend in Bay City. After the noon meal (*lunch* was an effeminate word) my uncle went "downtown" to a mysterious room with

9

a rolltop desk, and my aunt retired to her bedroom for an afternoon nap. This left only me and the cook (in fact, the maid of all work) alone in the house. As soon as might be, I therefore stole quietly outdoors, crept across the road to the lumber mill, and climbing a rickety ladder to the railway trestle, betook myself to the blissful business of managing a whole railway system—as engineer, signalman, fireman, brakeman, and all. There were, alas! no magnificent switches to turn, the frogs, wherever the track divided, being discoverable only by trial, error, and a bit of lifting and straining. It took a good deal of effort to get one of the carriages rolling, especially if, at the blowing of the noon whistle, the workmen had left it half covered with boards, usually twice as long as the car. I early discovered, at first to my alarm, that on the principle of inertia it also took a good deal of effort to get one of these things to stop, though fortunately there were rude bumpers made of four-by-fours at the end of any section of trestle. There were no brakes, but by rapidly dismounting just before the moment of catastrophe as a dangerous frog came in sight, I could on most occasions either switch the car to a longer stretch of trestle or, if necessary, shove a piece of wood under a forward wheel, usually with noisy results.

The great trick was to get the car moving rapidly enough to give one the sense of prodigious speed, mount it, pass illimitable piles of logs and lumber, switch to another part of the trestle, and get back again without hurt. I suppose that somebody during the history of the mill had once greased the axles of these clumsy carriages, but it must have been a long time before, for each of the several wheels gave out its own peculiar screech. Why I never woke the watchman I don't know. Perhaps he was both asleep and drunk. Perhaps he figured that I was apparently a son of the owner, or at any rate some blood relative, and that I was none of his responsibility.

I had no watch, and there were no five o'clock whistles on Saturday afternoon, but the light on the bay was a sort of chronometer, and besides, even a small boy gets tired. I usually grew weary about five and returned to my aunt's house, somewhat black as to grease and powdery as to sawdust; whereupon the cook, seeing me come in the back door, dropped whatever she was doing, uttered a smothered squawk, and hurried me upstairs to a bathroom, where she scrubbed me thoroughly, plastered my red hair down on my scalp, and reclad me in clothing that was not so noticeably clean and new as to attract attention. Whether my aunt ever knew of these guilty excursions I never learned, but as my uncle, a large man with a loud voice and a gold watch-chain, felt that I was puny, whereas all boys of five or six should be manly, he perhaps instructed my aunt (and the watchman?) to let me alone. It was on the whole one of the most highly satisfactory chapters of my life. I had a railroad and I ran it by myself; I was out of the house and therefore could not disturb my aunt; the cook took no further responsibility than getting me neat for dinner time; and I seem never to have got hurt: though I usually came home with a few cuts and bruises, they were no more numerous and no more serious, I surmise, than falls to the lot of most boys of my age.

A second great point in visiting Bay City was the annual wildfowl dinner, at which my parents and I were always present. I do not know what the game laws of the state of Michigan permitted, but every autumn my aunt's rather generous dining table expanded until it took up most of the dining room, guests poured in, a proper seat was made for me, and, flushed with triumph, the cook placed before each guest a whole wild duck or wild goose, whatever the hunt had produced. Nor, except that I always drew the smallest fowl, was I in any way discriminated against. If I had difficulty with the outer integument of the bird or with some of its bonier parts, the nearest adult took time off from his own problems to assist me with my surgery. I remember also a great deal of wild rice and enormous saucers, if not of cranberry jelly, then of some other pungent accompaniment to the birds, who disappeared in a wild crackle of bones. This main course was followed by apple pies— none of your store-bought pies inflated with an air-pump and only half-filled with imitation fruit, but pies of a classical structure, the crusts flaky and covered with cinnamon, cinnamon-and-sugar, or some other delectable flavoring matter, the interiors aflush with genuine fruit juices and stuffed with gobs of apples cut into great manly slices fit for a tugboat captain. Probably there were other sorts of pie too—we ate well in eastern Michigan—but for some reason the apple pie of my aunt (sounds like a phrase in a French grammar) remains forever shining, a whole disk or a generous sixth of a circle, on a blue plate of the Willow-tree pattern imported (let us be honest—smuggled) from Sarnia in Canada just over the channel from Port Huron.

Then there were the tugboats. I doubt if there were more than two or three of them, and I doubt that they ever did much more than push or pull a lumber raft to its destruction at the sawmill, but on those rare occasions when my uncle commended me to the care of the captain of one of those enchanted ocean liners, all other pleasures faded away. I was at first perched on the horsehair seat, circular and awkward, behind the wheel in the small pilothouse, where the pilot or the captain or the mate, if there was one, was supposed occasionally to take his weight off his feet. The horsehair covering of this lounging seat was stuck full of stiff hairs something like small black pins; and as in those days little

11

boys were still under the sartorial influence of that dreadful personage Little Lord Fauntleroy, these wretched needles-and-pins pricked me unbearably just under each knee. I could not complain because, in the first place, I was a guest of the boat, and in the second place, I was fearful lest, by shifting my weight, I might cause the tug to roll over. The tugboatmen were both laconic and kindly; and the man at the wheel would sooner or later say, "Sonny, why don't you go outside?" Probably he wanted to tell dirty stories. But he always added: "Stay behind the rail, and don't go aft." A tugboat, even a mere river tugboat, is so built that the pilothouse and the foredeck are protected by rather high railings, whereas the after part of the boat has virtually no railing at all, since the towrope must have free play if the river bends or the tug has for some reason to alter the course of the raft. I therefore went out "on deck," scarcely able to see over this formidable barrier; but still, it was a boat, I was, in my mind, in command of it, and if the tug headed in the right direction, there were the illimitable waters of Saginaw Bay and beyond them, invisibly past the deep blue line of the horizon, a foreign land called Canada. If we were returning to the sawmill, matters were still satisfactory: after an extensive foreign tour I was bringing my scarred but dauntless crew and vessel back to their native land. Alas! the tugs, if they float anywhere today, float in that land where there is nothing but apple pie and wild duck to eat and nothing but lumber-mill railways to push about and one is forever five years old.

Chapter II

On to Milwaukee

THE SIGNIFICANT CHANGES in one's life seem to me to fall into two opposite classes: those that are dramatically evident, such as those caused
by a death; and those that are only gradually evident. The significance of
the latter dawns slowly, and realization may not come until years go by.
I could not possibly know, when we moved from Saginaw to Milwaukee,
that my whole existence was now to be altered and that, instead of being
a son of the Wolverine state, I was to become a Badger and face until
later in life the westering sun and the southern sea and not know the
nostalgia eastern Michigan has for Cornell, or New York City, or Yale,
or Harvard (where, to be sure, I later turned up). To one who is only five
or six the changes between one abode and another are often imperceptible, time glides along with so lulling a stream, and the boys of one
young summer are so like the boys of another young summer that it is
virtually impossible to remark: "This was the landscape wherein my
whole existence was altered." How shall the young lad know?

I do not remember how the back yard with apple trees in Saginaw, the
house with the varnished landing, and the rescue from a watery death by
a kindly neighbor turned dreamlike into the idea of Milwaukee—at 309
Oakland Avenue, to be precise, a three-storey "flat," as such residences
were called (and there were hundreds of them). We lived on the top floor.
The owner, a workman, and his family occupied the ground floor, and a
pale, indeterminate family of uncertain lineage rented the second floor.
There was a back yard surrounded by a high board fence, and there was
some sort of gateway, coal bin, and tool shed in one corner of the yard.

The back yard was further complicated with clotheslines, some of which by an ingenious arrangement of hooks and pulleys could be rolled to the top back porch and let fall again without disaster.

The front of our new abode was to my eyes less interesting than was the back yard. The front presented, as did most of the block, a geometric row of three tiers of front porches, golden oak doors at the right-hand end of each verandah, and a large window placed firmly in the middle of the façade of every floor, each such window displaying a large table holding an enormous flowering plant that made me think of undertakers' offices. The front rooms were of course genteel, but the rear of any floor opened on an intricate set of three outside staircases, each flat having, so to speak, a separate box or cell of its own, the landings being regularly arranged so that the iceman could readily deliver blocks of ice to the refrigerators and the grocery boy leave his bundles. The back façade had a wild geometry that fascinated children and was good for games.

The owners were the Tinkers, plain, honest, warm-hearted, genial Germans who could never do enough for a small boy, particularly in the way of sugared doughnuts, and whose eldest son, a silent and serious youth of great mechanical aptitude, I followed about like an obedient dog. Herb had a job, but by some special arrangement he commonly got home before his father did, and without further ado, went at once to the tool house, kept carefully locked, where he was building a horseless carriage. He had taken the shafts from a pony cart, installed a one-lung gasoline engine under the seat of the cart, and attached driving shafts to both the rubberized rear wheels and of course somehow to the engine. He was now working on some way to steer the thing, should the buggy ever leave the tool shed. Stopping and starting were simple enough: you either cut off the gasoline (or was it kerosene?) or manipulated the choke before you jumped aboard the quivering vehicle. The great day came, albeit only Mr. and Mrs. Tinker, Herb, and I were privy to the event. He invited me to take a seat next to him. There was a vast roar, a great cloud of dirty smoke, and the buggy backed out—backed out, mind you!—from the alley into the street, startled a team of horses peacefully dozing near an opposite sidewalk, and proceeded to go around a whole city block. My recollection is that owing to some unforeseen difficulty in the steering apparatus we could only turn right, but we moved—we moved! Incredulous faces appeared at windows, people stood frozen to the sidewalk, a horse or two bolted, and one young girl tried to hide behind a telephone pole. I do not know when Henry Ford first circumnavigated a city block. It is sufficient for me that I was the first boy in knee-pants in all Milwaukee who rode in an automobile without mishap around a whole block.

This unprecedented miracle was the triumph of my Milwaukee years, but I was getting on in life and began to realize that we had come down in the world. A family which had once occupied a whole new house with a varnished stairway and a broad landing did not huddle without loss of dignity in the top floor of a three-storey Milwaukee flat. Early explorations of the Oakland Avenue neighborhood showed me that it came in social strips evident even to my juvenescent understanding. We were four or five blocks from the lake front, which was shut from public view by great iron gates, immense hedges, stone pillars, and topless towers of imitation Rhenish castles or houses of splendid Milwaukee cream brick, each in its own grounds, each lawn manicured, each tree as carefully tended as if it were a tooth being filled. Formidable men in uniform occasionally swung open the elegant portals when shining carriages of the latest mode, occupied by parasols and attentive derby hats, drove in or departed with equal majesty. There was, it is true, a railroad track somewhere too near at hand, whose Wagnerian whistle sometimes shattered the brooding silence, but the broad avenue on which these fantastic structures faced resounded only to the patter of coach dogs, the regular cloppity-clop of horses' feet, and, oh how rarely! to an ambulance or a police wagon.

Streets proceeding westward in geometrical order parallel with the drive along the lake monopolized by Grandeur steadily degenerated to the uses of common folk. One held a streetcar track. Our own street was devoted to city traffic. It had delivery carts and trucks to pick up rubbish. It bore painters' carts and cabbies among its flotsam and jetsam; there was an occasional ambulance and often a funeral, though it was not a route for parades. It had also in the summer ice delivery wagons, on which it was important to hang long enough to get a cooling and relatively clean sliver of ice into the mouth before being discovered by the driver. It had coal delivery carts (which nobody wanted to ride), and ice cream wagons (which of course everybody did). A little to the west of Oakland Avenue we came to the banks of a small, ill-kept river, and a street along this river bank was the farthest east of embattled Poland, which in gangs of ten or twelve came whooping through our chaster area with crass shouts of derision and occasional scuffles. They were on their way to Flushing Tunnel Park, a strip of land that stuck out into Lake Michigan and had something to do with the water system or the sewage or perhaps both, and which the baronial halls above the lake could do nothing to obliterate.

15

I was not allowed to join the Polish contingent. In the first place I was too small, in the second place I was "puny," and in the third place I could not speak their dialect, in which they conveyed fortissimo insults to Oakland Avenue and all its inhabitants. They went out with fishing poles, cans of live bait, and some hope of catching fish they would not have to throw back into the lake because of age or weight, and I think they were more often disappointed than not in their luck. But as they usually came back thoroughly wet, I assume they all fell into the water, sanitary or otherwise. There was apparently nothing the beer barons and the lumber kings could do to stop them from using Flushing Tunnel Park. If I happened to be in the back yard when they appeared, I was promptly called into the house (it was alleged for fear of being kidnapped), and I spent the time until their dripping return at a side window in the Tinker flat expectant, happy, and by no means feeling ill used. It was a living fragment of a medieval tournament, not a deprivation, and I recognized with a sigh that if there were Pagans and Christians in the world, I belonged irretrievably to the Christian tribe.

Like other midwestern cities Milwaukee had been laid out on the gridiron pattern popular since the days of William Penn, but Lake Michigan had only a distant respect for the principles of Euclid, and the sinuosities of the Milwaukee, Menomonee, and Kinnickinnic rivers, which conjoined their waters and flowed in an irritatingly devious way into the lake, had left little triangles and pinnacles of land wedged in among the more decorous squares. One such was Farwell Place, not far from our home, a sword-shaped piece of real estate useless for any purpose except the one to which it was wisely put. Some philanthropist had erected on this property all in one building a drug store, a newspaper and magazine stand, and an ice cream soda fountain. His cigars were, I was told, fresh; his cosmetics seemed to draw customers; his prescriptions were, I gathered, scientifically filled; and his ice cream, his ice cream soda, his remarkable tables and chairs apparently held together by bent copper wires that never collapsed, and his silver-frosted holders for delectable sodas have seldom or never been equalled in this world. I do not, I am ashamed to say, remember his name; it was sufficient to become possessed of a nickel or a dime, proudly announce that you were going to the drug store, and you were off on a visit to the Arabian Nights.

Our comedown in the world, whether by some catastrophe subsequent to the Saginaw fire and the panic of 1893 or by some slower drop into the decent if ungrammatical lower middle class, I never made out. Some fragments of former grandeur were solemnly preserved. The parlor contained pieces of "good" furniture stuck here and there, an umbrella stand stood in the hallway, and a Tiffany lamp flung its precarious light over the dining-room table, illuminating my mother and me and, occasionally, my father. I heard no more talk about stationery shops and printing, but an increasing rumble about a vast, cavernous structure "downtown" somewhere which was on the up-and-up and which my father, if all went well, was to represent as a traveling salesman in groceries and staple goods over a wide territory vaguely defined as central Wisconsin, which was in time to be vastly extended to the Mississippi and the Twin Cities. He took the post, I think, with misgivings, for he had to cover southeastern Wisconsin, mile after mile, with the hit-and-miss of local trains, interurban trolleys, and "local" mail wagons, or else make his way from one dim country hostelry to another by a hired and weary livery rig. My father had not been home much of the time in Michigan, and henceforth he was to be home even less, since transportation over country roads in Wisconsin weather and stops in country hotels with exiguous accommodations kept him away from Milwaukee for weeks on end. Moreover, the traveling salesman (drummer was a "literary" word) was expected to be one of the boys, to smoke with the best, to linger at the table, to drink at the bar, to gamble, to tell interminable stories and listen to longer ones, and to allow the local storekeeper an ample period of time in which to make up his mind, and sometimes an even ampler period to change it. I know, for I went on one of these trips to the detriment of my schooling and the wrath of my schoolmates, my absence having marred their perfect attendance record and deprived them of the reward of an extra holiday. But the country inns were by no means dens of iniquity. They were run under the severe eye of a German or Scandinavian Hausfrau; and if there were ladies of the evening, they came in discreetly by the back stairs.

With my father absent for days on end I do not really know what my mother did to pass the time. For me there was school—kindergarten and the first grades. I early learned the rudiments of German and once was escorted from the first-grade room to the second-grade room to demonstrate my superiority in some small problem in addition the second-graders seemed unable to solve. I think Mrs. Tinker and her clan regarded my mother as socially a cut above them. I do not recall that the Tiffany lamp shone on many social evenings. We lived in an uncertain part of town, and only when my father returned from one of his interminable trips among the Wisconsin storekeepers did things brighten up. In later years I have found myself guessing and guessing again at the long, gray grind of my mother's life.

In Port Huron and again in Saginaw she had been a girl and a young lady of importance, daughter of a family of some local consequence, possessing a clear contralto voice that sufficed for church quartets and

17

group singing. This placed her among the elite. I have a cabinet photograph of her and three other maidens (they deserve the noun) grouped gracefully on or around a bench supposed to suggest the isles of Greece, their hair bound up in Grecian fillets, their costumes the nearest Port Huron could approximate to Grecian robes, their eyes full of soul, looking expectantly at the photographer's skylight whence, it is evident, the god Apollo might momently descend. And yet one cannot make fun of them. There was something sweet, something intangible and fragrant that came to them out of Arcadia. They lived and sang in St. Clair County, but they dreamed, I am certain, of Daphnis and Chloe, if only for a few transient hours.

My mother believed in the Impossible and the Ideal. I think her life was a long disappointment heroically borne, from her early marriage to the engaging Frank Alexander Jones to her death in a dreadful nursing home near Boston. She was a person of innate refinement who never found her way, who, like so many other thousands of innate refinement, could never rise above refinement into—what shall I say? The grim courage of art? Philosophy? A real aesthetic? A genuine religion? A (God forgive the word) personal *Weltanschauung*? If she had sat at the feet of Margaret Fuller, I doubt that she would have understood a single word from that Delphic oracle, but she gloried in persons, she gloried in a job well done, and she was victimized, I believe, by the whole pattern of education for the refined middle class in the hurley-burley of the Middle West. My guess is that she would have dismissed Amos Bronson Alcott as so much poppycock, but she would have got a good deal out of Ralph Waldo Emerson, and puzzled over what he meant.

In the nature of the case I saw less of my father than I did of my mother, and moreover, he died while I was a boy in grade school. My memories of him are of a grave, attractive man utterly misplaced in life. Very likely—and how hard it is to revive across seven decades a personality that shaped one's life!—he was a gentle soul, never meant for the crudities of business in the wholesale grocery establishments or local cigar stores that he came later to manage.

I am sure I was scolded and on occasion spanked, but my memory is mainly of amiable family picnics to Gratiot Beach north of Port Huron when we visited there, or to an enchanted area in the north quarter of Milwaukee where the lake in a final squiggle against Euclid's geometry broke into a series of ellipses and beaches, bluffs and sandplots. At any small depression on the hillside or any crossing of the footpaths of Whitefish Bay, ingenious management had set a table shaped like a toadstool with a red trim, found room for a small wooden bench, and yet allowed space enough for young children to dig in the dirt and ruin each

18

other's shovels. White-aproned waiters hurried perpetually up and down these pathways, miraculously carrying seidels of foaming beer on trays that somehow managed to keep level with the horizon. There was distant band music, and there were girls in leg-of-mutton sleeves of the Howard Chandler Christy style, and there were beaux with limber canes. I was given lemonade, for my mother had scruples (she would!) against beer and what would the neighbors say? but it was small matter on an afternoon as beautifully and harmlessly *gemütlich* as one could imagine. Happy the day when my father returned at long last from some tiresome trip to Oconomowoc or Wauwatosa, rushed in, changed his clothes, ordered us to change ours, and, properly dressed for Whitefish Bay, took us there for a sunny and utterly useless afternoon.

I can but hint once more that my father was born in the wrong place in the wrong time. Michigan was in the throes of vast speculations about lumber and railroads and banks and real estate development, and as the offspring of a family of some standing in Port Huron, my father had to play the game. But I think he would have been happier as a teacher. He was bookish. He had inclinations to style in clothes. I think he longed for a less parochial culture than the Middle West then offered.

Other memories of my Milwaukee years come flooding back. Ordinarily the Jones family, when it revisited its ancestral home, made the trip from Milwaukee to Port Huron by rail, a journey that necessitated a hideous and interminable transfer in Chicago, where Parmelee bus drivers enthusiastically crowded us into the wrong buses for the wrong trains at the wrong depots. My father had his moments, and in one of these, while we were visiting in Port Huron, he discovered that there was a train ferry that ran across Lake Michigan from Ludington to Milwaukee. No Parmelee bus drivers, no change of trains or stations. You stayed on the sleeping cars and there you miraculously were! We stepped aboard our train at Detroit; we rode quietly across lower Michigan with its scores of lakes; we arrived at Ludington, where, with a little shuffling and some slight amount of being banged about, we felt the bump of the wheels as they slid onto the tracks of the ferryboat and some slight tremor as the boat took on the whole weight of our immense equipment. Towards the violet hour, the mighty pulses of the ferry engine began to throb, there were various commands, ropes were let go, and we moved slowly and with infinite majesty—even a car ferry can be impressive—out of the sheltering piers past the dirty inshore water into the deeper blue of the lake. We had been warned that Lake Michigan could be choppy in a cross breeze, but I do not recall anything except the regular throb of the engines, the receding shoreline, and the excitement of being simultaneously on water and on land.

Within reason we had for a brief time the run of the ship. I do not remember whether we ate in the silver splendor of the dining saloon or the more plebeian quarters furnished us by the ferry. Despite the most heroic resolves to stay awake and see the lake at midnight, the air made us sleepy, and when we woke the next morning we found ourselves dingily docked in some part of the Milwaukee River. But even then things were managed better than in Chicago. There was no mob of shouting Parmelee drivers; instead, carriages drove up in regular order, and we were safely sent away, whether to Oakland Avenue or to some more lordly address. At such moments my father was in his element. Even when there were no orders to give, he looked every inch able to issue a great many of them. Here was the princely role he was born for, and he got our bags and trunks and boxes as royally dispatched as if he were an important diplomat returning from a foreign tour.

One more moment of glory remains to be told, for it is to this day as vivid as it was in the eighteen-nineties. There was in Milwaukee a local German theater, and we were also visited from time to time by traveling companies out of Chicago. Some months after our settlement at Oakland Avenue, there came to Milwaukee a traveling company which staged *Superba*, a musical extravaganza, the chief feature of which was the hair-raising leap of a black horse from one mountain peak to another, the two tallest stage mountains ever seen in Milwaukee. I do not know what dark *diablerie* swung the horse from one mountain cliff across a dangerous pit to the top of another mountain, though I now suspect it was not unconnected with piano wire, but at any rate horse and rider leaped and rescued virtue in distress on the opposite peak. The black horse was led on stage at the final curtain for the last tableau and enthusiastic applause. I had been unusually "good" for some days, and after a solemn family conclave it was decided that *Superba* was the sort of theatrical entertainment I might be permitted to see. I was therefore taken to a vast and glittering "opera house," the largest theater in the city, all overflowing with seats in curves and tiers, gilt pillars, gold it might have taken the mines of California to produce, red velvet hangings in all parts of the house, people suspended in two and threes, in sixes and eights over my head in golden boxes, and a mixed aroma of cleaning fluid, perfume, peanuts, chewing gum, fur, and all the other combined smells of the theater. A smartly uniformed usher showed us to our seats, ran his flashlight along the backs of them so that we could make out our numbers, gave us programs without any wisecracks, and departed like a heaven-sent Mercury.

The Harvard College Library Theater Collection doubtless possesses somewhere in its millions of items a copy of the program of *Superba*, together with the names of the authors, producers, and principal stars. I have never looked it up. I never shall. I do not wish to know the name of the great hero who spurred his horse to that death-defying leap. I think it was Galahad, and I do not wish to be told otherwise. I am sure that somewhere a faded theater program gives the names of all the fairies and demons and perhaps even of the stage hands and the silver cornetist. I do not want to know who they were. To this hour, if there was a story line to *Superba*, I do not know what it was. All I remember is one vast mass of glitter and awe, a shining, glimmering, changing panorama of beauty from the first moment to the end. There were transformations. Scenery melted away and revealed robbers' dens or enchanted castles. There were songs and there were choruses. There were dances by creatures too lovely to have been spawned by mortal men. There were acrobatic stunts of varying degrees of improbability. And there was that black horse, led before the footlights at the last possible moment amidst volleys of applause. Experiences such as this are irreversible and unrepeatable. Such was my first breathless look at the Parthenon. Such was my first glimpse of the Grand Canyon. Such was my first sight of the Lincoln Memorial in Washington one early morning, there being nobody else present but a guard. Such was *Superba*.

Chapter III

La Crosse: Hometown

ANOTHER TURN of the wheel of fortune at the beginning of the new century sent the Jones family of three from Milwaukee to La Crosse, then as now a tidy midwestern city on the left bank of the Mississippi River halfway between Minneapolis and Dubuque. It is one of those smaller cities, such as Prairie du Chien and Winona, destined to develop as a trading post, grow as a lumber town, be nurtured by the railways, and then gradually diminish in importance as the airplane and the automobile took over traffic on land, and the barge system ended the run on the Mississippi of the river boats beloved of Mark Twain. La Crosse was to be my hometown so far as a wandering scholar has one; and as I look back on my boyhood and youth, I count it a piece of great good fortune to have grown up in a lesser city that might serve as a model of the melting pot. It had a population of about 30,000 when we moved there and acquired a house at 1632 Ferry Street, near enough to the eastern edge of the town to permit me to explore the prairie (ever full of sandburs) that stretched, with only occasional houses, from the Green Bay and Western Railroad a block or so east of our house to the great line of bluffs beyond. It also permitted me to learn about farming, since the richer lands at the bottom of the coulees had excellent patches of soil, and besides, it was no great matter for an active youngster to climb to the top of the bluffs, where the farms were more nearly continuous. Thus I came to know Bill Freehoff, scion of a farm family, my buddy in high school and later at the university, who rose to eminence as a liberal member of the Wisconsin legislature.

Bill was the essence of the second generation of immigrants who made Wisconsin what it was in the La Follette days. Generous, awkward of speech and manner, he yet radiated an instinctive inner integrity that won him election after election to the legislature shortly after he was graduated from Wisconsin in our class of 1914. The family farm was on top of the bluff country not very far from La Crosse, and it was there I learned something about hard work, the skill it takes to run a farm, and the profits and perils in raising dairy cows. The Freehoff family was not wealthy, but having the gift of thriftiness, they were well off and in no way led the grinding life of the farmer pictured by Hamlin Garland. Bill could bring home anybody he wanted to; and he and I either tramped our way or rode in the family buggy to and from the farm on many a weekend. Father and mother, reticent always, were nevertheless warm-hearted, as were the younger children; and the whole family—for that matter the whole neighborhood—was immensely proud of a farm boy who had gone to the city, attended the high school and then the University of Wisconsin, and come back home without a swelled head, but was knowledgeable about Wisconsin laws and the dairy industry. Their pride was justified. If Germany had been populated with more citizens like Bill and his clan, Hitler would never have been heard of outside a madhouse. I think Jefferson with his dream of a decent agricultural republic would have taken the Freehoffs to his heart.

My own family misfortunes aside, it was one of the happier periods of my life, as it was one of the happier periods of American history—I mean the years running from the advent of Theodore Roosevelt to the White House in 1901 down to our entry into the First World War. But here I must deal with what may seem a contradiction. It is the fashion among intellectuals, particularly those who know little of American life beyond the Hudson River, to look upon this era as the Age of Innocence, a period they sometimes extend through the twenties, and, given the usual concept of the Gilded Age and the Genteel Tradition, often run backward at least to the Cleveland administrations, and sometimes to the presidency of Rutherford B. Hayes. The phrase about innocence connotes a naive belief in goodness, in the progress of mankind and particularly of the United States, in reform by political action and constitutional change, general acceptance of the doctrine that human nature is fundamentally sound, and a mistaken belief that the majority of Americans are reasonable persons—an assumption that underlay La Follette's appeal to the voters. In Wisconsin these were the great days of La Follette and the Progressive movement. But all this, it now seems, was mere innocence.

It is argued with a considerable show of reason that the age of Teddy Roosevelt and his successors knew nothing comparable to the dreadful

23

destruction of the Jewish people by the Nazis (what about the Turkish massacres of Armenians in 1894–95?), the horrors of trench warfare in World War I (we shuddered at the savagery of the Russo-Japanese War and the three or four Balkan wars), the atom bomb (we did what we could by building the dreadnoughts and the airplanes and by perfecting the submarine), the assassinations and bloodbaths of the Bolshevik Revolution (we contented ourselves with "suppressing" the Indians, lynching the Negro, and recording bloody battles between striking workmen and the police, the militia, the Federal army, or all three). Before the time of the universal breaking-up of empires, we led the way by destroying the empire of Spain in 1898 and building an American empire on better lines, or so we hoped. Some of us, however, formed vigorous anti-imperialist groups.

All this is not to deny that the present time is one of the most violent and disorderly in history; it is intended only to point to the fallacy of supposing that before Pearl Harbor everything was simple, easy, and bright. I have lived through the Spanish-American War, the Russo-Japanese War, the Boxer Rebellion in China, the massacre of the Jews at Kishinev, various insurrections in Latin America, two World Wars, and much else. I do not know how to measure either violence or "sophistication" in proportion to the population or the damage or the wisdom it creates. Like the aged Longfellow, as Samuel Eliot Morison notes,

> I am too old
> To hope for better days,

but I have learned to distrust generalizations about history made by "advanced" thinkers and revisionist historians, especially when they contrast the simplicity of one epoch with the complex darkness of a succeeding period.

Let it not be forgotten that the Gay Nineties, into which I was born, may have been gay in terms of Koster and Bial's Music Hall, where moving pictures were first publicly shown, or of the Floradora Sextette, but they were not gay in terms of ordinary life. A business depression began in 1893 and lasted into the twentieth century. They were not gay in terms of Coxey's army, an attempt to organize the unemployed into a great protesting mob that was to march on Washington and demand relief from Congress—public works, road construction, and the issuing of half a billion in paper money. The characters in such contemporary works of Henry James as *The Turn of the Screw*, *The Wings of the Dove*, or *The Golden Bowl* are neither innocent nor admirable examples of morality. This was the age, it is true, in which William Dean Howells in *Criticism and Fiction* is said to have denied the possibility of realism in

American letters because American novelists are forced to "concern themselves with the more smiling aspects of life, which are the more American," a dictum perpetually quoted out of context. Modernists might be cheered if they would read the preceding sentence in Howells's essay, which declares that the more admirable traits of American life are all changing for the worse. This was in 1891. In 1907 Henry Adams printed the story of his own *Education*, which, following his misreading of Willard Gibbs, proves by an absurd mathematical formula that the world must come to an end by about 1925 at the latest. William Graham Sumner did not believe that progress was possible except as the blank universe willed it, and Thorstein Veblen demonstrated with ironic logic in 1899 in *The Theory of the Leisure Class* that all the leisure class got for its exertions was conspicuous futility. Josiah Royce, a philosopher admired during the innocent era, said grimly that life was valuable enough to be tragic, a strange commentary on the more smiling aspects of existence; and in the nineties smart young people were reading Max Nordau's *Degeneration*, which proved that all modern art was corrupt. Mark Twain's pessimism grew with the years, reaching its climax in the nihilism of *The Mysterious Stranger* of 1916.

This is not a book about the history of thought or of literature, but I observe that in the midst of the Genteel Tradition, much misunderstood, Ed Howe brought out, in 1883, his merciless *The Story of a Country Town*, Jack London by and by produced *The People of the Abyss* and *The Iron Heel*, Stephen Crane's *Maggie: A Girl of the Streets* was taken up and praised (somewhat overpraised) by Howells, and one of the best sellers of the time was Mrs. E. L. Voynich's disturbing attack on the Christian Church ("God is a thing made of clay, that I can smash with a hammer; and you have fooled me with a lie"), *The Gadfly*, which in these later days is being reprinted. And what about Upton Sinclair's *The Jungle?*

All this seems to contradict what I have said about the La Crosse of my boyhood and youth, but the contradiction is apparent, not real. I learned about the tougher thinkers of my time when I went to the university. The fatuity of small-town life as set forth in Sinclair Lewis's *Main Street* (1920) I never knew, and if I did not read Ibsen and Strindberg until I went to college, I read widely both at home and in books checked out from the La Crosse Public Library, where I graduated from the children's room to the level of an adult's card.

As La Crosse was an important railway junction (five roads came together there in my lifetime), we had admirable traveling shows which stopped for a night between Chicago or Milwaukee and Minneapolis or St. Paul, for like every city of our size we had an "opera house." I saw the aging Modjeska in Schiller's *Mary Stuart*, which, years later, I produced at the University of Texas. I saw the younger Joe Jefferson revive *Rip Van Winkle* in honor of his father, the elder Jefferson. I saw Robert Mantell and his traveling company do *Hamlet, Macbeth, The Merchant of Venice*, and other Shakespearean plays; and if, as the phrase goes, he hammed his parts, at least I was introduced to Shakespeare in the live theatre and not buried in a schoolbook. I saw light opera—*The Pink Lady*, for example—and I saw grand opera when the tireless San Carlo Grand Opera troupe came to town to stage all the familiar war-horses that a limited company and a limited orchestra could manage. It is fashionable to deride this company, but their missionary work in music was beyond praise. I remember, too, that Oberhoffer brought his Minneapolis Symphony Orchestra to La Crosse, playing a standard repertoire, but a standard repertoire was precisely what we needed. We also had a tent Chautauqua; and though it is possible to deride the Chautauqua (I have done it myself) with funny remarks about William Jennings Bryan and the Swiss Bell-Ringers, one has only to turn to Theodore Morrison's sympathetic history of the Chautauqua published in 1974 to know how valuable it was as an institution. We also had university lecturers from Minnesota and Wisconsin and other institutions of higher learning; and because there were so many Germans and Scandinavians in La Crosse, we had choral societies and amateur chamber music and a number of excellent music teachers. I "took piano" from Charles Weiss, a pupil of Leschetizky, who, while I played a sonata by Clementi, would sit in a chair by my piano stool, knitting or crocheting because he was an impatient man and frequently put out of temper by the performances of his pupils.

If I seem to have gone at this chapter backward instead of proceeding in due chronological order from our leaving Milwaukee, it is because the stereotype of town life before television, the automobile, and the radio needs to be destroyed. In retrospect, I now know that the public schools of La Crosse were excellent, that the little city, though it was out of what Goethe would call the great world, nevertheless developed a curiously interesting life of its own, that without any fancy pedagogical theories the teachers I had in the grade schools and in high school sensed what I was good for and encouraged me to develop my talents, whatever they might prove to be, on lines congenial with my situation in life.

I do not know what led my father to leave Milwaukee. In the few remaining years of his life (he died in 1906), he was for a period a traveling salesman for a wholesale grocery in Milwaukee, an agent for a life insurance company that was later heavily involved in the Hughes investigation into insurance scandals, and for a time owner of a pool-hall and cigar stand.

I do not know much about my father's financial life, but he somehow found the money to buy the corner lot at Seventeenth and Ferry streets and the big red house and barn that stood on it. He remodeled the living room in a style vaguely suggestive of William Morris. There was a chimney cater-corner to the entrance into the dining room; there was a comfortable chest under the windows on the east side of the room and flowered cushions on which to loll; there were built-in bookshelves along another wall, and wide double doors leading to the parlor, where the upright piano stood, and at right angles another pair that opened on the dining room. I have mentioned my bookishness and my belief that my father would have been happier in some scholarly post than he was in the business world. How else explain a dictionary stand made out of gilded metal I long took for gold. There was a wooden lectern on its top huge enough to carry an unabridged Webster, and a gilt shelf below, which bore Ridpath's *History of the World*. Unfortunately the dictionary stand operated on some sort of clumsy spring-lock (all gilded), to the continuing peril of anybody's fingers, including mine.

Upstairs were four bedrooms of decreasing importance leading to the rear of the house, where the smallest room was obviously intended for a maid or a cook who was to sleep there and go down the back stairs into the kitchen. I do not recall that we rose to the glory of maidservants, and this room became the sewing room, for in those days a "sewing lady" came and stayed with a family until she had completed making or mending clothes for the year.

There was a big back yard shaded by oak and maple trees. In the yard was one of those wooden double swings, with seats and a platform all hung from a wooden frame by various ingenious bolts, nuts, and cross pieces to keep the contraption steady, and a device that prevented youthful energy from swinging so furiously that the whole swing would collapse. This was useful as a railway, a steamboat, a pirate ship, or whatever else required motion. There was also a small vegetable garden that I was supposed to take care of; and the back porch, which was latticed, held an icebox and an ice cream freezer which I cranked when required to do so on a Saturday afternoon, the reward being that I was allowed to lick the dasher when it was pulled out of the finished cream.

One other feature of our La Crosse residence is worth cataloguing— the furnace. This burned slabs from the lumber mills, of which there were still two or three near the Mississippi River actively cutting up logs; and when we were about to run out of slabs, we phoned (an old-fashioned wall telephone that you had to crank) for a fresh supply. A horse-drawn truck came, dumped a couple of cords of slabs by a cellar window, and drove off after chewing up the grass, leaving me the chore of hurling the slabs into a cellar bin under the window. A slab makes a very satisfactory racket as it lands on a cellar floor or on some brother slabs below, though from time to time I had to go down into the cellar and straighten them out. In cold weather, after my father's death, I set an alarm clock for 3:00 A.M. and went down to feed the furnace before the pipes froze. Winter temperatures hovered around the zero mark or below it very frequently in La Crosse.

I have said that La Crosse was a model of the American melting pot. The block above Ferry Street was occupied by Norwegians, the adult males being employed in one or another of the lumber companies, and the clatter of their dinner pails as they went to or came from work was a cheerful warning to families that dinner had jolly well be ready. The first house across from ours on Seventeenth Street was occupied by the Lysaker family, whose children, Emma, Paul, and Elmer, liked to play in my yard and were called home for meals by their mother in stout Norwegian, which I, alas, never learned. The house next to us on our side of Ferry Street was occupied by the Kepplers, a German couple who made sauerkraut on the back porch. Next to the Kepplers was a strange dwelling, a wooden product of the Gothic revival. This was inhabited by the widow of a Confederate army officer, Mrs. Mars, and her old-maid daughter; was always dark and mysterious; and seemed to open for visitors only once a year. The house terrified all the children, and I later used it in a prize-winning short story, "Mrs. Drainger's Veil," which has appeared in several collections of short stories, including *The Best Short Stories of 1919*. Beyond lived the Tuteur family, who were Jews, Mr. Tuteur being, as I recall, in the liquor business. Beyond the Tuteurs was Judge Higbee, unmistakably of English stock, and on the other side of the street were the Olsens, who were Swedes, and the Oeschgers, who were Germans. A little later a new house was built almost opposite our own and was occupied by a French-Canadian family. But nobody thought anything of this conglomerate; we had in La Crosse Norwegians, Swedes, Bohemians, Poles, and representatives of other races, including a few blacks. The mayor of La Crosse was then named Skaar, and the congressman from our district was John H. Esch, joint author of the Esch-Cummins bill for greater control of the railroads.

Winter in La Crosse could be severe, and the Mississippi froze to a depth of several feet. Ice-cutting was a picturesque occupation, to be viewed, if you were very warmly dressed, from the bridge that spanned the main channel of the Mississippi. A special ice-saw cut out the blocks

28

of ice, three or four feet square, and a pair of horses dragged these to a chute rising from the bank of the river to the top of an enormous wooden icehouse. These beautiful pieces, like glittering, gigantic diamonds, were hauled up by an endless belt, which discharged them into the icehouse. There another crew embedded them in sawdust from the lumber yards.

The level of water beneath the ice sometimes sank and, along the edges of the islands or the marshes, left ledges of snow-free ice some twenty feet wide and three feet thick, on which one could skate endlessly. You had of course to be wary of a break in the ice-ledge, and there were safer ice rinks in town, but I used to rejoice in my solitary excursions along these shelves. I also tried skiing, a sport which had not then reached the perfection of the present age. Our skis were little more than stout, hard wooden boards properly shaped and varnished, with a rubberoid pad for the foot and a stout rubberoid or leather strap into which you slipped your foot. We had no ski poles. We had no special ski slide, but went out to the bluffs and slid perilously down some sloping hillside, hoping we would not hit a rock or barbed wire or a nasty bit of root buried just beneath the surface of the snow. I once hit a rock, laid open one knee, and had to stagger back as well as I could to the St. Francis Hospital, where a sympathetic nun and a kindly interne bound up my wounds.

The Hogan School across the Green Bay tracks held only five grades, and I had to transfer to the Third Ward School to finish my grade school education. This school was a mile from our house, but like other pupils I walked or bicycled this distance four times a day whenever school was in session, for there were no school lunches. We had occasional fights along the way or on the school grounds, but those commonly left no ill-will and, aside from a few black-and-blue bruises, did no physical harm.

On my father's death, my mother was left with a large house and a boy on her hands and virtually no income. She managed, however, to secure training in what was known as the Marinello method of scalp treatment, hair washing, and kindred arts, and set up a practice among the wealthier families in La Crosse, trudging from house to house with a black bag that held the necessary equipment for her customers' needs. As her practice grew, she was necessarily away from the house more and more, leaving me (what else could she do?) to my own devices. Our house had a huge attic, and I had somehow acquired a variety of lead soldiers and a passion for playing war games on the attic floor, outlining, with chalk "lifted" from school, seacoasts and cities and rivers and islands, and using strawberry boxes turned upside down for forts. I do not know where or how I got on to this—perhaps I had picked up H. G. Wells's little book on war games or some other at the public library—but I worked out a most elaborate code of rules, pushing a small kerosene lamp over

29

the attic floor in order to see, for our house was illuminated by gas, and there was no gas jet in the attic. I could not interest any of my contemporaries in my fantasies, so I was again a loner.

Since I was now old enough to earn a little money, I took to mowing lawns and selling *The Saturday Evening Post* to regular customers or to passers-by at some street corner. Either in the eighth grade or in my first year of high school I acquired a paper route, carrying the evening paper, the *La Crosse Leader-Press*, through one of the older parts of the city— the small and tidy red-light district, several breweries, and wards largely inhabited by German-Americans. Of the red-light district I recall only the amiability of the girls, and I was especially grateful for the corner saloons and the breweries on cold or rainy nights. The saloons always had a free-lunch counter where the hungry newsboy could help himself without reproach, and the breweries—that is to say, their boiler rooms— were snug and warm.

Every afternoon I rode my bicycle either from home or from school to the newspaper office, which was near the river, bought a five-cent apple pie from a consumptive-looking vendor or her pale daughter, who served these unsanitary delicacies and others out of a shed attached to the wall of the newspaper building, got my pile of papers, put them in my paper-bag, and cycled my route. I usually got home about six or six-thirty, by which hour my mother had returned, rested, and prepared supper. Ah, but I slept as I have not slept since.

On Saturday mornings I had to collect ten cents from each customer. My German customers seem in my memory to have lived only in one-storey houses with a front door which nobody ever entered except on formal occasions and a back door commonly opening on a trellised porch. In the rear of any such house there was a pathway down to a "summer house" in the middle of the back yard, a pathway which divided the vegetable garden from the flower garden. On Saturday morning you knocked at the back door, and by and by the mistress of the domicile appeared, recognized you and your errand, sang out in the voice of Brunhilde, "Papa! Papa! Der Pressbube ist gekommen," and pointed to the summer house. You made your way thither, where the man of the house, taking his ease of a fine spring or summer morning, would recognize you, slowly take his pipe out of his mouth, after gigantic efforts extract a black leather coin purse from his pocket, open its silver catch, extract a dime, put it in your hand, say "Ach," somehow get the purse back into his pocket, and resume his meditations. Although I was reasonably punctual in making my Saturday rounds, I never knew one of these German households to have their dime ready for me.

One of the events of my boyhood was the sight of what was supposed to be the last lumber raft come down the Mississippi from somewhere about St. Croix, Wisconsin, modest enough when compared with the giant rafts in the *Adventures of Huckleberry Finn*, but still big enough to require a stern-wheeler to push it and a bow-boat lashed sideways across its downriver end to assist the unwieldy thing in getting around bends in the river without breaking to pieces. This raft, with its stern-wheeler and its bow-boat, marked the end of an era. The lumber industry was dying in Wisconsin as it had died in Michigan, leaving behind a ravaged landscape in the northern half of the state. One by one the lumber barons were losing their grip on the state government. New industries were coming to Wisconsin, not merely in the industrial area around Milwaukee, but also in smaller urban centers, of which La Crosse was one.

Somewhat confusedly, but nevertheless steadily and, in later years, with better organized political and economic strength, Wisconsin was becoming a dairy state. Not only Scandinavians and Germans but later immigrants as well (I write as of 1910, when I was graduated from high school) were slowly turning the ghastly areas left by the lumber industry into productive agriculture—raising not only milk cattle but also fodder and eventually vegetable crops and grains. No longer dominated by the lumber barons, the legislature was legalizing dairy cooperatives, boosting butter and cheese as products of the state, frowning on oleomargarine, reducing intrastate railroad rates, and improving rural education. The needs of the new economy remade the College of Agriculture at the university. The "short course" for young (or for that matter, for older) farmers, offered during the winter months, increased the knowledge of scientific agriculture. The county agent likewise was abroad in the commonwealth, and from the university itself came regular issues of pamphlets intended to improve everything from public health to the growing of mushrooms in damp cellars.

Not that politics miraculously disappeared overnight. The dominant Republican party split into the Stalwarts and the Half-Breeds, supporters of the La Follette idea. Moreover, the uneven distribution of population in the state created an almost insoluble sociological problem, the bigger cities being principally in the southern and middle counties, with the northern parts of the state but sparsely populated. One of the social consequences was the vast puzzle of what constituted a fair distribution of educational opportunities for urban dwellers and country folks, old "Badgers" and new immigrants, industrialists, and labor unions. Wisconsin already had in 1910 more state colleges ("normal schools")

31

than it needed; yet a new one sprouted in La Crosse. Were all these schools to be supported by state money, and if so, how was the money to be proportioned? Were they all to be equal as schools of higher learning, at least for the two years that constituted their usual curricula? Would it not be wiser either to have each such school specialize in something, or should all simply imitate, though with thinner resources, the first two years of the university at Madison? What about equality of libraries? Of laboratories? Of recreational facilities?

A solution to part of the problem was the installation of a common purchasing agency, but this in turn threatened the freedom of individual teachers to experiment with new books and new laboratory equipment. Another was to put all the state colleges under a common board of regents. A third might have been to give the charge of the entire educational system of the state to a single body like the Regents of the University of the State of New York. Wisconsin did not accept this Napoleonic solution, but only recently it made all the state colleges into state universities and then merged these with the University of Wisconsin into one enormous institution with many campuses.

These and other forces, including radical changes in systems of transportation, have altered the Wisconsin of my youth. By 1914 or thereabouts the Scandinavian farmers and others, having got what they wanted in the way of legislation, were inclined to resist what now seemed to them "radicalism"; and though the son of the elder La Follette had his brief day in the political sunshine, less than a quarter of a century after the death of the great Progressive leader, Joseph R. McCarthy was to become a senator from the state that had once been liberal, and to begin his career as a demagogue who did infinite damage to public confidence in the government of the United States. McCarthy is disgraced and dead, and Wisconsin has better men to represent it these days, but when on occasion I revisit the state—at Madison or Milwaukee—I feel I am walking in the country of ghosts. All, all are gone—the old familiar faces.

BOOK TWO

EDUCATION

Chapter IV

Classes,
Railroads,
Verses

I DO NOT RECALL any ceremony when we were graduated from the eighth grade, though it is possible the superintendent of schools visited us and said something graceful. The superintendent was John P. Bird, and we knew little about so august a personage except for his peculiar way of pronouncing the letter s. Irreverent youth therefore referred to him as Johnny P. Whistler. This we thought excruciatingly funny, the more so because we were sure to be reprimanded by any passing teacher who overheard us. In that distant day pupils were awed by their teachers, and teachers were not afraid of their scholars.

I entered the La Crosse High School in the autumn of 1906, while my mother continued her rounds as a shampooist and masseuse and I continued to carry papers. My first year in high school was spent in an aboriginal building of the General Grant era, all over cornices and mansard roofs, but in my second year we moved into a new building about six blocks from my home. It had among other modernities an auditorium, wide and cheerful corridors, modern desks, comfortable chairs, lockers, a gymnasium, a lunchroom, clean toilets, and other evidence that La Crosse was an up and coming town.

Transition from grade school to high school was, I discovered, a true rite of passage, though I would not then have called it so. Instead of being confined to a single room, you went from class to class as your study card directed. Bells rang. You moved with your comrades from place to place for Latin or typewriting or physics. You met all your fellow students only at "assembly," when we were called together to listen to some visiting fireman, to commemorate Lincoln's birthday, or to cheer on the football team. In your sophomore year you confronted the necessity of working out a studies program under the supervision of a counsellor and of choosing among a dazzling variety of offerings. I went in for four years of Latin, stenography and typewriting, American history, and, as I remember, German. But above all and most thrilling, teachers no longer called you "Howard" but addressed you as "Mr. Jones." The benefit of my course in stenography and typewriting was immediate and practical, but the intellectual benefits of my four years of Latin were immense, if remote. I thought then and think now that my high school education was excellent.

I cannot pass the entire staff in review, but in memory Miss Lena Heidemann, who taught American history, was tops. She was an old maid, tall, thin, and angular. Her nose, that rudder of the mind, was of a commanding style, and her eyes could subdue you with a single glance. She had innate dignity, and she expected dignity in others. She also possessed that mysterious quality developed in certain personalities of subduing you without arousing resentment.

The interval between classes was seven minutes, during which time you were supposed to have proceeded from one room to another. Usually there was a buzz of conversation and some mild horseplay even after the teacher had entered the room. Not so in Miss Heidemann's course. The moment she opened the door, conversation ceased, and we respectfully watched as she marched to her desk, wrote a name or a date on the blackboard, turned and surveyed us, announced the assignment for the next session, repeated it for the benefit of the slow of wit, and then proceeded to the business of the hour. If the topic was, say, the French and Indian wars, and if she called on you for information about the battle on the Plains of Abraham, you were expected to answer with precise information. Either you knew that the British general was named Wolfe or you did not. If you did not, she did not scold; she merely gave you a silent glance, and passed on to someone else. She occasionally expressed verbal approval of a good answer, and that made your day. She had complete command of her subject, she was not afraid of dates, she did not surmise that by requiring you to know something precise about the American past she was smothering "creativity." Writing had to be exact and clear, and how many hours she spent reading our slovenly prose I shudder to contemplate. She violated all the rules or rather lack of rules for schooling nowadays, and we adored her for the simple reason that she assumed as a matter of course that she was there to teach and we were there to learn. She remained a fixture of the school for years; when at last she retired and it was learned that her legal pension would not keep her in comfort, some sensible person in La Crosse wrote to as many of her former students as he could locate, explained her situation, and asked for contributions. The response was instant, and the checks were accompanied by letters of appreciation.

I joined the Lincoln-Douglas Debating Society. In Wisconsin during the La Follette era you were early exposed to public issues. The Lincoln-Douglas Debating Society was given the use of a classroom one evening each week, where it conducted its meetings with meticulous regard for parliamentary decorum. I was once president of it, and I know I never went to a meeting without a copy of Robert's *Rules of Order*. Indeed, we set so high a value on decorum that once a month (our meetings were weekly) we set aside half an hour for parliamentary practice, and woe betide the president who could not rule rightly and firmly on some tricky point in parliamentary law. The president had also to confine speakers to the time allotted them (usually fifteen minutes), cutting them off, if necessary, in the middle of a sentence, a Spartan practice that has fallen into disuse.

Football was of course our major athletic passion, and I was at one time elevated to the post of cheerleader; that is, I became a cross between an expert rabble-rouser and the conductor of a chorus. I stood on the football field immediately in front of the bleachers devoted to our rooters, and there, megaphone in hand, I ordered the crowd to sing or yell. This was supposed to encourage our team. How making these noises encouraged our team I never learned; and I remember that a friend who played quarterback at La Crosse complained that our yells often drowned his signals and compelled him to give them twice, to the deep gratification of the opposing eleven. The cheerleader was instructed to keep one eye on the playing field and the other on the bleachers, a difficult thing to do since it required perpetually turning one's back on either the game or the rooters. When we played in foreign territory—say, Sparta or Viroqua—the cheerleader went along as regularly as did the coach, and was supposed to draw from the little band of the faithful who accompanied the team as much noise as he could elicit, this commonly being drowned by the tintinnabulation of the opponents' band. It is a curious American custom. "Training" cheerleaders and their assistants had as yet not come in, nor had women cheerleaders or drum majorettes. My activity as cheerleader and a mild course in a German Turnverein were my sole athletic accomplishments. Carrying papers furnished quite enough exercise.

Opinion in my day in Wisconsin enthusiastically applauded the existence of high school debating societies. There were district and state debating contests. In La Crosse our orators were usually male and drawn from the Lincoln-Douglas Society, though sometimes rivals appeared, one of them a team of girls who roundly defeated us in a local debate. If our team won, or, as once happened, swept the entire state and not the district only, we tasted briefly of the cup of glory. Public contests at home or abroad were conducted under a rigid protocol. They were chaired by some prominent adult; there was a jury of three or five adults; each speaker on either side had fifteen minutes for a main argument and five minutes for rebuttal; the jury retired—sometimes, it seemed, for an infinity of time—then returned and announced its verdict. The losing team was supposed to congratulate the winners, and the chairman, having thanked everybody, adjourned the meeting.

In high school I discovered a shy talent for writing and contributed to the school paper and the school "annual," that preposterous volume supposed to record everything of consequence during the school year, together with photographs of every important event and individual pictures of each member of the graduating class. I also wrote some sort of play, which the faculty was petitioned to put on and which it wisely declined to do.

Besides selling *The Saturday Evening Post* (five cents a copy, of which I kept three) and carrying papers, I began my career as an amateur typist. During the summer vacations I worked as a part-time secretary for the legal firm of Woodward & Lees, attorneys for the local division of the "C.B.&Q" (Chicago, Burlington and Quincy Railroad), where I typed letters and took copies of them in an old-fashioned letter-press. There I also learned the infinite increase in the value of a stray cow inadvertently hit by a locomotive. Then, through one of my mother's customers, I became secretary to Hamlin Garland, who had a summer house in West Salem, about twelve or fourteen miles northwest of my town. I owned an old-fashioned, flatbed Royal (this preceded the days of portable typewriters), which I tucked awkwardly under one arm, trudged or took the streetcar to the Milwaukee station, rode on the noon train to West Salem, walked to Garland's cottage, arriving in a somewhat sweaty state, and sat down at a table in his study, a room which was at any rate cool. From the famous author I took dictation, directly at the machine. Fortunately, words came slowly to the great man, who commonly paced the room while I typed what he said. The first part of each session invariably consisted of letters to Gifford Pinchot, Theodore Roosevelt, and others of that ilk, since Garland had given up local color about farming for a series of potboilers supporting conservation and describing life on the Great Plains. I never saw the replies to these letters, albeit I suspect they were not as frequent as he desired, since it seemed to me that over a period of, say, six weeks, I was always typing the same sort of thing. The letters being done, we then turned to literature. I am under the impression that I typed a good deal of either *A Son of the Middle Border*, *A Daughter of the Middle Border*, or one or more of their sequels on my flatbed Royal. Or perhaps it was cowboy stories, which he turned out for popular magazines for mere cash. I had to stop at an hour early enough to get back to the West Salem railroad station and catch the down train for home. Once home, I took the rough copy Garland had dictated and recopied it neatly and cleanly on fresh sheets of paper, which I brought him on my next excursion to West Salem. I might as well add at this point that, when I entered the new normal school, the president, Fasset A. Cotton, learning of my talents, gave me a part-time post in his august presidential chambers, where, it now seems, I spent endless hours copying paragraphs out of his annual reports made as former superintendent of education in Indiana, which he solemnly delivered as addresses at meetings in Wisconsin. It was not my duty, I thought, to examine the ethics of this procedure, which I now publicly confess for the first time.

After being graduated from the La Crosse High School in 1910 (I think I was a commencement orator), I entered next autumn the newly created La Crosse Normal School (Teachers College as it later became before it turned into a branch of the University of Wisconsin). I enrolled in it partly because the tuition was low, partly because I could not at this point afford to go to the University of Wisconsin at Madison, and partly because the school was supposed to offer not merely a curriculum that led to a teacher's certificate but also the equivalent of the first two years of university education.

I find it difficult at this distance in time to be either accurate or just about this institution. It was on a large piece of unattractive land not far from my home, and has since 1910–11 increased its buildings, enriched its landscaping, and, though it is intended to concentrate on the training of teachers of physical education, enriched its curriculum as well. It was only a couple of years old when I entered its doors, and it was then housed in a sort of enlarged version of the new La Crosse High School; its president and its faculty were new to their situations (many of them were from the Hoosier State); and it was rather badly split into three not wholly harmonious sections: the college preparatory courses, the courses which led to a certificate enabling its holder to teach in a Wisconsin high school, and a third, somewhat vaguely outlined program that granted certification to the holder to teach for a year in an ungraded country school. (I still have mine.) Its clientele was necessarily local and ranged from the relatively urbanized graduates of La Crosse High School to products of rural schools in the adjacent counties, almost wholly agricultural. I remember a blind girl with red hair who was ceaselessly chaperoned, as it were, by Susan Ceranska (I think that was her name), a great, motherly creature who wore pink waists and purple skirts, possessed all the Christian virtues, and had an eighth-grade reading ability. I remember a boy who financed his way through the curriculum by sleeping at nights in an undertaker's parlor so that no one would disturb the corpses. At the other end of the spectrum there were students who would have fitted into any well-established college, Ivy League or otherwise.

The new normal school took on shape with a miraculous rapidity possible only in America—the development of the library under the direction of Florence Wing and Gertrude Dickens; the organization of a confused and sometimes contradictory curriculum; the shaping of athletics (always fundamental to an undergraduate education), with extraordinary difficulties arising from the awkward fact that girls outnumbered boys eight or nine to one, with consequent pressures on lockers, gymnasiums, and toilets; and also I take it, the inner adjustment of a faculty assembled from all sorts of places, Germany to Indiana, and having to adjust mutually hostile theories of education to the uneven preparation of the students. Most of the students were plain, simple country boys and girls, the majority of the latter wanting to qualify for a state certificate, teach for two or three years, then retreat into marriage, a home, and the rearing of children. Professional courses in pedagogy and "psychology for teachers" had of necessity to be so elementary—I remember one week-long discussion about separating the boys' and girls' outhouses in country schools—as to drag down the intellectual level of the whole institution; yet the "collegiate" courses I took were, by and large, well enough, except that the science courses had to be taught on so simple a level that I got nothing out of them. Two members of the English department, David O. Coate and Bessie Belle Hutchinson, could have qualified for any liberal arts position in any American college; and though now all I can remember of a course by J. E. Engelmann, the vice-president, is that the reason a dog wags its tail is that he has no other use of it, Engelmann was, apparently, a leading educational psychologist. Moreover, before I was graduated, I wrote an outdoor musical entertainment, *The Masque of Marsh and River*, a protest against the further destruction of a noble bluff by a stone-crushing company, that was produced by the whole school, faculty and students, with considerable zest and a real concept of what the thing was all about. (Percy Mackaye had recently made the masque a popular dramatic form.)

On the doctrine of any port in a storm I am grateful to the La Crosse State Teachers College, but I doubt that the school was really good for me. There were too many girls and too few boys, and it was far too easy for a boy of any small degree of talent to shine. That I was an only child, that my father died when I was young, that the conditions of my mother's employment (and for that matter of mine) left me little time for recreation, and that my temperament was, as I have suggested, that of a loner, make me feel that the queer distribution of sexes in the State Normal School was not right for me. I needed blunt male companionship, and I got very little of it there. I was blatantly a "writer," one who "swallowed the dictionary," and that set me off from most of my contemporaries, male or female. The work was undemanding, as, indeed, it had to be, because of the nature of the student body. I got sick of girls, had virtually no love affairs, remained thoroughly virginal, and paid heavily for this later.

On the other hand, some of my summer vacations during my high school and state college years left me no opportunity for going with girls and were as extraordinarily male as my school years were female. Through my work at Woodward & Lees and through the chance of knowing some railroad men, I got a job as timekeeper on construction gangs working for the C.B.&Q. out of La Crosse northward along the Mississippi. I was supposed to record the hours worked by three construction gangs who were "laying steel" along the main line; that is, they were ripping out the existing tracks, putting in new ties where they were needed, and substituting heavier rails for those then in use, after which they regraded the roadbed. One of my gangs was Greek, a second Italian, and a third hobo. I had no trouble with the Greeks or the Italians, since their own foremen helped me check their names and their hours, but the Americans were an endless source of trouble. They arrived on an early morning work train out of Chicago, most of them either drunk or sleeping off a jag, and they had no foreman. Many had no intention of working on the railroad, immediately deserted, and took to tramping the roads and frightening the farmers' wives or doing odd jobs for the farmers in return for meals or sleeping in the hay. I was supposed to get their names as soon as they arrived at camp, but after once or twice discovering that the railroad had hired Abraham Lincoln, Weber & Fields, or Jesus Christ, I learned to wait until the deserters had fled and those who wanted a paycheck were willing to give a plausible family name.

My second duty was to see that in tearing up the rail we did not delay the stately journey of a transcontinental train on its way to or from Chicago. For this purpose I had a portable telephone in a white box suspended from a large hook and cable, by which it was hung from the company telephone line. It was a heavy apparatus and usually required four men to hang it up or take it down. This was the first thing to get done every morning and one of the last things to undo every evening. Once the connection was made, I rang up the stationmaster at each end of the block we were working on, to learn from him the latest reports on the progress of through trains. I reported this to the foreman, who could then calculate how much time would elapse before he had to close some gap in the tracks with temporary rails in order to let the Pacific Limited go by. He was expert at this, and we rarely delayed any train.

The foreman, the assistant foreman (the "straw boss"), the crew of the work engine, and I lived on our work train. A work train was composed of a locomotive at one end, a caboose at the other, and a string of ancient freight cars in between. These last were converted into sleeping quarters. One or two of them became dining cars. The living quarters were simplicity itself: bunks were built along the sides, a space was reserved for washing and hanging up clothes, and sometimes there was a stove, though in the summer this was not necessary. The dining car had a long table down its length and benches on either side of the table. The cook worked in an adjacent freight car with a cooking stove, various pots and pans, and of course shelves and boxes for the storage of provisions. We aristocrats had the caboose.

The work train puffed along the main line until it reached the passing track nearest to our location, switched onto it, and except when the locomotive was needed for getting a carload of ties or rails to us, stayed until it was time to move forward. We went to work on handcars. On Saturdays the bosses and I boarded the caboose, which was then hurled towards La Crosse by a fireman and an engineer eager for home and family, or for recreation and a girl. You have not lived until you have traveled in a caboose, one of the lighter cars on any railroad, hitched to a work engine under the control of a fireman and an engineer who want to go somewhere in a hurry. On any one of these weekends we never knew whether the caboose was on the track or in the air.

The food was hearty, coarse, and abundant. The cook and his assistant were given to baking biscuits, but as the flour bin in the kitchen car was lacking in such elementary virtues as tightness of fit, the flour developed weevils, and in consequence you ate your biscuit with solicitude. Lunch was *al fresco* unless it rained; and at what Whittier would call our nooning, the laborers sprawled in the shade. Noon was also a convenient time for patronizing the portable toilets, which had to be transported to a new location as we moved on. We were instructed to screen these indecent things from the gaze of passengers on the Burlington trains, but almost invariably two or three men would be urinating in full view of a parlor car as a liner crawled carefully over our improvised track. Week after week, invariably indignant ladies would write indignant letters to some company agent, who forwarded them to the superintendent of the division, who would in turn write or telephone a reproof either to me or to the foreman.

Some episodes of my railroad summer are vivid in my mind. The Greeks, for example, had a goat, which went to work with them hitched to the center post of the Greek foreman's handcar. When payday came around, the goat would disappear, but in two or three days his replacement would be hauled back and forth from the work train to our new location until the next payday, when it suffered the fate of the first goat, which was to be roasted. The Greeks trooped in a body to some spot not far from the work train, taking the goat with them, slaughtered the goat, roasted it, cut it up into portions, and washed the portions down with beer or occasionally wine. Where they got the wine I never knew. The Italians, like the Greeks, were a relatively stable group, partly because such English as they had learned had a Sicilian flavor to it that made it unintelligible to the rural American ear. They tended on any payday to explore the small towns along the railroad, I suppose looking for female companionship, and I suppose they found it. After any payday the hobo gang would be decimated, and we would have to ask for another unreliable supply out of Chicago.

One day we were laying steel over a swamp somewhere near Trempealeau, Wisconsin, with a thunderstorm rushing towards us from one direction and a gasoline-driven handcar from the other. We had not been apprised of the gasoline car. Fortunately the straw boss, seeing the oncoming storm, had hurried us, so that the steel on the trestle was already laid. He saw the car coming and warned the workmen on the trestle to get out of the way. They did so in safety with one exception. The exception was a conscientious Greek who, having given a final turn to the nut of a bolt, stepped back on one of the middle crossbeams of the trestle, thinking he would be safely out of the way of the approaching handcar. Unfortunately, the signalmen to whom the car belonged had placed the large wooden blade of a track-switch horizontally across the car, in which position it stuck out by about three feet. It swiped the Greek and tumbled him into the swamp below. Simultaneously the storm broke over us, the car went on at increased velocity to avoid any ructions, the gang yelled and shook their fists, and the straw boss and some of the Greeks climbed down into the swamp. The victim had fallen into a pool of water under the trestle, where he lay unconscious. He was dragged out. His heart was still beating, and the foreman ordered me and four other men to get him to Trempealeau. We laid our injured friend on the handcar, I got on, the four men got on, and we started pumping, there being just enough room for the six of us. The rain increased, the lightning flashed, the thunder banged and clattered and bellowed, and we pumped and pumped and pumped. I think I have never again been so wet as I was on this wild ride.

A little before we reached the station platform, our patient began reviving; and when we got to Trempealeau, a doctor was waiting at the little depot, the straw boss having telephoned to the telegraph operator to get help. After we had put the injured Greek into the doctor's buggy, it ceased raining. The doctor assured my four pumpers that their comrade would not die; and we found some beer somehow and pumped back to our gang, the exercise serving in some degree to dry us off.

It is time, however, to go back to school. The head of the English department at the normal school was a soft-spoken, roly-poly man named David Orland Coate, whose wife was also roly-poly and soft-spoken, and to my maturer vision they seem to have been invented by Charles Lamb. They had come from Indiana, brought to Wisconsin by the first president of the college.

Now it must be repeated that in the opening decades of this century we of the Middle West were being indoctrinated with the virtues of regionalism, a cultural theory parallel to the Progressivism of La Follette. To the regionalist the brazen tyranny of New York over the arts in America was self-evident. We wanted to move the cultural center of the republic to Chicago. Poets, novelists, musicians, and painters were to give out the new gospel from the several states. And the new gospel was already being enunciated—by Zona Gale in her saccharine *Friendship Village* stories; by William Ellery Leonard, who wrote a drama about the Wisconsin Indians called *Glory of the Morning*; by Lorado Taft, the sculptor, who lived in Chicago; by Hamlin Garland, who summered in West Salem; by Thomas H. Dickinson in Madison and Laura Sherry in Milwaukee, who established the Wisconsin Players, and got plays published, too, under the title *Wisconsin Plays*, First Series, and *Wisconsin Plays*, Second Series. I had a play called *The Shadow* in the second collection of these one-act dramas, and I also wrote, later on, another one-act play, *The Blue Gods*, which was produced by the Players, though I never saw the production. The weakness of my pieces was that they smelled of Maeterlinck, not of the Middle West.

Under the encouraging eye of David O. Coate, who found in me more talent than I knew I had, I continued writing verse. My earliest published work was a small pamphlet of thirty pages entitled *A Little Book of Local Verse* with a foreword by Mr. Coate and a dedication to my mother. Here is a sample poem characteristic of local-color enthusiasm. Midway, I should explain, was a village not far from La Crosse, and it must be remembered that automobiles were still a rarity in 1915, at least where I lived, and that all the country highways were dirt roads.

CERTAIN REFLECTIONS AT MIDWAY

At Midway town, at Midway town
The dust-white road goes up and down,
And flashing past and to and fro
All summer long the autos go.

They seldom stop at Midway town,—
The place is small and dead and brown,
A store, a station, and a hall,
A dozen houses — that is all.

'Tis true the meadows are as fair
At Midway town as anywhere,
And overhead in August skies
The clouds careen like argosies.

The black-eyed Susans by the way
Curtsey and dance there every day,
And from the wheat fields joyously
I heard the blackbirds mock at me.

Surely at Midway one can feel
At night the cruising planet reel,
And see in heaven the milky wake
Of star-dust its propellors make.

And yet — and yet — at Midway town
The silver road goes up and down,
And flashing past and to and fro
All summer long the autos go.

Chapter V

Madison

HAVING SAVED UP enough money for tuition, I entered the University of Wisconsin at Madison as a junior in the autumn of 1912. The Chicago, Milwaukee, and St. Paul Railroad (as it was then), and the Chicago, Burlington, and Quincy ran their main lines through La Crosse to the Great West, whereas the Chicago & Northwestern regarded us as an inferior region and took a more direct route to the Twin Cities. One therefore had to board a local train to get from La Crosse to Madison by rail, and the coaches always kept that queer smell that accumulates on local trains—a combination of orange peel, human sweat, peanuts, and heaven knows what else. I bade farewell to my mother, who thought I ought to complete my education but who looked forward with some anxiety to so long an absence of her offspring. About this time, I think, she was employed by the normal school as a sort of housemother or counsellor for the girls, an experience which many years later got her a similar appointment in a dormitory at the University of North Carolina.

I learned that the university was vast and confusing, the student body, it was said with delight or consternation, numbering about 4,000. (As I write, the number is just under 40,000.) William Freehoff, who had been my buddy in high school, had entered the university as a freshman when I enrolled in the normal school, and he now looked after my room and board, introducing me to a sort of student cooperative called The Cardinal Cat. Later on I was to transfer my room to the top floor of the YMCA, a building which stood on the lake shore, and take my meals at Ye Gath Inn, a pleasant boardinghouse whose patrons were about equally divided between men and women. Not having been a freshman at Madison, I was necessarily cast once more in the role of oddball, since class distinctions were still important to the hierarchy of student values. I was never hazed, I did not have to take the compulsory drill (Wisconsin came under the provisions of the Morrill Act requiring military training in return for governmental aid to the agricultural college), and I had no course in Freshman English, the writing course required of all entering undergraduates.

In those days the university had on its faculty such men as John R. Commons, Edward A. Ross, Richard T. Ely, and other representatives of "progressive" social thinking, some of whom had come to Madison after having, it was said, created "trouble" at other universities. They were lured to Wisconsin by the bright promise of the La Follette era and by the pledge of the Regents to maintain academic freedom. This pledge had been made when the Regents in 1894 had refused to dismiss Ely, charged with being a radical friend of labor. At that time the Board of Regents had adopted a ringing resolution which stated in effect that whatever constraints might be placed elsewhere on freedom of thought and of discussion, the "sifting and winnowing" of thought for the purpose of ascertaining the truth should be forever unhampered at the University of Wisconsin. This declaration may still be read on a bronze plaque by the chief entrance to Bascom Hall, the main building of the university at the top of "The Hill."

I was assigned an adviser, learned that I was supposed to "major" in something, and chose English for my bailiwick. But this did not mean I could not do work in other departments. I enrolled in a lecture course given by Ross, a rather large class which met in an appropriate lecture hall that sloped from a row of high windows at the top downwards, like a serrated roof, to the floor, where the lecturer stood. Our text was, as I recall, Ross's *Introduction to Sociology*, or it may have been some other of his renowned publications. At any rate each chapter was followed by study questions. Ross did not usually lecture; instead, he made these study questions the issue of the hour in a game of question and answer, somehow overcoming the usual timidity evident when an undergraduate is called upon to speak in a large lecture room. I have never seen a class more skillfully managed than was this one. But I came to the conclusion that sociology was not my cup of tea.

I also enrolled in E. B. McGilvary's "Introduction to Philosophy," which began with John Locke and came down to the contemporary world. I have no reason to suppose that Professor McGilvary made any great splash in the philosophical world, but a more charming, a more cultivated, a more luminous lecturer I have never met. He made you see the inevitability of the ordering of the philosophers—like a baseball game, Locke to Berkeley, Berkeley to Hume, Hume to Kant, and so on. He was determinedly impartial, and to this day I do not know what school of thought he represented. But he made you feel that whether you were an idealist or a pragmatist, a Stoic or a Christian, the important thing was the life of the mind, and the important way to enrich the life of the mind was to accustom it to general ideas. It was a heartening example of undergraduate teaching at its best.

I was more at home in the departments of English and of history. Oscar James Campbell had recently come to the university from Harvard via the Naval Academy at Annapolis and was destined to introduce Max Eastman to a university audience during World War I—that is, in 1917, after the Regents, in violation of the sentiment on the famous bronze plaque, had voted to deny this Socialist the use of any university building. I enrolled in "O. J.'s" course in the development of the English novel, another great force in my intellectual development. O. J. wrote out every lecture he ever gave, and these lectures he read aloud. But he read so vivaciously that, although we knew he was peering through his spectacles at his manuscript, he seemed as spontaneous as he was informative. At moments of high intensity he would seem to wrap one leg around his lectern in order to get as near to us as possible. He was opposed to bifocals and always carried two pairs of spectacles to the classroom, one for looking at us and at his manuscript, and the other for reading out of a book. To witness the swift changing of these spectacles, especially as he popped the second pair on his nose and ears, was as good as a comedy. Great moments came when by accident he had lost his marker from the novel out of which he wanted to read and had to hunt around for the relevant paragraph or page. He would grumble to himself while he thumbed through the pages, some of us unconsciously leaning forward to assist him in the hunt. When he found what he wanted, he would utter an exasperated "Yah!" and read the passage to us with undiminished delight. He was assisted in the course by E. H. Gardner, under whom I once did some writing in an advanced course in composition. He, too, was good in his way, but his way was so totally different from O. J.'s, it was clear that the faculty was made up of all sorts and conditions of temperaments. But the point is not merely the engaging personality of an attractive scholar; the point is that this was the first time I had been introduced to a meaningful history of a literary form and shown the cause-and-effect relationship between the age and the work on the one hand and the experience and temperament of the author on the other.

I also studied under Norman Foerster, a disciple of Irving Babbitt, who was as reserved as O. J. was open and joyous. This course was one in American literature, and as I was at the time all for regionalism, I had looked forward to taking it, only to be disappointed in its conduct and its content. We used Foerster's one-volume anthology of selections from the major writers and W. B. Cairns's one-volume history of the national letters. This latter was a dull, if accurate book, but as all the available histories of American literature were elementary manuals for a beginning course and frequently apologetic in their tone, this shelf of mediocre volumes cast a pall over academic discussion of American writing. They occupied the field until the appearance of John Albert Macy's *Spirit of American Literature*, a short but influential study that deplored the ancestor worship given the New Englanders and denied that writing in America was a mere branch of British literature.

Another striking personality in the English department was William Ellery Leonard, poet and linguist, whose extraordinary sonnet sequence, *Two Lives*, unjustly forgotten, was one of the earliest examples of self-analysis in print. His autobiographical book, *The Locomotive-God*, which came out in 1927, two years after *Two Lives* had been privately printed, is also a searching piece of self-analysis, tracing the agoraphobia from which the poet suffered to his being frightened at the age of two when a huge locomotive came thundering past him just as he had strayed some distance from his mother's protecting presence. In the years after I left Wisconsin, Leonard's area of freedom grew more and more circumscribed and was eventually reduced to the familiar area of his home, his office, his classroom, and the faculty club. In my undergraduate days he was still able to take long walks along the shores of Lake Mendota, sometimes inviting me to accompany him. I was puzzled to understand why we never went beyond an insane asylum that fronted on the lake. I knew nothing of the tragedy of his wife's suicide nor of the blame which her family threw, as it seems unjustly, upon him. I was fascinated by his conversation, his bearing, his resolution to live his own life in his own way. He was at the center of more cultural conflicts than any man I ever knew. In the main a product of the eastern part of the United States and of Europe, with German university training and a doctorate from Columbia University, he was now in the Middle West without any particular belief that the regional movement in the arts had any meaning. He was a Unitarian, but he preferred Lucretius, whom he translated, to William Ellery Channing, for whom he had been named. Amidst the middle-class population of Madison and of the university, his wide bow tie, always a vivid color, was fiercely defiant. Trained in old-line philology, he was a *Dichter* after the German manner. As a public figure he was fiercely an individualist, who, among other unpopular convictions, would later oppose our entry into World War I.

Another course which stirred me as O. J. Campbell's did was a course in the history of the Crusades offered by Dana Carleton Munro a little while before he left Wisconsin to go to Princeton. I did not know at the time that he was one of the foremost medievalists in the United States, nor that his *A History of the Middle Ages* (1902) was not merely the best textbook in its field but also an original and fresh interpretation of a great historical period. After the feckless manner of undergraduates I elected the course because it came on Tuesdays and Thursdays at a convenient hour, and I needed something to fill a gap in my credits towards a diploma. The students were few, Munro's attitude was modest and sympathetic, and as I knew nothing about the Crusades except that they had occurred, his course was a revelation to me. He made the whole matter of historical research come alive, and he demonstrated the way by which a great teacher-scholar can challenge the curiosity and gain the sympathy of neophytes. Some humanist in the Renaissance, asked why he was leaving Italy to go to Asia Minor or Greece, responded, "I go to wake the dead." Munro not only waked the dead; he alerted the living by taking us with him on the crusade. As the term neared its end, I was really filled with a sort of excitement. Would we conquer Jerusalem or would we not? We were each expected to take on some small research project of our own; and I wrote a paper on the treatment of the First Crusade by one of the medieval chroniclers (at this distance in time I don't remember who he was), by Torquato Tasso in *Jerusalem Delivered*, and by Edward Gibbon in *Decline and Fall*. I remember toiling over this assignment as I had never toiled over a piece of writing before, but I was rewarded by the approbation of the master and the grade of A. The fusion of literary analysis and historical perspective required for this essay was perhaps a portent of the lines of inquiry I have followed as a university professor.

I played the piano, rather badly, and in Madison I had small opportunity to keep alive the little skill I had acquired. I took a course in music appreciation one semester, which was naive to a degree and which illustrates how far we have come in the teaching of a major art since I was an undergraduate. The class met in the auditorium of a former church at the base of Bascom Hill. I forget who taught it. I am sure he did the best he could in view of the fact that the class consisted of students without any musical training whatsoever and was often elected by members of one or another of the university athletic teams. He had on the platform a piano, a pianola (that is, a player piano), the rudimentary phonograph of the era, a collection of records none of which lasted more than a few minutes, and at the back of the platform a screen for the showing of lantern slides. He explained the major and minor keys and their relationships and said something about harmony; he explained what a sonata was supposed to be and what a symphony; he went on to tone poems and musical romanticism; and he attempted to do something with opera. One of my most vivid memories is his presentation of "The Ride of the Walkyries," to which we were introduced by a transcription on the pianola and the simultaneous appearance on the screen of slides of the scene as produced in an opera house, alternating with replicas of paintings of the Walkyries by various European artists.

I add another name to my memories of the Wisconsin faculty. This is that of Rollo L. Lyman, professor of public speaking, who, as I had continued my amateur career as a debater or declaimer, coached me for various oratorical and debating contests. Debate was still taken seriously at the university, so much so that just after Charles R. Van Hise became president in 1903, he aroused a great deal of wrath when he took over the room hitherto assigned to the Philomathia Society and turned it into a classroom. I became prominent as a student speaker and in fact was the student orator at the commencement of June, 1914, addressing myself to the importance of poetry in modern times, a topic I was totally unfit to handle. Lyman took a great interest in me and, when I was about to graduate, urged me to follow him in the fall to the University of Chicago, where he was to join the faculty of the School of Education and edit *The School Review*. I was to be his assistant in editing the magazine—at a modest salary, but one which I could live on as a graduate student. My mother and I held some sort of consultation by mail or when I was home, and since I was finding more satisfaction in literary scholarship than I could as a newspaper man, I agreed. Rollo Lyman made no pretense to the advancement of learning, but he had a homely wit, great good sense, and broad sympathies; and he and his wife, when we had all removed to Chicago, virtually threw their modest home open to me.

Outside the classroom what I most enjoyed at Wisconsin were the meetings of The Stranglers, an informal group of faculty members and students who came together to hear one of the members read aloud from a book or present some literary effort of his own. We usually assembled at the home of O. J. or that of Ned Gardner, and our interests were sufficiently varied so that nobody quite knew what to expect at any meeting. I remember a student named A. Harcourt Mountain holding us enthralled one evening by his reading of Henry James's *The Turn of the Screw*, virtually my first introduction to that novelist. The reading was followed by a heated discussion of the purport of the tale, and I recall how late we adjourned and how shaken we were by the story. The refreshments were kept simple, and the give and take between students and faculty was always pleasant. This club got its odd name from one of our diffident associates, who stuttered. One rainy evening when the members were tardy, this chap declared indignantly that he did not like the way his associates came "strang—gn—ling" in.

I earned my way through the university by secretarial work. I became an informal aide to Professor Joseph Jastrow, a psychologist who was also chairman of the university lecture committee and whose correspondence with similar chairmen at other Big Ten universities, and with railroads, lecture bureaus, lecturers, and the heads of various departments at Wisconsin or elsewhere, was varied and rewarding. His brother, Morris Jastrow, an archaeologist at the University of Pennsylvania, was convinced that the Book of Job originated as a Greek play written by a Hellenized Jew. He turned it into an English drama, which was produced by the Wisconsin Players. Horace Kallen was Job, and I drew the role of Bildad the Shuhite. Along with my fellow counsellors I had to sit on the stage wrapped in a sort of bed sheet, looking as mournful as I could while Kallen recited the despairing cadences that made up most of his role. When it came my turn, I assured him with great calm that God would bring avenging justice down on the heads of tyrants and hypocrites. As there was no action in the drama but only speeches, I never felt it to be a theatrical success.

Professor Jastrow was a friendly man and tolerant of my imperfections as a secretary, but he kept our relations on a strictly business basis. Not so my other standard patron, Professor Thomas H. Dickinson, head of the local group of the Wisconsin Players, who carried on a miscellaneous correspondence with all sorts of people and saw to it that the Players carried their offerings on occasion to other towns and cities. This was in accord with the "Wisconsin idea"—the university in the service of the people. Besides teaching and directing the players, Dickinson was at this time getting together the material for his influential anthology *Chief Contemporary Dramatists* (First Series), published in 1915. This involved correspondence with dramatists, stage directors, actors, and publishing houses both here and abroad, and introduced his student secretary to the complexities of copyright, permissions, translation rights, and so on. A second volume came out in 1921, and a third in 1930. The third included my own translation of Sam Benelli's *The Love of the Three Kings* (*L'Amore dei Tre Re*), which I was to make at the University of Texas, where I had the help of Alfred E. Trombly, E. J. Villavaso, and Benjamin F. Woodbridge in getting over some of the more difficult passages in Benelli's rhetorical verse.

The world of ancient Hellas was divided between the Greeks and the barbarians, and campus life at the University of Wisconsin was similarly split in two. The Greeks were the fraternity crowd and the sorority girls; and the barbarians were the democrats. I was one of the barbarians, though in my senior year I was asked to join a fraternity, I forget which one, on the ground that the brethren needed a student who could lift their scholastic level and so preserve their Wisconsin charter. I refused. I couldn't see what good the fraternity would do me or what good I could do the chapter; and also, being a Progressive of the La Follette persuasion, I refused from conscientious political motives. The fraternities and sororities seemed to us democrats to have altogether too strong a hold on elective offices in the student government, on the staff of the *Daily Cardinal* (the student newspaper), in the honor societies, and in other centers of power in our miniature society. I do not know where the sympathies of President Van Hise and Dean E. A. Birge lay in this important problem, though I suspect they were divided, since the fraternities and sororities, if they were in a sense antidemocratic, took responsibility for board and lodging for a notable fraction of the student population off the shoulders of the university. The administration and the faculty, however, kept out of the rumpus and let us fight our political battles in our own way. The issues may now seem trivial, but they introduced us to the politics of power. At any rate I was elected to Iron Cross, the secret honor society in my day, just before I was graduated.

One curious central problem seldom surfaced. By tradition men who were Greeks chose their female friends from the sorority sisters, whereas we democrats got our girls from among the occupants of the women's dormitories or of the lodging houses. This created certain embarrassments which even the building of the Wisconsin Student Union could not quite eradicate. A fraternity man could take his girl at permissible hours to the frat house for dinner or a dance or a conversation or study help or minor lovemaking, provided he took her "home" before curfew. The undergraduate who was a barbarian—i.e., not a Greek— had nowhere to go except to a few rooms in the Union Building or an occasional parlor in a rooming house. In consequence, as night stole over the lawn and buildings and the lake shore with its paths and the lake with its canoes, if it were not too cold, an observer might discover pairs of shadows under trees or in protecting doorways or in boats on the lake.

In my day "going steady" was known as "two's-ing," and two's-ing was a favorite outdoor sport except in freezing weather. A dreadful rumor would ever and again sweep through rural Wisconsin to the effect that twenty or thirty illegitimate babies had been born to Wisconsin coeds during the last academic year; but as this story seemed always to be revived just before the legislature took up an appropriation bill, this legend, together with the charge that the institution was teaching atheism, or anarchism, or socialism, or something else dreadful, did not seem to have much basis in fact. Perhaps my generation of undergraduates was less sexually charged than the current crop is supposed to be. Certainly the sexual mores of my time were not those of the present.

My own sexual adventures during these years were, I think, modest. On his deathbed my father had struggled to make me aware of the facts of life, but he had himself been so genteelly raised that he lacked the right vocabulary, could not call a spade a spade, and left me more puzzled than enlightened. My mother had all the inhibitions of her upbringing. I got from somewhere a copy of Dr. Sylvanus Stall's once popular volume, *What a Young Boy Ought to Know*, but I think it told me nothing I had not picked up from somewhere else, and failed to inform me of other essential matters. I found things out as most youngsters did, in the most disorderly way. I had the usual passing crushes for this, that, or the other girl, but the more permanent star of my existence during these years was a sensible, attractive, and modest Norwegian girl with whom I went through high school, the normal school, and the university. She had wonderfully blue eyes, a throaty and charming voice, a quiet intelligence, and much laughter. But no engagement was possible because her family did not approve of her marrying out of the clan, and I had no money nor any prospect of money. In those Arcadian days unions by young persons without the ceremony of matrimony were virtually unknown. I left Wisconsin for Chicago; she embarked on a teaching career in the public schools of the state and by and by rose to be something of a political power in the commonwealth. She married a lawyer of Norse ancestry.

I recall only one or two mild misadventures during my undergraduate years. One was the canonical beer shampoo which virtually all male undergraduates had to endure. The victim was lured by an invitation to a picnic at some point on the shores of Lake Mendota, went willingly enough, and at some period during the meal, had to suffer a beer shampoo; that is, a bottle or two of beer was poured, foaming, over his head while he was firmly held in a sitting or lying position. Thoroughly drenched with this liquid, he was faced, when he got back to Madison, with the necessity of ridding his scalp and his clothing of a persistent beery smell, a process that commonly took some hours.

My second incident, if it be a misadventure, promised to be more serious. I had as roommates two engineering students, one named Perkins, a product of Massachusetts, and the other named Dewey, from Colorado. The usual undergraduate grind finally got under Bob Dewey's skin one fine March day. He proposed a two- or three-day canoe trip as a refresher, and when Perkins refused, asked me to go. I was not much of a canoeist, but a monotonous round of stenography, typing, and class instruction had made me amenable to any change. I consented. We rented a canoe at the Lake Mendota Boat Club, got ourselves some cold lunches, and departed late one morning. We coasted along the shore of Lake Mendota until we reached the mouth of the little canal that connects it with Lake Monona, traversed the canal, and reached Lake Monona, to the southeast of the university. Thence by a succession of small waterways we expected to go through Lake Waubesa to the last of the four connecting lakes, Lake Kegonsa.

A mild breeze was blowing over Lake Mendota when we started out, but we paid no particular attention to it; and as we went through the little canal that brought us to Lake Monona, the trees along the canal protected us from the wind. But when we reached Monona the wind was vigorous, waves of considerable size for that small body of water were lapping the shores, and the middle of the lake was filled with whitecaps. What to do? Dewey was big, vigorous, and athletic. We resolved to brave it out and pointed our canoe straight across the middle of the lake. Bob Dewey was at the stern, and I had the bow paddle. My duty was to keep us pointed right in spite of the wind. I think I never labored so hard in my life. Occasionally the bow would veer a bit, when I could catch glimpses of the city side of Lake Monona and of spectators watching these young fools attempt the impossible. Just as a rescuing expedition seemed about to embark, we fortunately reached a mildly sheltered cove on the side of Lake Monona we were headed for. With our last ounce of strength we hauled the canoe up on the beach and fell, exhausted, on the sand. How long we lay thus I do not know. But by and by we arose, got our little craft into the water, and paddled along the quiet little stream that fed into Lake Waubesa. Again we stopped, hauled our canoe ashore, and, after the proper pioneer method, tried to sleep on the ground under the overturned canoe with our blankets under our heads. The flies and the mosquitoes troubled us all night long. We awoke, or at least ceased trying to sleep, got up, and looked around. We spied a small railroad station and made for it. Bob lay down on the boards of the platform, and I tried the hard bottom of a baggage wagon. By and by we recovered enough energy to haul the canoe to the platform and again went to sleep until the whistle of a train awaked us. Fortunately it was a local passenger train. We somehow got the canoe into the baggage car and crawled into the smoker, aching in every joint. I have never cared much for athletic exercise since those memorable thirty hours.

Chapter VI

Chicago

MY MIND DRAWS a blank when I try to recall how I went to Chicago in the autumn of 1914, how I registered, or how I happened to draw a room in Hitchcock Hall, at the time of its construction (1902) the largest and most prestigious of the university dormitories. It had rooms for ninety-three students, the university preacher, and a head resident or master, Professor David A. Robertson, who later became president of Goucher College. Hitchcock Hall is composed of five contiguous but not connecting oblong blocks four storeys high, a set of four rooms and a bathroom opening on each floor in each oblong. The only entrance to any block is on the ground floor, where the doors open on a cloister along the south or campus side of the building. One therefore tended to associate in the main with the occupants of one's particular oblong. Among the students I came to know best were Maurice Block, who had some connection with the Art Institute and later joined the staff of the Henry E. Huntington Library and Art Gallery in San Marino, California, and Leslie and Norman Parker, law students, sons of a prominent lawyer in Evanston, Illinois.

The University of Chicago is organized on the quarter system, an inheritance from its first president, William Rainey Harper, classes normally meeting four or five times a week for each of the three-month periods. The quarter system has its strengths and its weaknesses. It compels the student to concentrate on the substance of the course in which he enrolls, but it also allows him much less time for general reading and reflection and for human contacts during any quarter. It is true I may be prejudiced, since I had to spend a due proportion of my time in the office of *The School Review*, located in the Educational Quadrangle, some distance from my dormitory. There my duties seemed mainly to consist of reading any manuscripts submitted for publication and rejecting the impossible ones, and also supervising the book reviews written for the periodical. I discovered with a morose bewilderment that most learned writers had no style and little grasp of how to organize an essay, and also that clear and accurate English was no necessary function of academic status. Almost at the same time I discovered a queer paradox about the University of Chicago—namely, that members of the faculty whom I came to know were engaging personalities outside the classroom, yet, confronting a graduate class in some scholarly subject, they turned, or at least many of them turned, into dull individuals.

Thus, I enrolled in the course required of all candidates for higher degrees in English or comparative literature, "Introduction to Graduate Study," taught during the quarter I took it by that formidable scholar John Matthews Manly. The class was scheduled for one-thirty in the afternoon, a deadly hour in any university. Mr. Manly was apparently accustomed to lunch very well. I sat in the front row immediately before the instructor's desk, along with John Henry Hobart Lyons, later of Columbia. Once Mr. Manly had come in and seated himself, John would sniff delicately and whisper in my ear, "Burgundy!" or whatever else he detected on the instructor's breath. Manly would ever and again give a lecture that sparkled with dry wit and fascinated by its insight, but for the most part he had the air of a man conscientiously fulfilling a distasteful duty. He was always a little late. One day he was very late. He came to the classroom door, paused, looked us over with a remote, inquiring eye, asked of the universe in general: "Is this the class in Chaucer? Hell, no—it's the class in graduate methods," and left. We waited and then silently dispersed. He was not seen for two or three days. Yet, when you came to know Manly outside the classroom, you discovered his kindliness, his Southern courtesy, and his readiness to put his vast store of erudition at your disposal.

I also enrolled in a course taught by Charles R. Baskerville, who was rumored to have read every play written in Great Britain from the *Quem Quaeritis*, which stands at the wellspring of the British theater, to the beginning of the eighteenth century or beyond. He must have done so, to the destruction of coherence in his teaching. One theme would suggest another, one title remind him of another play in a remote century, one commentary recall its rebuttal by some other specialist. The result was a kind of erudite chaos, an academic anarchy filled with allusions, play titles, writers, theater bills, source materials, and learned references. About halfway through the course this became so unbearable that a group of us decided that if we were going to pass an examination, we had better set up an orderly reading list of our own devising and drill ourselves by some sort of question-and-answer game in the substance of the plays.

Again: Robert Morss Lovett taught a course in Milton, inherited, I believe, from his deceased friend and collaborator William Vaughn Moody, poet and dramatist. Outside the classroom, Lovett had a puckish humor and a charming personality; but once in the classroom, or at least in this particular classroom, he shredded Milton as if that genius were wastepaper. Philip Schuyler Allen, with whom I was later (1928) to publish *The Romanesque Lyric*, was chairman of the German department. I never heard him speak German, and any course of his was likely to turn into something else. There was a legend, probably apocryphal but pointing at truth, that one student enrolled in Allen's course in German lyric poetry had written a term paper on Henry James. Yet Phil Allen was a vast and sympathetic individual, a Rabelaisian, a beer drinker, a friendly giant who went out of his way to help the undeserving and who aided me in a most unexpected fashion.

There were, of course, exceptions—for example, William A. Nitze, whose teaching of the literature of the French neoclassical period exemplified French clarity and the *esprit gaulois*, and Ernest Hatch Wilkins, later president of Oberlin, whose face duplicated the features of his beloved Dante and who analyzed the literature of the Italian Renaissance with a clarity and a precision reminiscent of the organization of the *Divine Comedy*. I suspect, though I do not know, that the curiously flat graduate instruction I received was the product of three forces: the quarter system, which compressed everything; the distinction the university maintained between graduate and undergraduate instruction; and the austere belief, coming down from Harper's time, that the essence of superior scholarship was impersonality and objectivity. Because graduate students are usually unhappy, I may be wrong.

I gained my best instruction from these same men outside the classroom. Since in my capacity as editorial assistant to *The School Review* I was, however remotely, at least on the fringe of the faculty, or perhaps out of sheer good luck, I came to enjoy an extracurricular friendship with many of my instructors. This did me a world of good. I have earlier hinted that their rich and happy existence off the campus, or so it seemed to me, made me realize, however imperfectly, that many of them represented the Renaissance quality of humanism. They led, or seemed to lead, exuberant lives. They seemed to gloss in the best sense the distich attributed to Luther:

Wer liebt nicht Weibe, Wein, Gesang,
Er bleibt ein Narr sein Leben lang,

and the fullness of their existences gleamed the more attractively against the cloud of war. For the guns of August brought death into the world and all our woe a month or so before I entered the University of Chicago. I can remember a week in the summer of 1914 in La Crosse when I bicycled from home each day to the office of the *La Crosse Tribune* to read on its bulletin board the name of another country that had declared war. In the remoteness of the Middle West this ghastly conflict then seemed to be nothing more than a human chess game, for our notions of battle were strictly those of Rudyard Kipling and Theodore Roosevelt. But were we alone in our error?

I was also educated by the city of Chicago. It is often forgotten that during any year from 1893, when the World's Columbian Exposition opened, to 1929, the year of the Wall Street crash, Chicago was about to become the cultural center of the United States according to all regional theorizing. And Chicago so far substantiated theory that it drew to itself until World War I or later an extraordinary variety of talent from the Middle West and the South, a process described in such novels as Hamlin Garland's *Rose of Dutcher's Coolly* and Theodore Dreiser's *Sister Carrie*. New York was far away; Chicago was near at hand and bursting with opportunity in business, in philosophy, in publishing, in education, in the arts. My two years there as a graduate student were a revelation to me of how rich life had been made by modern culture.

I went to the Art Institute and saw Impressionist and Post-Impressionist paintings. I attended concerts by the Chicago Symphony Orchestra, then conducted by Frederick Stock, who—as Guy Maier, the pianist, once told me—had the ear of God himself. I heard the entire *Ring* from the second gallery of the Chicago Auditorium, as well as other notable operas mounted by the excellent Chicago Grand Opera Company. I sat in Maurice Brown's Little Theater in the Fine Arts Building on Michigan Avenue to witness his remarkable production of *The Trojan Women*, the first Greek play I had ever seen. I went to the Cort Theater, which specialized in farces, such as *It Pays to Advertise*. I wrote my first professional book review for *The Dial*, which began publication in Chicago in the 1880s and lingered there until 1918. My interest in the theater was strengthened by Chicago's Drama League and by its publication, *The Drama Magazine*. I was made conscious of the movements in modern verse by Harriet Monroe's *Poetry: A Magazine of Verse*, printed and edited in Chicago from 1912 onward. I visited a sculptor's studio for the first time when I met Lorado Taft, the creator of the *Fountain of the Great Lakes* near the Art Institute and of *The Solitude of the Soul*, housed within that amazing building. I ate in (to me) strange and exotic restaurants when they were not too expensive— Greek, Italian, German, French. I met all sorts and conditions of students, despite the curious constraint I have noted resulting from the architecture of Hitchcock Hall. I went to the Indiana Dunes, and I rode on the Chicago and North Shore interurban trolley. And to my intense astonishment I had my first book published in Chicago, virtually without my knowing it. The story is incredible.

Dating back to my school days in Wisconsin, I had been attracted by the bittersweet poetry of Heinrich Heine, particularly by his expert use of line and by the way he practiced *Stimmungsbrechung*, that is, the abrupt breaking off of a passage of lyricality or any other serious mood through a calculated descent into mockery, satire, or realism. At the University of Chicago I was a candidate for a master's degree, which required the writing of a master's thesis, supposed to exhibit one's acquirement of at least the rudiments of scholarly methods. I had been tinkering with a translation of Heine's two poetic cycles, *Die Nordsee*, trying (and sometimes succeeding) for the identical line lengths, rhythmic cadences, and verbal colorings of the original. I was, moreover, in 1914–15 still in a transitional stage between my curiosity about the history of cultures and my impulse to become a writer, an impulse that had some justification since I was asked to write an ode for the celebration of the twenty-fifth anniversary of the founding of the university. I did so—an endless thing, too long to be recited, so that the university printed it as a pamphlet distributed to the seats of the audience participating in the celebration. Free verse was in 1915 an "advanced" poetical form, and Heine's poems were an early and beautiful instance of the variety and vividness possible in any such prosody. It seemed to me also that an accurate and sympathetic translation of a German masterpiece into English verse—and Phil Allen and Paul H. Phillipson encouraged me to think that my version had these qualities—would manifest both scholarly attainment and aesthetic interest. I submitted the idea to my faculty advisers.

Translation, it appeared, however excellent, did not imply scholarship. Numerous conferences, I am told, were held regarding this extraordinary proposal among the representative of the English department, a representative of the German department, Tom Peete Cross of the comparative literature faculty, and a representative of the graduate dean's office; and it was finally agreed that a candidate for the M.A. who knew German so well he could "do" Heine into equivalent English meters might qualify, provided he also exhibited some more conventional sign of scholarly worth. I learned of this stipulation from Tom Peete Cross, who suggested I write a critical introduction to my translation. I remembered my early admiration for Swinburne's "By the North Sea," magnificent if monotonous. I reread Swinburne, revived my enthusiasm, discovered that both Heine and Swinburne dealt not only with the North Sea but with cosmological speculation, managed to produce some forty pages of critical prose on this topic, and was duly admitted to candidacy for the degree, which I received in 1915.

In 1916 Phil Allen, acting on his own, obtained a copy of my thesis and generously took it to Paul Carus, the director of the Open Court Publishing Company in Chicago, to whom he submitted it for publication. I was occupied with other interests, nor did I know anything about the matter, until one day, on arriving in my dormitory room, I found a huge package. On opening it I found the entire text of my thesis, together with the German original of the poems, in galley proofs, and a request that I return the whole thing, read and corrected, within ten days. I was dazzled, dropped everything else to read the proofs, and sent them back, being so innocent that it never occurred to me to ask for a contract or for royalties. Some months went by. Again a large package arrived, containing twenty-four copies of *Heine's Poem "The North Sea"* translated by Howard Mumford Jones, bound in blue cloth and exhibiting on the cover a circular design involving seagulls and a breaking wave. The work, to my astonishment, is still in print, for I recently received copies of a paperback edition brought out in 1973 by the same publisher, now removed to La Salle, Illinois. Somebody on the staff of that company wrote me at the same time to say that the office could not find a copy of the contract for this book, and would I please send them a duplicate? I couldn't. There never was a contract. But I find with pleasure that I dedicated the volume to O. J. Campbell and Ned Gardner.

I received my master's degree in June, 1915. The university kept to the ancient custom of an oral examination of candidates for any higher degree, and the rule then was that the candidate be seated alone in a classroom with the door shut while a faculty committee one by one revolved among the classrooms. All I remember of my examination was that Robert Morss Lovett came in, his chin quivering as it often did, sat down, looked at me for a long minute, then asked: "What was Milton's theory of church government?" "Presbyterian," I answered promptly. We sat and looked at each other for a minute or two more; then he abruptly arose, nodded, and walked out. I later learned that Lovett despised all oral examinations as futile. He and Phil Allen once served together on a committee appointed to examine a candidate for the doctor's degree in comparative literature. Lovett sat for a time, then scribbled a note to Allen and left the room. At the end of the questioning the candidate was excused in order that the committee might deliberate *in camera*. The members naturally thought that Lovett had left a written vote for Allen to record. What he had written, however, had nothing to do with the candidate. The note read: "Phil, you and I are the best-looking men in the room."

In 1915 I still could not determine what I wanted to do. Lyman was willing for me to continue on *The School Review*, but it was important for me to launch out on something more permanent. Fortunately James Weber Linn of the English department, who was in charge of the required freshman writing course, got me appointed to the staff of instructors on whom he rode herd, and I returned to Hitchcock Hall in the autumn of 1915.

Academic life, however, was now affected by serious national and international issues, especially by the so-called Preparedness Campaign that dominated a good deal of public discussion before our entry into World War I. The argument was that the country's defense had been allowed to fall into weakness. Accordingly, men of the temperament of Newton D. Baker and Teddy Roosevelt launched a national propaganda movement, or rather, movements. One thesis was a demand that the president and the Congress build up the navy and the army. Another was a demand for the creation of imitation military camps—such as that at Plattsburg, New York—and even an imitation navy. Some state legislatures voted money for short courses in military instruction, some colleges and universities established ROTC programs, and a few institutions won special *réclame* for imitating, as far as they could, West Point or Annapolis. The third idea was through meetings, publication, and parades to awaken the country to its lack of preparation for a modern war.

The preparedness movement naturally affected us in Hitchcock Hall. Maurice Block was an ardent dove. The Parker boys were as ardent in their Republican activism. Sincerely believing that we ought to be ready to fight for our country if the need arose (and the threat of war grew bigger month by month), they became members of the First Illinois Cavalry of the state militia, later known as the National Guard. As Maurice had to spend a good deal of his time at the Art Institute, and as the study of law and military drill cut deeply into any free hours the Parkers had, I found myself more and more isolated in Hitchcock Hall.

There were probably more doves than hawks on my stairwell, but although I could see the dovish point of view, I felt increasingly uneasy. Having grown up in Wisconsin in the days of Bob La Follette, who preached service to the state, even though he was against our involvement in the War, I was caught up in the infection of preparedness and battered by the appeals of the Parkers that I join them in the cavalry. I finally did so. The experience made no sense, but I would not have missed it.

As a cavalryman I was no worse than Samuel Taylor Coleridge, who, it will be recalled, enlisted in a cavalry unit of the British army under the appropriate name of Silas T. Comberbacke. But the regiment needed recruits and would have accepted anybody. The First Illinois Cavalry had its barracks on the Near North Side between Schiller and Goethe streets (the latter thoroughfare being variously announced by streetcar conductors as Gerty Street, Go-thee Street, and Go-eethy Street). I asked to be in Troop M, the unit to which the Parkers belonged. The colonel was Milton J. Forman, who continued to command the regiment when, after our declaration of war, it was turned into an artillery unit, since the colorful but futile appearance of German hussars on the plains of France proved conclusively that the cavalry was useless in modern combat. I did not last long. I assisted (in the French sense) in keeping Pancho Villa's Mexican raiders out of Springfield, Illinois; but by the time our regiment moved from the Springfield fairgrounds to Texas and the Mexican border, I had been discharged for bad eyesight, which I had had all along.

Troop M of the First Illinois Cavalry was one of the most curious organizations I have ever joined. It was composed of a few students, principally graduate students, members of blue-blood families from the North Shore, and a picturesque variety of men from the riffraff of Chicago. One of my fellow patriots recognized only the number eleven and had to be put into the eleventh place of a line for any count-off. Theoretically the state of Illinois furnished our chargers, but it is one thing to have a cavalry regiment and another thing to maintain mounts for 800 men. The state compromised; and since only two troops drilled on any weeknight, the state maintained a stable for two troops only. The horses had nothing military to do all day long; accordingly some financial genius saw to it that they went out during the daytime for the pleasure-riding of civilians. The consequence was that when the troops drilled at night in Jackson Park, no command requiring us to gallop ever sufficed to get the whole mass into rapid motion. The horses were too tired.

We rode as a regiment only on such special occasions as the Fourth of July or the preparedness parade. For that occasion those brave soldiers not fortunate enough to draw a regimental horse were supposed to hire their own steeds at the Chicago stockyards. One rented such a horse as he could get; in our troop, as I remember, the tallest private seemed always to ride the littlest horse. Beyond directing an admirable stream of profanity against the horse, the rider, the state of Illinois, and military stupidity in general, there was nothing the top sergeant could do to improve this misfit except to try to conceal the incongruous horse and rider in the middle of the troop as we rode up or down Michigan Avenue. But this concealment seldom succeeded, and the cavalryman appeared to be walking on the avenue with a horse walking under him.

We were, I think, an interesting example of the melting-pot process at work. The captain of Troop M was a quiet, gentlemanly man, something of a scholar, who read Latin. One of the lieutenants could have passed for an illiterate Hercules. The captain, unfortunately for me, overheard me using some Latin expression when we were drilling (why I used it I do not know), called me in, cross-examined me, found out I could use a typewriter, and made me troop clerk. This was not bad on a week-to-week basis, for all I had to do was a perfunctory checking of the roll, but when the regiment was sent to Springfield and mustered out of the service of the state of Illinois into the service of the United States, the job meant that I literally typed for twenty hours making out duplicate muster sheets and checking every polysyllabic Polish or Lithuanian name about three times. I was also supposed to discover the residential address of every trooper; and if their paychecks did not arrive on time, it was not the fault of my honest endeavor. Then I was also to make out certificates of honorable discharge for soldiers like myself, whose substandard eyesight, weight, height, or other defect led the national government to reject them. I went back by train to Chicago and Hitchcock Hall, and struggled with the War Department, the state of Illinois, and the United States Post Office to get the few dollars due me for my patriotic endeavors. The state of Illinois still owes me carfare from Springfield to Chicago.

I ought to add as a coda to this account that the Illinois cavalryman was supposed to be armed with a rifle and a sabre. I do not remember that we ever carried our rifles while we drilled in Jackson Park, but we invariably buckled on our sabres before we trotted out to drill. The sabre seemed to me the most useless weapon ever invented by man, although I suppose the wild horsemen of the Russian steppes or the Arabian deserts must have wielded a curved sword with a skill not known in the United

States. When we first set out for drill, the sabre reposed quietly in its scabbard on our left thighs; but when the command "Draw-aw-aw sabres" came to our ears, we grasped the reins firmly in our left hands, reached across ourselves, and withdrew the shining blade from its sheath. This was supposed to be done with a great, sweeping motion brought to an end by a smart stopping of the sword at the right shoulder blade, the tip of the weapon pointing to the sky. The difficulty in our troop, and I suppose in other troops likewise, was that our chargers did not like this swishing of something over their heads, and as we did not wish to cut into their ears, the beautiful curve required by the regulations was seldom achieved. Even worse was the command to sheathe the wretched weapon while the horse was in motion. You were supposed to reverse the action of drawing the sabre, but getting the blade back into the minute opening of the scabbard while the horse was trotting or walking my comrades and I found impossible to achieve. No amount of instruction by the top sergeant, no amount of cursing, no amount of reproof, could teach the gallant members of Troop M to recover their weapons with either grace or unanimity.

In the late spring of my second year as a graduate student, I was invited to a wedding at Evanston on the North Shore. At the wedding brunch, or whatever it was, I drank more champagne than I had ever drunk before (it was not my usual tipple), and departed in midafternoon, feeling agreeably hazy, for Chicago. After a long while, late in the afternoon I found myself back in my room at Hitchcock Hall, confronting three or four urgent messages to the effect that Professor Lovett wanted to see me at once in his office. Vaguely troubled by the thought that some calamity had occurred, I dowsed my head in cold water, changed my clothes, endeavored to look as self-possessed as might be, and went to Lovett's somewhat dingy cubbyhole in the depths of Cobb Hall, oldest, I think, of the university buildings. I knocked, I was told to enter, and I found Lovett in the company of a man whom I had never seen before, but who was obviously a Southerner if his voice and manner were any test. I was, though I did not know it, at another turning point in my life.

The voice belonged to a middle-aged gentleman of energetic but benevolent aspect. He had a large head, quite bald, a firm and somewhat portly body, an equally firm grip of the hand, and spectacles over eyes that twinkled as Mr. Pickwick's are supposed to have done. He also had a slightly impatient air, for he had, it was clear, been waiting a longer time than he had wanted to for my arrival. His impatience, though evident, was restrained by his courtesy. His voice was pleasant and emphatic. Lovett introduced him to me as Dr. William James Battle, acting president of the University of Texas, and then seated himself in his chair in the character of an interested but slightly amused spectator. I could make nothing of his attitude.

Dr. Battle came to the point at once. "Dr. Lovett," he said, "thought you might be interested in a position we have at the University of Texas." Texas up to this moment was a thousand miles from my thought. I was speechless, but fortunately I did not have to say anything. Dr. Battle's unconquerable energy carried him on. I learned that the president of the university had recently resigned and that he, Dr. Battle, was acting as a *locum tenens* until the regents could find a successor to Sidney Mezes. (I did not know it, but President Mezes had resigned two years earlier to become president of the College of the City of New York, and the regents had still been unable to find his successor.) The university had an English department, and up to a few years back, Stark Young had been a member of the department. But Mr. Young had not been comfortable in the English department and had threatened to resign. President Mezes, however, had felt that Mr. Young would be a loss to the university, and understanding Mr. Young's dissatisfaction—Dr. Battle hesitated a little over this term—with the English department, he had created a special department for Mr. Young, the Department of General Literature, with Mr. Young as its chairman. (I found out later that he was not only the chairman; he was the entire department.) Now the wish to go to New York had again overcome Mr. Young, and he had really resigned, forcing the acting president to look about for somebody to replace him. Mr. Young, it appeared, had been "creative," and Dr. Battle wanted somebody who was "creative" for the post. Dr. Battle had been impressed by Dr. Lovett's description of my talents, and he was prepared to offer me a position. What was "general literature"? Well, it was—it was, so to speak, well, it was literature in a general sense, it was not literature confined to any single—er—department.

I fear I continued to be speechless, for Dr. Battle went on. He could not, of course, offer me a post or a salary comparable to that Mr. Young had held, but he was prepared to make me Adjunct Professor of English and General Literature at a salary of $1,800 a year. I spoke, I think, for the first time to inquire what sort of post an adjunct professorship might be. Dr. Battle informed me that this term had been invented at the University of Virginia and transferred to the University of Texas some years earlier by scholars who had gone from Charlottesville to Austin, and that the more usual term was "assistant professor." I then was moved to ask why, if Mr. Young had had a department all by himself, I was to be made an adjunct professor of English and general literature. It appeared that Dr. Battle regretted the split-off of general literature from English, though he was apparently not inclined to extinguish general literature, and that if I took the post I would be in a sort of olive-branch position. He then hoped I was interested.

Eighteen hundred dollars in 1916 looked as big as eighteen thousand dollars would nowadays, and I was also aware that a suckling teacher was commonly appointed to an instructorship, not to an assistant professorship, however disguised at Mr. Jefferson's university. I looked at Lovett. His face was impassive. I then signified my acceptance of the post. Dr. Battle uttered a loud, emphatic "Good!", shook my hand heartily, and said he would welcome me to the university. I then made the gaffe of a lifetime. "Where is the University of Texas?" I said in my bewilderment. Lovett looked at me, Dr. Battle looked at me, smiled and said gently, "It's at Austin, the capital of the state." I blushed, I thanked him, I thanked Robert Morss Lovett, and I withdrew. I hope I do not misrepresent Dr. Battle in this shorthand report of our conversation, my first with a representative of the Southern way of life. If I do, I apologize to his genial shade. But it was at this short notice that I unwittingly embarked on my twelve-year career as a damyankee in the former Confederate states. I say "twelve years" although I did not go to the University of Michigan until 1930. But I was exiled for two years of this period—two years I spent at the State University of Montana because of the hostility of Governor James E. Ferguson to the University of Texas— as will presently appear. I also add as a sort of postscript that Dr. Battle did not deceive me in anything he said, but he had not expatiated on the qualities of the English department which created so lasting a dissatisfaction in the bosom of Stark Young. Probably he couldn't. This I was to find out for myself.

BOOK THREE

ON THE ACADEMIC FRONTIER

Chapter VII

Do You Want
to Be a Texan?

I WAS TO GO to Texas in the autumn of 1916, and the prospect seemed to me like an excursion into a foreign land. Hitherto my farthest trip south had been to Springfield, Illinois, and my notions of the Lone Star State, aside from the pleasantness of the genial Dr. Battle, were gleaned principally from the juvenile novels of Edward S. Ellis. The La Crosse Public Library, naturally, did not specialize in the literature of the Southwest. Here, then, was a real turning point, since not merely was I going farther away from home than I had ever gone before but I was also undertaking to teach courses I was ill prepared for, in an institution I knew nothing about, and accepting responsibility for subject matter laid out by a man I had never seen. The purpose of the Department of General Literature was as foreign to me as the aim of the Buddhist scriptures. I found that Stark Young's mainstay had been a yearlong study of the development of tragedy from its beginnings in ancient Greece, and this he seems to have alternated with a parallel course in comedy. He wrote plays himself, and it will be recalled that in later years he became a leading theater critic in New York.

I scrapped the comedy course for two very good reasons: I could not possibly get up the entire dramatic history of the Western world in three and a half months, and I discovered that a perpetual diet of plays the jokes in which had to be explained in learned footnotes was more tedious than funny. Then, there was the awkward business of my odd relation to the English department. This, however, soon simplified itself: all I had to do was to teach one section of Freshman English, a job that the paternal tutelage of James Weber Linn at Chicago had prepared me for. But I was supposed to teach three courses. What was the third to be?

As I had recently been reading in Ibsen and Schopenhauer, it seemed to me that the smart thing to do was to offer instruction in the literature of pessimism, among other reasons being the fact that in the summer and autumn of 1916 pessimism was very much in the air. This was the era of the failure of the British at Gallipoli, the slaughter of British and Canadian forces at Passchendaele, and the nine indecisive battles of the Isonzo as the Austrians and the Italians bloodily wavered back and forth in the Trentino. It was likewise the year when the spineless Kerensky government in Russia was tottering toward its fall. So far as my specialty was concerned, it was also the era when the death of Henry James ended one great line of American literary development, and the demise, in 1914, of James Whitcomb Riley had marked an end to another—that of cheerfulness, homely things, a general belief in progress, and the dogma that however wicked Europe might be, the United States was the country of peace, plenty, and prosperity. Unfortunately, in the summer and autumn of 1916 there was nothing tranquil along the Mexican border, and though Woodrow Wilson was to be reelected in November principally because of the emotional appeal of "He kept us out of war," his high-toned attempts to mediate hostilities in Europe got nowhere at all. The next year, in February, he was compelled to sever diplomatic relations with Germany; and in March, following the failure of his appeal to Congress to allow American merchant vessels to be armed, he was sourly to say that "a little group of wilful men," senators all, "have rendered the great government of the United States helpless and contemptible." Such was the stormy atmosphere wherein my adult teaching career was launched. These terrible months seemed an appropriate time to analyze pessimism. But the legislature of Texas was to think otherwise.

Civilization was breaking up, but my immediate problems were two, one of them practical, the other theoretical. The practical one was how in God's name, with no more resources than those of the La Crosse libraries at my command, I was to master at least the rudiments of the history of the stage in preparation for teaching at a university I had never seen. In my work at Madison and Chicago I had learned something now and again about drama in English, but I knew nothing about the plays of the Greeks and the Romans. I got hold of an invaluable manual by A. E. Haigh, *The Attic Theatre*, read it by day, and studied it by night. I also hunted down some standard translations of Aeschylus, Sophocles, and Euripides, so far as I could find any, and I had to consider what translations were available in cheap editions for classroom use. I reduced the Roman theater to two meetings of my course, one on the theater itself, the other on that dullest of all tragic writers, Seneca; and I planned to move into the medieval world after "doing" Seneca as quickly as possible. At Chicago I had performed in medieval mystery and morality plays.

I remember that in the case of Aeschylus I had to use a dreadful translation by a Scotch scholar, John Stuart Blackie, principally because it was available in Everyman's Library, the volumes in which were cheaper than they are now. I still have my copy. The reader can judge of the quality of Blackie's verse when I cite the concluding lines of the first strophe of the chorus in the *Agamemnon:*

> Sing woe and well-a-day! But still
> May the good omens shame the ill.

I took on the translations of Sophocles by Sir George Young, which, if not inspired, are at least not thus banausic; and of course—this was fifty years ago—I planned to use some of Gilbert Murray's versions of Euripides. These I can scarcely read today, but in 1916–17 they were the latest thing in turning that dramatist into a smart anticipation of George Bernard Shaw.

While I labored at these necessary tasks, another and profounder problem intruded upon me from time to time. I had earned two academic degrees. I was the product of three institutions of higher learning in the Middle West. I had done some writing—journalism, verses, plays of a sort, prose narratives, criticism—and I was also, as I have hinted, steeped in the theory of regionalism. Amidst the clash of nations and the fall of empires I had now, or so it seemed to me, extended the original meaning of regionalism to include the national letters and, so far as I understood such things, the national art, the national music, and the national history as well. Why, then, had nothing in my academic preparation outside the exiguous course in American literature taught by Norman Foerster prepared me to expound the meaning of American culture to a world at war, or even, for that matter, to a world at peace? And why had my predecessor as the chairman of the Department of General Literature, himself a writer in the American vein, done little or nothing in his curriculum to expound either the origins, the history, or the governing principles of the arts in America? American literature had not been ignored either in La Crosse or Madison or Chicago and was, I soon discovered, taught at Austin by a scholar like Killis Campbell, who knew all there was to know about Edgar Allan Poe, and a teacher like Leonidas Warren Payne, Jr., who had written a textbook on the subject and who, as the *Letters of Stark Young* (1976) have since revealed, continued to keep in touch with that rebellious spirit long after Young had left Texas. Yet in these four schools and, as I was to discover, in the country generally, American literature remained what I called it in an address of 1935, "The Orphan Child of the Curriculum."* "The significant fact about American literature," I said at that time, "is not whether its three centuries outweigh the ten centuries of British literature, with Chaucer, Shakespeare, and Milton thrown in; the significant fact is that it is an important literature and that it is American." "Why," I asked, "should it be thought that disentangling the political allegory of *The Faerie Queene* is an important critical problem, whereas disentangling the political allegory of the *Knickerbocker's History of New York* is not?" I was not saying that the artistic merits of the one work were on a level with the artistic merits of the other—merely that the relevance of the problem set in the one case was remote, but its relevance in the other case immediate.

It was some years before I worked out what seemed to me a philosophic answer to this question; meanwhile here was I getting up the dramatic history of a people infinitely more remote in time than Edmund Spenser, and puzzled to know why I seemed to have accepted a position in which all the literary world was my province except American writing. As a partial professor of English I could not intrude upon courses taught by elder colleagues like Campbell and Payne, but as a more than partial professor of general literature I could encroach upon the province of virtually anybody else.

As the date neared when I was to go to Texas, my mother was trying to reconcile herself to my probable death by pistol shot somewhere in the western wilds, a barbaric and distant country, desolate and arid, growing only cactus plants and mesquite, and populated by gun-toting cowboys, treacherous Mexicans, savage Indians, and desperate outlaws. In vain I tried to reassure her by saying that Dr. Battle did not wear warpaint nor have spurs on his boots and seemed to me a thoroughly civilized human being. I assured her that the catalogue of the University of Texas, which I opened before her eyes, indicated a high level of intellect. I also showed her a gracious letter from Professor James Finch Royster of the Department of English, welcoming me to Austin and asking where and how I would arrive so that he could meet me and take me to his home. But she was like Rachel weeping for her children and would not be comforted.

My initial journey to Austin was during the golden afternoon of American railroading, that magnificent system of transportation now in

---

* Published in *The English Journal* (College Edition) 25 (May, 1936): 376–88.

rust, bankruptcy, and ruin. In September, 1916, I boarded a Burlington train at La Crosse and rode most of the day down the Mississippi to St. Louis, where I descended at Union Station, that majestic structure I have always esteemed as one of the masterpieces of the national architecture, which was in the days of its glory filled with trains, passengers, baggage trucks, porters, brakemen, firemen, newsvendors, lights, enormous confusion, and general happiness. I searched along the innumerable tracks until I found a sign indicating that the magnificent steel serpent behind the sign was the Sunshine Special, the crack train of the International and Great Northern Railroad, alas, long since vanished into memory. There it was, a giant metal snake in ordered segments, its head a panting locomotive longing to be gone. It was a splendid train—mail cars, baggage cars, day coaches, a long succession of Pullmans, a dining car through whose windows one saw snow-white linen, shining silver, and glittering lights, and a club car, glowing at the end of this steel monster. I found my Pullman, found my berth with the aid of a porter who had learned his manners in some ducal hall, and then, when the train slowly and easily backed out of the depot, made my way to the majestic diner, which was already filling up. A Chesterfieldian head-waiter ushered me to a neat and orderly table. I do not remember what I ordered and ate except that this was my introduction to that unique creation of the Confederate South, beaten biscuits, of which the kitchen seemed to have an inexhaustible supply. In the midst of dining I peered out of the window from time to time, but between the reflection of the table lights and the increasing speed of the train, I glimpsed only lights in stores or houses or at street crossings, or the red and green eyes of the railway switches as we slid southward.

I finished my meal, paid my check, left, I hope, a proper tip for the waiter, returned to my Pullman, and found that the porter, in my absence, had made up my berth; wherefore I walked the length of the train to find a seat in the club car, where I listened with eager ears to a variety of accents—western, midwestern, southern, and southwestern—I had never heard in one place before. These were spoken by assured and sophisticated voyagers, who chatted, smoked, and drank, all of them easy and familiar with long-distance travel. By and by, feeling both awed and weary, I went back to bed, sleeping soundly until a long stoppage of the sense of motion awakened me. The train had pulled up at Texarkana, on the border between Texas and Arkansas; and once we left the station, I got my first look at the immense commonwealth which was to be my home. I breakfasted, I lunched, I watched the endless rolling plains of central Texas disappear from my vision, I meditated on teaching; I thought about life, death, and eternity.

Then late in the afternoon, we reached Austin. I descended from all this magnificence to the soil of Texas to discover that my train had stopped at a street crossing and was blocking a wide avenue, on one side of which a small brick-red railway depot with yellow trim was being held up by four or five silent Negroes (Black had not become beautiful), their hands in their pockets, their shoulders firmly keeping the wall in place, their eyes gazing at nothing, their lips utterly sealed.

When at length the train rolled on, the Negroes, their duty over for the day, disappeared; the station still stood upright, the passengers departed; and I looked north along a rising street and saw, blocking my vision, the largest capitol building I had ever known. I was, emphatically, in Texas. The stately width of the avenue led in the right sort of proportion to the capitol grounds, though the two sides of this boulevard were, I regret to report, less impressive than they should have been. Farther away from me there were business blocks, most of them having a sandstone look and none of them of any particular individuality; and nearer the station, the street was lined with a steadily dwindling row of buildings, two or three storeys high, most of them of either gray or yellowish wood. These shops or stores had wooden awnings spanning the sidewalk in front of them, one end fastened to the building, the other to metal or wooden uprights on the curb. These reduced the blinding sun and mitigated the heat, which weighed on me like a blanket.

I looked about for any academic-seeming person who might be named Royster and found none—in fact, I found nobody. Silence seemed to have descended from the skies on the tracks, the boulevard, the platform, and the station. I sought the advice of the ticket seller, who was just closing his window; he told me to walk up the avenue three or four blocks, where I would find the Driskill Hotel, the pride of Austin, only a door or two away on a cross street. I went, only to learn that the state convention of something or other was occupying every room in that hostelry, but the clerk suggested I try the Avenue Hotel some two or three blocks farther towards the capitol. I toiled onward toward that stately edifice.

I was to find replicas of the Avenue Hotel in central and western Texas over my years there, but this was my first introduction to a structure common enough in the American Southwest. The hostelry was built of wood having a color somewhere between yellow and orange. It was two storeys high and had a flat roof. The generous entrance was wide enough for trucks, carriages, horsemen, and pedestrians, and led immediately into a central courtyard open to the sky and surrounded by railings to which horses could be—and had been—tied. Both on the ground floor and on the balcony above, all the doors opened upon this central court or on to the veranda along its periphery. With some difficulty I found the office; wrote my name in an old-fashioned hotel registry book mounted, sloping, on a central swivel; was handed an enormous door key and told that my room was on the second floor and that the "boy" would bring up my bags, such as they were. I was then left to my own devices to find the room assigned me. I went up an outside staircase and tramped from door to door, for scrubbing, the rain, or the friction of masculine shoulders had worn away a good many numbers to invisibility. At length, however, I found my proper chamber. It was spare, rather dusty, and sparsely furnished. There was a brass bed with straw ticking, a bureau slightly lame in one of its four feet, a looking glass so warped I meditated on the horrors of shaving, a couple of chairs, and two electric light bulbs dangling from the ceiling, one by the mirror and one over the bed. I had asked for room and bath. There was a bathroom with a basin, and an ancient metal tub mounted on splay feet but no stopper for the drainpipe of the tub. I turned on the water, which was at first the color of rare roast beef but presently softened to a sort of saffron hue. In those days Austin drew much of its water from the Colorado River (the Texas stream, not the river of Grand Canyon fame), which deserved its name.

A considerable time after I had asked for it, the "boy" finally brought me a rubber stopper for my bathtub, and I was half undressed for my bath when there was a knock on the door and James Finch Royster appeared, full of apologies. He and his family had been out for the day, the car had broken down, their return had been unduly delayed, and he had searched the hotels until he found me. Briskly he ordered me to dress, picked up my bags, had a word or two with the clerk, and piloted me to the curb outside, where his car and the faithful, the incomparable Negro Jim stood waiting for us. I shall come to James the professor in a minute, but I must first say something about Jim, a storybook Negro, the kind that, I fear, infuriates the "affirmative action" people today.

As a small boy on a plantation Jim had fallen off the tailboard of a cotton wagon and broken his leg, which had been so awkwardly set by a local doctor that he had a permanent limp, a defect that excluded him from a good many jobs. Somehow or other, either in North Carolina or Texas, he had attached himself to the Royster family. He had become their guide, philosopher, and friend, their factotum, shopper, weather prophet, cook, and housekeeper, their all. If the two Royster children when small had to be taken to school, Jim took them; if Mrs. Royster (Carrie Belle) was not feeling well (she was a rather delicate woman), Jim took care of the house; if there were guests, he looked after the guests; he watched the lawnmower, the sprinkling system, the plumbing, the automobile; he got the meals when necessary; and he managed the domestic economy with scrupulous care. Carrie Belle would ask him of a

Monday, "Well, Jim, how much money do we need this week?" and Jim, having gone through the refrigerator and the pantry, would promptly announce the amount; the money was given to him, and no questions were asked until the following Monday, when the formula was repeated. I have never known a more competent human being.

James Finch Royster, a graduate of Wake Forest in North Carolina and a Ph.D. from the University of Chicago, had come to Texas in 1914 from the University of North Carolina, brought to Austin for the purpose of modernizing the English department at the university. His principal interests were linguistic, but he had a wide sympathy with modern writing. There were two children, a girl and a boy; when the Royster family finally went back to North Carolina, Chauncey, the son, returned to a family tradition and became a doctor like Dr. W. I. Royster, a leading surgeon in that state. The Royster family was to become famous in North Carolina not only for its varied abilities but for the oddity of naming its offspring after states of the union. Virginia Royster was well enough, but the distinguished surgeon, who was christened Wisconsin Illinois Royster, stuck to "W. I."; whereas Vermont Royster was—and is as I write—an editorial writer for the *Wall Street Journal*, living in retirement at Chapel Hill.

The Royster household in Austin was hospitality itself. The head of the household took me over the forty-acre campus of the university and introduced me to various personages, initiated me into the Faculty Club, where I was to have meals, and then suggested that he had tentatively reserved a room for me in a house near the university managed by the relict of a Confederate army officer, who took in paying guests. As Royster's judgment had been impeccable in everything else, I accepted the proposal, and he brought me to the house in question. The room was comfortable; the hostess, though reserved, seemed courteous; the rules she laid down were sensible; and I was installed the next afternoon. It was, it appeared, the custom of my hostess (I dare not call her "landlady") to welcome each new paying guest at breakfast the morning after his arrival. I went down the next morning to join her at the table, which was set with a certain old-fashioned elegance. But when she learned I was from Michigan and Wisconsin, the conversation seemed to stiffen and even freeze. Unable to find any congenial topic, I expressed admiration for the heavy silver setting at my place. My hostess stiffened even more. "We would have had more of them," she said, "if you Yankees had not stolen our forks and spoons." I refrained from telling her that my maternal grandfather had been a Copperhead Democrat and that my paternal grandfather had never enlisted in the Federal army, nor did I press the point that since I was not born until 1892, I was scarcely responsible for larceny committed in the 1860s. I never breakfasted with her again; and as soon as I could, I found other living quarters. Such was my introduction to being a damyankee (one word in the South). Years later—in 1931, to be exact—I published in *Scribner's Magazine* an essay "On Leaving the South," in which I tried to give a balanced view of my experiences in that part of the United States, and I remember that Ellen Glasgow found it an impartial and sympathetic analysis; but I still remember (and the essay recalls) the queer shock I felt at being charged with stealing spoons.

The University of Texas is now one of the wealthiest universities in the country, its book and manuscript collections fabulous, and its architecture impressive. But the state of Texas was run in 1916, and still is, under a constitution dating from 1876. This constitution was adopted at the end of the Reconstruction period, and it contains every conceivable gadget for cross-checking the expenditure of money that political ingenuity could devise. The income for the university was (and is) principally derived from public lands originally belonging to the Republic of Texas; and in my day there, before the discovery of oil, this income was principally composed of rents for the grazing of cattle on the plains. Since the cattle lobby saw to it that these rents were never high, and since even this small income could be spent only for physical upkeep and not for salaries, actual building could be undertaken only when the state treasurer had accumulated a sum large enough to justify a new structure. In 1916, therefore, the famous forty acres looked rather desolate. There was one fine modern building, used as a library, designed by Cass Gilbert. There was a relatively modern girls' dormitory built through the generosity of Major George Washington Littlefield, an ex-Confederate, ex-cattleman, and ex-banker who lived and died in a hideous red brick house on the edge of the campus. There was a heating plant of the usual sort—a huge brick chimney attached to a sort of undistinguished yellow barn. There were a law school with high steps, an engineering building, also of brick, and a men's dormitory of rather extraordinary shape known as B Hall. But the most conspicuous building, since vanished, crowned the hill: this was "Old Main," a tall, high-shouldered brick edifice with an enormous tower, supposed to be Spanish Gothic, and to a large extent unusable. My friend Dr. Battle retained an office near the top of the tower, where he carried on an intermittent warfare with bats; and the English department was housed in a series of wooden cells along an enormous basement corridor derisively known as the "English Channel."

During the war innumerable wooden sheds were put up here and there to accommodate the ROTC and other military units, in one of which I taught Dante's *Inferno* in the heat of a Texas spring. The forty acres were bounded by churches; religious dormitories, such as Newman Hall for the Roman Catholics; Bible Institutes, which taught courses for which university credit was given; the usual campus bookstore and stationery shop; and clothing stores, pressing establishments, drugstores, soda fountains, quick-lunch places, and all the other small and frequently transient establishments that line most university campuses and justify the phrase "academic slum." There were also fraternity and sorority houses, commonly set back a block or two from the avenues bounding the campus. But the skies were an incredible blue, the sunshine put a gloss on everything, I found meals at the Faculty Club pleasant, and the library facilities were competent. The outlook seemed promising.

Chapter VIII

More Texans

MY LECTURE COURSE on the history of tragedy drew something like a hundred students, a large class in those days, all of whom were girls except for four or five men, who huddled together during class and escaped in a body at the end of each session. English was not, apparently, a subject for males. The students seemed unusually attentive, but it was not until some weeks had gone by that I discovered through an assistant that one of the reasons for attention was my midwestern accent, which, I suppose, they got used to eventually. There was no projector in the room and of course no lantern slides; and as God has not given me a gift for draftsmanship, I still wonder what curious concepts they may have imbibed from me about the theater in ancient Athens. Although Texas was run on the quarter system, the summer session being the fourth quarter, a "whole course" might occupy an entire academic year; and I therefore split my instruction into thirds. I took up classical drama and the medieval stage in the first quarter, the Renaissance and the eighteenth century in the second, and nineteenth-century and modern writers in the third.

I am not sure that I brought Aeschylus alive, although I had better success with *Oedipus Rex*, and much more with Euripides, who, even in Sir Gilbert Murray's saccharine verse, seemed more like a human being than his two heroic rivals. Seneca was a total flop. I discovered that medieval plays required so much explanation of Biblical theme and story that I began to wonder precisely how much the Bible institutes were really accomplishing. Once we got to Marlowe and Shakespeare, interest

81

picked up; and of course when we reached Oscar Wilde, Shaw, and their contemporaries, there was no lack of liveliness. There were also some American plays, but texts, I found, were then hard to come by.

The course in pessimism drew a small group of campus intellectuals and could be taught virtually as a seminar. My section of Freshman English was, I infer, representative, but it brought me one surprise. Each instructor was furnished with a class list just before the course began, and on the first day I called the roll. When I came to "Billy Hogue," I naturally asked for "Mr. Hogue." No answer. I repeated the name. Perfect silence in the room. Then I said, "Is Mr. Hogue in the class, or does anyone know where he is?" A sweet feminine voice responded, "Perhaps you mean me. I am Miss Billee Hogue." In Texas as elsewhere in the South, girls are sometimes given boys' names either out of parental disappointment at their sex or to perpetuate some name traditional in the tribe. (Family names were also sometimes used for Christian names. I still wonder what her classmates called Miss De Rugeley Pearson; and why the distinguished Virginia family whose last name is Cocke did not think their way through the ambiguities of the name when they christened a daughter Pensive.) Nowadays the newspapers are filled with laments that as a result of television and radio the reading habits of Americans have sunk to about an eighth-grade level. I did not find this to be true at Texas, but the writing was abominable and revealed then as now the frequent failure of our secondary schools to teach ordinary prose, spelling, grammar, syntax, punctuation, and vocabulary.

The faculty of arts and sciences there as elsewhere was organized into departments, but these departments were again brigaded into divisions, each division with a chairman. I belonged to the Division of English, General Literature, and Public Speaking. To the English faculty, public speaking was apparently a detestable thing, and the members of one department seldom recognized the members of the other. I found myself by default, green though I was, elected chairman of the division, since the English department thought of me as one of themselves, or at least as one-third of one of themselves; the public speaking people regarded me as neutral; and I was the entire Department of General Literature, I could not influence anything. The result was one of the queerest patterns of parliamentary behavior I have ever known. The chairman of the English department would call a meeting of the department at, say, four in the afternoon, which I dutifully attended, although whether my vote counted as one vote or a third of a vote I never found out. We discussed whatever it was we discussed, and then somebody moved to adjourn so that the division might meet. The door opened, and the Department of Public Speaking filed in. I now left my seat in the rear row, moved to the platform, occupied the chair just vacated by the chairman of the English department, called the meeting of the division to order, and asked for the minutes of the last meeting to be read. This took about one minute. I then inquired whether the chairman of the English department had anything to report; he in turn called on the secretary, and I listened to a brief account of the meeting I had just attended. I then asked the chairman of the public speaking department whether he had anything to say. He never did. Then I reported that things in the Department of General Literature were unchanged, somebody moved to adjourn, and we all filed out after a ten-minute session. I think I had then to report to the dean of the college, my letter usually running to one brief paragraph. But the proprieties had all been observed.

When I had been long enough in Austin to have made a few confidential friends, I inquired into the origin of this Gilbert-and-Sullivan farce, and I was told, with what justice I cannot say, that it dated from Sidney Mezes's time and was an effort without seeming to do so to break the iron grip of Dr. Morgan Callaway, Jr., on all literary instruction. Dr. Callaway, whether he was titular chairman or not, ran the English department. Born in Georgia in 1862 shortly after the battle of Antietam or Sharpsburg, he was the son of a Methodist minister who later became an artillery captain in the Confederate Army and, after that, a professor of English at Emory University. The mother died when the child was four, and he was sternly brought up by a deeply religious foster mother. He may have had playmates, but like Gilbert's "Precocious Baby," he must have been born old. After various teaching jobs, he acquired or inherited enough money to send him to The Johns Hopkins University, where he became the prize product of English philologists like Bright and Bloomfield and was awarded the first Ph.D. in their subject. He was called to the University of Texas in 1890; in 1898 he became a full professor; in 1920, at the age of 58, he married; and in 1925 he was more or less retired as university research lecturer. He died in 1936. The only scholarly indiscretion he ever committed, so far as I know, is that in his callow youth he published *Select Poems of Sidney Lanier* (1895), but his maturer masterpieces were *The Appositive Participle in Anglo-Saxon* (1901) and *The Infinitive in Anglo-Saxon* (1913). The latter recorded all the infinitives he could find in that venerable language, but he missed two, as James Royster later pointed out.

Dr. Callaway was diminutive, sported a yellowish moustache, seemed mildly cross-eyed, spoke in a curiously high voice with great carrying power, had no use for the post-Victorian world or anything in it, and was seldom seen without an umbrella, a briefcase, and a pair of rubbers. The definitive biography in the *Dictionary of American Biography* speaks, as it should, of his Southern courtesy. Courteous he was, but courtesy with him was a weapon, not a value, and he was notably adroit in announcing that any change proposed in a faculty meeting or some remark by a colleague antagonistic to the unbreakable conservatism of Dr. Callaway's philosophy of graduate study had wounded him deeply by implying that his (Dr. Callaway's) professional training was faulty or incomplete. The only colleague to beat him at his own game was James Royster, who, whenever Dr. Callaway announced that he was wounded, promptly arose to say that he was even more deeply wounded by Dr. Callaway's assumption that the previous speaker had had any wounding intention.

The curious power of this little wizard was incredible. I have seen a row of his colleagues, quite as erudite as he and quite as mature, sitting on wooden chairs outside his office until the Great Philologist opened his door, beckoned to one of them, and said in what he intended to be a whisper, pressing a piece of paper into the hand of the colleague, "Dr. So-and-so, would you be good enough to meet the class in Milton at eleven o'clock in Room 24?" As Dr. So-and-so had been down in the printed catalogue for some months as giving this course, the question was not even rhetorical, but according to the customs of the department the assignment was not wholly legal until the whisper and the piece of paper. Among Dr. Callaway's pet detestations were Walt Whitman, modern fiction, cowboy ballads that J. Frank Dobie had been praised at Harvard for collecting, the modern theater, and Negro spirituals and worksongs, the special pride of John Avery Lomax, in whose house I once briefly lived. Tyrant though he was, you could not get at the secret of his despotism, but you were forced to admire a man around whom the philological universe he had been taught to regard as changeless was crumbling into ruin. It will be imagined, however, that there were only a few matters in which Dr. Callaway and I saw eye to eye.

I inherited the direction of The Curtain Club, the student dramatic society founded by Stark Young. The university had no theater, and we were forced to produce our plays wherever we could, sometimes in the moldy "opera house" in downtown Austin. Sir Henry Arthur Jones was then in vogue, and I thought his problem drama *Mrs. Dane's Defence* was possible for undergraduates. It is a harmless play, the plot of which turns on the question, Has a woman with a past any future? Mrs. Dane had had a past and protected her future with great skill until the last act, when in a tremendous courtroom scene an adroit lawyer manages to reveal most of it. Rehearsals were well under way when I was suddenly called to the office of the president of the university, a new man, Dr. Robert E. Vinson, who had been transferred from the presidency of the

Austin Presbyterian Theological Seminary to that of the University of Texas in 1916. He was to become one of the principal targets of Governor Ferguson in the war against the university which shortly followed, but at this time I had never met him.

Our interview was brief, but it was pointed. "You are," he said, "the director of The Curtain Club?" I admitted that I was. "You select the plays they produce?" I answered that I was merely one of a committee to choose the plays. "Why," he said suddenly, "are you putting on a play about a prostitute?" I stared at him in astonishment. When I recovered my voice, I asked with total incredulity, "Are you referring to *Mrs. Dane's Defence*?" He was. "It is by Sir Henry Arthur Jones," I remarked, "one of the leading English playwrights of our time." "Why," he repeated, "are you training undergraduates in a play about prostitution?" "Dr. Vinson," I replied with some heat, "Mrs. Dane is not a prostitute and never was one. She is a woman who committed a fault early in life and has been struggling ever since to rehabilitate herself." "What was that fault?" he wanted to know. "She had had an irregular love affair," I answered. "What kind of fault?" he insisted. "Dr. Vinson," I said, controlling my temper with difficulty, "have you read the play?" He had not. "You are," I went on, "I believe, a minister of the gospel?" He said he was. "Have you ever heard of the forgiveness of sins?" This time he stared at me. "Then," said I, "I suggest you practice a little of it in the case of Mrs. Dane and that you do not condemn something you have not even read." I walked out of his office. The play was produced, and neither the world nor the University of Texas collapsed.

There is not space enough to speak of the dozens of unusual personalities I came to know that first year in Texas—H. Y. Benedict, dean of the College of Arts and Sciences and later president of the university, who never overcame his Southwest drawl and never tried to, and who suggested the cow country as firmly as his associate, Hanson T. Parlin, a bachelor always well turned out, suggested the cosmopolite; Paul Batcheldor, a mathematician, incarnate New England, the silentest man I ever knew; Eugene Campbell Barker, a historian who knew more about the Texas past than any other living man but whose reputation therefore was not as national as it should have been; Killis Campbell, who refuted the charge that Poe's weakness as a poet was that he "didn't know enough" by assembling in one book all the references he could find in Poe about what he read, failing, I fear, to realize that reading is not necessarily knowledge and that Poe, like Herman Melville, pretended to have mastered books he had merely looked into; James Blanton Wharey, whose academic background included colleges and universities in North

Carolina, Maryland, Tennessee, and Berlin, whose specialty was John Bunyan, and who was as fat as his friend and colleague, Robert Adger Law, was tall and thin. These last two I especially remember because, to show the students that the faculty was patriotic, we formed a faculty company that drilled regularly on the football field. Credited with vast military experience because I had been in the Illinois cavalry, I was made top sergeant, whose first business was to dress the company. If I dressed it (that is, lined it up) from the front, most of Wharey stuck out in the rear; if I dressed it from the rear, much of Wharey protruded a good many inches beyond the lank body of R. A. Law.

Then there was Charles W. Ramsdell, known in his day as the "dean of Southern history," one-time president of the Mississippi Valley Historical Association, the most genial of men. And there was Frank Burr Marsh, a Michigander, whose extensive writings on ancient history won him international renown, but whose excellent course in the history of Rome drew very few takers, so that he spent his leisure hours in reading detective stories and memorizing the names of all the presidents of all the Latin American republics, God knows why. I became a member of a shop club that met monthly for dinner at the Driskill Hotel, and at those meetings I learned the gossip of the university and listened to professional papers by scientists, economists, law professors, and others. I think Max Handman, a refugee from Rumania and an important economist, got me into this club. But these and others are, alas! mostly dead and gone, dear reader. The university has altered beyond belief, and I feel like the servant in Job: I alone am escaped to tell thee.

Members of the faculty were expected as a matter of course to serve the state by giving public addresses. One day in the middle of the year John Avery Lomax, secretary of the Texas Ex-Students (i.e., Alumni) Association, made his solid way down the English Channel, knocked at my door, came in, and inquired: "Dr. Jones, are you willing to give a high school commencement address?" (Every faculty member, whether he had a Ph.D. or not, was "Doctor.") I signified I would and inquired where and when. The school was in Mission, Texas, then a sleepy town in the Rio Grande valley, and the address was to be in June. I put the problem aside for a while in order to think about a suitable theme, and after some weeks, John Avery Lomax appeared again to ask: "You are still going to give that commencement address, aren't you?" "Yes," I replied with surprise, "Why do you ask?" "Well," he said, "Mission has a new principal, and he wanted to be sure." I reaffirmed my determination to make the speech, and set about finding a subject. Utterly ignorant of Texas high schools, I thought I might take as a text Milton's famous sentence that the primary purpose of a generous education was to prepare the student to perform justly, skillfully and magnanimously all the offices both private and public of peace and of war. After all, there was a war going on.

Airplane travel had not yet come in, and Mission, with a population of about 2,500, could be reached only by railway. On a hot June day in 1917 I took a train from Austin to San Antonio; transferred at San Antonio for a night ride to Corpus Christi; at Corpus Christi boarded yet a third train for Brownsville; and at Brownsville found I was to be carried to Mission, some sixty miles up the Rio Grande, by a single steel coach, gasoline driven. Mission had had railroad connections with the outer world only since 1907. Irrigation began in that year, and by 1930, Mission was to be in the heart of the grapefruit country, but in 1917 it had been incorporated as a town for only six years.

When I boarded the sleeping car at San Antonio, I had casually noticed a scholarly looking man who took the berth across the aisle from me; at Corpus Christi he got on the same train as I did; and we waited together to board the dinkey that ran up the Rio Grande Valley. We descended at Mission, a railway depot built in the adobe style; my fellow traveler went in the passenger entrance doorway ("For Whites Only"); and I, for some unknown reason, went around to the baggage room, which also had a door. We met squarely in front of the ticket window, which was shut. There was not a soul in sight, and the little town lay shimmering in the heat a distance from the depot. "I expected to be met," said I. "So did I," he responded, "by the high school principal." "What!" I exclaimed. My fellow sufferer was a professor of education at Rice Institute, as it then was, in Houston, and had been called to give the commencement address at Mission. So, it later appeared, had representatives from two other colleges, neither of which, fortunately, had responded. As there seemed to be nothing else to do, the heat being too great for a long walk with our suitcases, we sat down and exchanged information.

By and by, about half-past one, a car drove up; and a sweating, red-faced Texan came in, full of apologies. He had, it appeared, been called out on some sort of errand earlier in the day, felt it was inappropriate to send a subordinate to welcome the commencement speaker, and had been delayed. But he looked at us with some bewilderment. Which of us was the commencement speaker? We announced that we had each been asked. (It later appeared that he was the man who, in order to be sure of having one speaker, had applied to four institutions.) We all got into his car, and the argument began. I wished to yield to my Rice acquaintance as being the older man and, moreover, an expert in things educational. But he insisted on yielding the place to me because I had come farther.

Inspiration struck our sweaty principal. "You will *both* give commencement addresses," he announced, and could not be shaken from this resolve. The car drew up at an adobe hotel in the little plaza at about two o'clock, and we were shown to our rooms. Dinner (served at noon in that part of the world) was long over, but our host thought he could find us some cold pork and tea. The principal departed to his own dinner, after announcing that he would return for us at four in order to show us the countryside, and that commencement was at eight.

The principal returned promptly on the hour with his car, and we drove through an endlessly uninteresting growth of mesquite for some miles until we reached a square brick building, where we stopped. The principal pulled at a doorbell, a black-robed friar sleepily appeared, and we received permission to mount to the flat roof of the edifice, some sort of Catholic retreat. The principal led us to the western parapet of the roof, called our attention to a muddy flow of water at our feet, and pointed to the continuation of uninteresting mesquite growth beyond it. "This is the Rio Grande," he said, "and over there is Mexico." My companion and I gazed respectfully into a foreign land. We inspected some ruins and then went back by the same road to Mission and the hotel. My impression is that the Catholic retreat occupied the site where formerly an early mission, long since destroyed, once stood, but I do not know. We thanked our host, who was obviously doing the best he could, retreated to our rooms, bathed as well as we might, had something light to eat, and were called for again at a quarter to eight by the principal in his car. Then we drove to the hall where the ceremonies were to be held.

The hall was an unadorned shoebox, built of brick. Its interior walls had undoubtedly once been a cheerful green; but the green had faded to a hue that suggested fungi and decay, and the ceiling was crisscrossed by lines of varicolored paper rings, evidently the relics of a dance held a good while before, since fly specks on most of the rings indicated a certain antiquity. There was a boxlike vestibule where four girls were awaiting us, and at the other end of the shoebox was a stage with six steps rising to it from aisles on either side of the building. The principal's arrival immediately started action. The four girls lined up in a row, a high school band below the platform played a squeaky version of the "Triumphal March" from *Aïda*, a superintendent of schools materialized to lead the procession, the principal fell in after him, we fell in after the principal, the four girls fell in behind us, and a minister closed our small parade. The four girls were the entire graduating class except for four boys, who had been drafted into the army. On our slow way to the platform I saw that the hall was filled with sweaty humanity, a considerable fraction of it made up of nursing mothers, and that about half

88

of the audience, whatever their sex, were Mexican, or seemed to be Mexican, for the lighting of the auditorium left something to be desired. There were exactly enough willow chairs on the stage to seat most of the procession, but the central feature of the little stage was one of those square bamboo tables with a matting top, the kind you find in certain types of photographers' studios. On the table top were four small paper cylinders, each tied with a ribbon. After we had seated ourselves and the superintendent of the Hidalgo County schools had made some remarks, the principal stepped to the lectern and announced that the Reverend So-and-so would give the opening prayer.

He did. His address to the Almighty resembled a prayer described somewhere in *The Adventures of Tom Sawyer*. He begged the Lord to bless the meeting, the superintendent, the principal, the teachers, and the graduating class; and he called God's special attention to the four boys who would have been present except that they were fighting for Christ and America against the detestable Germans. He prayed for the success of the war, for the president of the United States, for Congress, for the country at large, and especially for the state of Texas, the governor, the legislature, the county, and the town. He also prayed for the commencement speakers. Fans swished, babies squalled, the audience shifted uneasily in its seats, but the prayer went on with the deadly precision of a funeral march. It did at last conclude; and the principal, in order to waste no time, announced with pride that Mission was especially fortunate this June in having *two* commencement speakers. My friend from Rice, at my pleading, rose first, and poured forth statistics enough to fill an elementary treatise on how to run a computer. He knew the exact number of teachers in Texas, the total number of scholars, the cost of the entire school system as a whole and by parts, the amount of money that was spent for chalk, erasers, blackboards, and books; he compared these statistics with those for the entire country, and he at length sat down. The audience was visibly impressed; they had not received so much concentrated information in any previous thirty minutes in all their lives. I, on the contrary, was depressed. How could my feeble speech about Milton's or Huxley's or Dewey's philosophy of education hold up its head against a volume of the United States Census Reports? I glanced around and noted an American flag posted in its proper place at the edge of the platform. I therefore threw my carefully prepared notes to the winds of heaven, and taking the flag as my text I orated. I tore the feathers out of the American eagle; I pictured Kaiser Bill as Anti-Christ; I spoke of bravery, wounds, and patriotism; I prophesied the missing half of the class would return alive and victorious; I lauded Hidalgo County and Mission for its contributions to the war effort; and I returned to my willow chair to the only applause of the evening. It was sheer demagoguery, but it worked.

When the applause subsided, somebody moved the bamboo table to the front of the stage, the minister stood behind it, the principal at one side of it, and the four girls stood up. The minister then took up one of the paper sausages, inspected the name on it to be sure it was the right diploma, handed it to the principal, who called out the name; one of the four girls stepped forward, received the diploma in her left hand and shook the principal's hand with her right, walked all around the side and back of the stage, and solemnly sat down. Each of the remaining three graduates repeated the same solo march. Then the principal applauded, the minister applauded, the man from Rice and the man from Austin applauded, the audience applauded, the four girls rose as one, and sat down, the band burst again into the "Triumphal March," and the commencement procession left the stage, this time in reverse order. The audience suckled its last baby and slowly dispersed, and my first dreadful triumph as a commencement speaker came to an end. I was later to appear, solo, in such flourishing places as Oil City, which could be reached only by a mail truck, at some town in central Texas where I had to perform in a Methodist church in the midst of the tools and trappings of a revivalist's week of saving souls, and in my riper years at various institutions north and south, east and west; but to this day nothing has ever equaled the memories of the ceremonies of 1917 at Mission, Texas.

Chapter IX

Fergusonianism

AT THE OPENING of *Huckleberry Finn* that great hero declares: "You don't know about me, without you have read a book by the name of 'The Adventures of Tom Sawyer.' . . . That book was made by Mr. Mark Twain, and he told the truth, mainly." Autobiographers try to tell the truth, mainly, but their difficulty was long ago rightly phrased when jesting Pilate said, "What is truth?" and would not stay for an answer. I was too new at the University of Texas to be more than an amused and rather bewildered observer, but the actual effects of the Ferguson War upon both my personal and professional life were far-reaching and cannot be ignored.

Before I arrived in Austin, William James Battle had quit as acting president of the university because of a conflict with the governor of the state, James E. Ferguson. Ferguson had been elected in 1914 and again in 1916 for his fateful second term. He was a high school dropout of Bell County in east central Texas, one of five children born to a Methodist preacher, farmer, and gristmill owner, who died when the boy was four. Like Pip in *Great Expectations*, the boy was, I fear, mainly brought up "by hand"; and at the age of sixteen he departed for the Pacific Coast, where he did various odd jobs, moving back to Bell County in 1896. There he worked as a farmer and studied law. Admitted to the bar in 1897, he married Miriam Amanda Wallace, known as "Ma" Ferguson, by whom he had two daughters, one of whom, named Ouida, eventually wrote a small, prejudiced, but readable little book designed to vindicate her father's memory. "Ma" Ferguson was twice elected governor (1924 and 1932) to "vindicate" her husband, though she was defeated in 1926, 1930, and 1940. The Fergusons had moved to Temple in 1900, where Jim opened a law office and where, in 1907, he was instrumental in organizing the Temple State Bank. He had never held public office of any kind when, in 1914, he announced his candidacy for Democratic nominee for the governorship. To the astonishment of the regular Democratic machine he won both the nomination and the election as "Farmer" Jim on a populist platform that included tax reforms intended to aid the tenant farmers (a tribe that constantly increased), prohibition (Jim was later found guilty of not revealing that he had borrowed some thousands of dollars from a brewery), an anti-woman suffrage plank, and—the one lasting result of his administration—improvement in rural education. He had mastered an oratorical style of marvelous demagoguery, which grew by what it fed on. He talked about the "Belshazzar revels" that a "rich crowd" was carrying on at the university, an institution that was, in his view, chiefly staffed by "butterfly chasers," "day-dreamers," "educated fools," and "two-bit thieves." A biologist at Austin had studied some rudimentary hair follicles on that hard-shell animal the armadillo, a discovery that did something important to its zoological classification as an edentate; this Jim described to his favorite audiences in the pronouncement: "My deah friends, do you know what they air doin' down thar at Austin with the hahd-earned money of you tax-payehs? They're payin' a man named *Pattison* ten thousand dollahs a yeah to prove that you can't grow wool on the back of an armadillo!" He frequently informed his auditors that the "gr-r-r-eat state of Texas" had gone "hog-wild over higheh education." The response of the crowd was uniform: "Pour it on 'em, Jim, pour it on 'em!"

William James Battle had since 1914 been generously working as acting president and had been assured that he would be made president. The governor's message of January, 1915, seemed to favor a good president and an independent board of regents as defined in the state constitution, but political pressures led the Board of Regents to pass over Battle for the presidency and to select the Reverend Robert E. Vinson in April, 1916. Ferguson, it is true, had said little about the university in his earlier addresses to the legislature and had vetoed no financial item concerning that institution; but he had been disturbed when Battle had made some necessary changes in the budget inherited from the former president, in whose place Battle was acting, and he now was furious that the regents had not consulted him when they chose Vinson.

What further causes there may have been for the Ferguson War on the university remain unclear. Austin gossip about this or that moral or financial peccadillo at the university? Charges made against the university in "a concealed packet of letters" that so far as I know has never been revealed? Political cronyism? (A charge the less unlikely when one learns that as soon as he could find or create a vacancy on the Board of Regents, Ferguson filled it with a henchman.) Whatever these further causes, antagonisms arose out of a conflict of personalities, not a clash of principles.

Ferguson soon let it be known that he thought Vinson was no proper president because (a) Ferguson had not been consulted about him; (b) Vinson's only administrative experience was at a small theological seminary in town; (c) he was an ordained minister who occasionally preached denominational sermons; and yet the institution over which he had just been called to preside was filled with luxury, fraternities, gambling, lewdness, card-playing, and Heaven knows what else. Furthermore, Ferguson charged, the business practices of the faculty were rotten with petty corruption. In the fall of 1916 the governor selected five members of the faculty for instant removal from their positions; and when President Vinson and the regents did not discharge them, the governor bluntly told the president and board:

Whenever you get the idea in your head that you will make one of these teachers out here bigger than the Governor or the legislature, it is just like a cash boy in Mr. Sanger's store telling Mr. Sanger [one of the regents] where to head in. . . . I got information that a professor of this school went down and presided at a county convention with a crowd that refused to endorse this administration. Now you have made the issue. You never criticized [Professor R. E.] Cofer [of the Law School] for going down and participating in politics in a county convention. You kept him, and you kept Will Mayes [of the School of Journalism], editor of a paper that skinned me from hell to breakfast. You have expected me to be satisfied and you believed me checkmated, but the biggest fight is on you ever had if you undertake to put this thing over.*

The special session of the legislature in 1917 voted relatively generous sums for the various state institutions, but late in May of this year the governor asked the regents to meet in his office. There, Ferguson began reading them a long message, charging various members of the faculty and of the administration with financial wrongs against the state, demanding that the "stately mansions" of the fraternities be abolished so that their less fortunate fellow students could live in less "crowded

* Ralph W. Steen, "The Ferguson War on the University of Texas," *The Southwestern Social Science Quarterly* 35 (March, 1955): 358.

boardinghouses," and declaring that the institution was made up of "fads and fancies" and "grossly mismanaged."

Texas is an enormous state, but it can on occasion be aroused. The Texas Ex-Students Association had gone to work; leading newspapers in the state had gone to work; the undergraduates had gone to work; the faculty had gone to work. A procession had been organized by the student government, and on that day in May hundreds marched in order from "Old Main" on the campus to the state capitol at the head of Congress Avenue, where the crowd flowed like a tidal wave not only around the building but also through its corridors precisely as the governor was addressing the regents in his office. He ordered out some Texas Rangers, but the Rangers, after looking at the band which headed the procession and the football team which followed, declined to do more than keep a sort of order in the capitol grounds. The only person properly to describe this demonstration was the governor himself.

As he was reading his message to the board (he recounted in his proclamation vetoing the university's appropriation) about the snobbish fraternities, the do-nothing professors, and the cost of academic education in contrast to that in the rural schools,

we heard the music of a band resounding in the corridors of the State Capitol. Upon looking out of our window we saw the student body of the State University which had formed on the University campus about a mile from the State Capitol and had marched en masse to the State Capitol behind a band and carrying banners reading: "The University's future is at stake." "We fight autocracy abroad, can we tolerate it at home?" "We are with the Board of Regents in the opposition to the Governor's unconstitutional demand," "Kaiserism is a menace abroad and likewise a menace at home." . . .

This parade marched down the walk in front of the Capitol and in about fifteen or twenty minutes returned by the same route, to the State Capitol and came directly in front of my office, where I was then conferring with the Board of Regents and in turn exhibited said banners directly in my face and within twenty feet of where I and the Board of Regents were conferring. And while said banners were being flaunted in my face, various students of the University called to me in derisive tones to read the banners. And said body of students remained in front of my office window for twenty-five minutes, and the howling and yelping were of such degree that further deliberation of myself and the Board of Regents was absolutely prevented. . . .

After said student body had left the State Capitol, the Board of Regents in my office decided to hold at once a meeting at their office at the State University to determine who was responsible for said parade. So far as I am concerned, it is immaterial who is responsible. The fact remains that the parade took place and that the banners were carried. If the young men who carried the banners did so of their own volition, the said sentiment and idea expressed on said banners were the result of the teaching and influence which they have received at the State University. If they carried them under the instruction of the faculty, then I unhesitatingly declare that the State University should be abolished, and never reopened with a faculty who would permit such facts.

On June 2, 1917, Ferguson announced his veto of the university's appropriation. But he had been a little hasty and careless. An important plank in both his campaigns for governor had been the itemization by the legislature of everything appropriated for state expenditure, the result being that the public records showed what everybody earned, from the janitor and the nightwatchman up to and including the governor. In proclaiming that he hereby vetoed as much of the state appropriation as ran from the top of page so-and-so to the bottom of page such-and-such, Jim failed to do two things: (1) he failed to veto the appropriation for the dean of the faculty of arts and sciences, which was at the bottom of a previous page, and, more disastrous still, (2) he failed to turn over the final page, at the top of which the entire appropriation for the maintenance of the university was given in a lump sum. This error was discovered by State's Attorney General B. F. Looney, who wrote President Vinson that Ferguson had vetoed the itemization but not the total sum appropriated and so had defeated his own ends.*

The counterattack against Ferguson continued. When Jim had used up, worn out, or otherwise got rid of members of the Board of Regents who refused to do his bidding, he put in "Old Doc" Fly of Galveston as chairman of the board, who now saw to it that six faculty members were dismissed. The former chairman, Will C. Hogg, had resisted the governor's original demand that five faculty members be fired with the cool announcement to Ferguson's face: "I had rather go to hell in a hand-basket than to submit meekly to your demands to discharge members of the faculty without a hearing."† Appointed secretary of the Texas Ex-Students Association after his term as Regent, Hogg challenged Ferguson directly:

To call our thimblerigging, swashbuckling, swaggering Governor a common garden liar would be the grossest flattery. . . . How far this cheerful and con-structive autocrat will be able to travel the rocky road of his mad career is measured entirely by the forbearance and apathy of the best citizenship of the

---

* The Ferguson case extended, of course, beyond the campus of the university, although the episode is often (and rightly) known as the University-Ferguson War. The documents from which I have quoted, beyond those cited in the other notes to this chapter, are in H. Y. Benedict, ed., *Source Book Relating to the History of the University of Texas*, University of Texas Bulletin no. 1757, Oct. 10, 1917 (Austin).

† John A. Lomax, "Governor Ferguson and the University of Texas," *The Southwest Review* 28 (Autumn, 1942): 15.

State. . . . Farmer Jim is a farce, and my prediction is that he is riding to the biggest fall, personally and politically, in the short and simple annals of the misguided politicians of Texas. *

In the meantime there was no appropriation for the university, but the legislature was moving toward the impeachment of Ferguson. Between 1915 and 1917 he had issued 2,253 pardons, and Jim's misuse of the pardoning power became, along with a dozen other matters, a strong reason for getting him out of office. Under the constitution he, and he only, could call the legislature into a special session for a specified purpose, but the Travis County grand jury nevertheless called the governor in for questioning not only about his own grocery bills and bank deposits but about some mysterious thousands of dollars, the origins of which were never made clear. The grand jury indictments never got into court, but about the time Ferguson announced his candidacy for a third term as governor, the Speaker of the House, one F. O. Fuller, sustained by the opinion of the attorney general, called the House into special session to consider bringing articles of impeachment against the governor. At first Ferguson pooh-poohed the idea that a quorum would attend; but when it became evident that a quorum would be present (a question for which he employed the Texas Rangers as spies), he hastily called a special session of the entire legislature. The House began its session on July 23, 1917; Ferguson called the whole legislature into being on August 1, expecting to be vindicated. He guessed wrong. The House presented twenty-one articles of impeachment to the Senate, the formal trial before the Senate sitting as a court began on August 30, and by September 25 Jim had been found guilty on ten of the charges, by majorities greater than the two-thirds required under the constitution; and he was forever after barred from holding any office of public trust within the gift of the state of Texas. Nor, despite the gallant efforts of his wife in this direction, and of many supporters, has his name ever been cleared.

The university's situation remained confused, however. Ferguson had vetoed the entire appropriation for the university, or so he (and most people) thought in early June; and despite the attorney general's reassurance that the governor was in error, for much of the summer the faculty did not know whether they had jobs or not. What was I to do?

* Steen, "The Ferguson War," p. 361.

Chapter X

Incredible Montana

THOUGH HE LIVED many years in Boston, New Hampshire-born Thomas Bailey Aldrich, editor of *The Atlantic Monthly* (1881–90), once announced that he was not a Bostonian but only Boston-plated. After nine months in Austin I could not claim to be even Texas-plated. I was a lost soul, having scarcely money enough to go back to Wisconsin. There were wild schemes for holding university classes in private houses and charging tuition, but I didn't have a house. At this juncture, with an abruptness possible only in life and melodrama, I received from Professor George R. Coffman, head of the English department at the State University of Montana at Missoula, the offer of a place as assistant professor of English at $2,200, more than a 20 percent increase over the salary I had just lost. In 1917 I knew less about Montana than I knew about Texas in 1916, but I did not pause for inquiry and accepted at once. I went back to Wisconsin for the summer; and in September of the year we entered World War I, I took a train for Missoula and entered upon two years even more feverish and fateful than my solitary life as a Texan. But to make both my academic difficulties and my domestic life understandable, I must say something about Montana as it then was.

The classic historian of the Great Plains, Walter Prescott Webb, writing in *Montana: The Magazine of Western History* (Winter, 1958), has this to say about books on American history:

It is extremely difficult to change the focus with which people are accustomed to viewing their history or their land. The conventional view of the West is from the

East, the direction from which the viewer approached it. The West should not be looked at from the outside but from the inside, from the center. The West is concentric, a series of moisture circles extending outward from the arid to the semi-arid, to the subhumid, finally to the humid land.

Mr. Webb continues:

The Great Plains to the east of the mountains are the burnt right flank of the desert. . . . Once the desert is recognized and accepted as the dominant force in the West, what goes on there among animals, plants, and men makes sense.

Almost three-fourths of Montana lies east of the mountains—that is, east of a line drawn through Great Falls and Bozeman—and though river valleys and occasional lines of hills interrupt the enormous sweep of the Great Plains as they gradually rise from about 2,000 feet to about 4,000 feet at the base of the Rockies, the general effect is one of enormous distance and endless space, which, when the Americans first came to know it, seemed a level plain of green grass promising to become an agricultural paradise. The western part of the state is mountainous with a decreasing number of flat valleys until, about fifty miles from the Idaho line, one comes to the pleasant area of Missoula, a town on the flat surface of a former lake bed, the eastern approach to which is through a canyon called Hell Gate. The term derives from the tremendous gales or gusts of wind that unexpectedly sweep through this mountain pass to disturb the milder climate of the university city. Once, when I was producing a pageant of Montana history on the football field, such a sudden blast swept Fort Missoula (made out of canvas) off the ground, tossed it into the air, and abruptly ended the show as the spectators fled from the bleachers.

Montana was admitted to the union in 1889, only three years before I was born. Its territorial history is confused and hectic. It had been successively a part of the territories of Louisiana, Oregon, Washington, Nebraska, Dakota, and Idaho before it set up for itself as an autonomous political unit. This it did in 1864, a significant date because into the 1870s Montana was being invaded by Missourians and ex-Confederates, some of whom dreamed of setting up a new Confederacy in the West (had not Brigham Young done well in Utah?). In the early sixties, southern Idaho and southwest Montana were for some of these years dominated by the notorious Plummer gang, the head of which banished the sheriff of Bannack County and got himself elected as a replacement. Henry Plummer and his men robbed or murdered more than a hundred persons. He was finally hanged at Bannack on a gallows of his own erecting; twenty-four of his men were also caught and summarily dispatched and eight others banished by vigilantes in 1864. The historian of this "Western" episode was a gentle-minded graduate of Oxford University, T. J. Dimsdale, whose book, *The Vigilantes of Montana* (1865), is one of the classics of the Great West.

In the same decade rumors that western Montana was rich in gold and silver and, eventually, copper, induced a succession of rushes to get rich, creating places like Bannack, Virginia City, Alder Gulch, Confederate Gulch, and Last Chance Gulch. Some of the lodes were soon exhausted, leaving ghost towns and scarred landscape as their heritage; but Bannack, in southwest Montana, Virginia City, fifty miles eastward, and finally Last Chance Gulch, rechristened Helena and about a hundred miles east of Virginia City, became the successive capitals of the territory or the state.

The influx of miners into western Montana annoyed the Indians, as did the coming of cattle and sheep ranchers into eastern Montana; and the future commonwealth became the stage for most of the last great Indian wars, including "Custer's Last Fight" on the Little Big Horn River. The severe winter of 1886–87 killed an incredible number of cattle and induced a good many second thoughts about the proper use of land and water in eastern Montana, especially when sheep grazed the grass so close as to kill the spring crop. As the day of the cowboy waned, crowds of homesteaders were drawn westward by railroad advertising, business depressions in the East, floods of immigration, and land laws passed by a succession of Federal Congresses, the members of which were for the most part utterly ignorant of the environment for which they were legislating. These homesteaders thought they had found a new Eden. The majority of them knew nothing about farming, or if they had any knowledge of it, they knew nothing about the irregular cycles of humid and dry weather on the plains. The result was an agricultural disaster so great that as late as 1920–30 Montana was the only state in the nation to lose population. Out of the thoughtless applications of Eastern notions of farming to eastern Montana came the creation of the dust bowl. Water, as one historian remarks, is more important than land in the West.

The continuing mining boom attracted the attention of great Eastern speculators, who saw to it that the mining industry was not unduly burdened by legislative taxation and who had paramount influence when the state constitutional convention was held in 1889. As early as 1888 the great Daly-Clark copper war began, to last for over a decade. Marcus Daly, an Irish immigrant, discovered that a silver mine he had bought at Butte really overlay a rich vein of almost pure copper; and wealthy himself, he persuaded rich California friends, including George Hearst, to go in with him. Thus was formed the famous Anaconda Copper Mining Company, the corporation that, under various reorganizations, was and is in Montana always "the company." Daly bought up or built coal beds, forests, a railway from Butte to Anaconda, banks, power plants, irrigation flumes, until in twenty years he was worth millions. William A. Clark had been one of his fellow magnates, but they became, for reasons still debatable, bitter enemies. Clark had political ambitions that Daly wished to deny, and the latter defeated Clark for the Democratic nomination for the U.S. Senate. Clark was not one to stay beaten. Both contestants bribed legislators and judges, and when Clark was finally nominated by a corrupt legislature, he was thrown out by the U.S. Senate itself on charges of illegality involving bribery. An acquiescent acting governor immediately appointed him an interim member of the Senate. In 1901 he was legally elected and took his seat.

In the meantime the struggle between the two men had convulsed the state and the Democratic Party. A peculiarity of mining codes is the so-called apex law, which means that anybody who discovers a lode on the surface is entitled to follow and work the lode virtually wherever it leads. Between 1900 and 1906 the Anaconda situation was therefore further complicated by a virtual state of war between the company and F. A. Heinze, who turned the apex law to his profit. As a result, men fought and killed underground, mines were dynamited, and bitterness between capital and labor increased. A raw exhibition of money power in Butte and Helena, and in western Montana generally, created much support for various liberal or radical political and social movements— the Non-Partisan League, the IWW (the Wobblies), and the Progressives. There were dynamitings of offices, fighting in the streets, and the dreadful lynching (1917) of Frank Little, an IWW organizer who was taken out of a sick bed and dragged over the streets of Butte by a rope tied to the rear axle of an automobile; his body was then hanged from a railroad testle. Butte was put under martial law in 1917, not lifted until 1918.

Such were some of the disquieting episodes in the history of the state in which I was now about to teach. The "company"—which was by 1917 an amalgam of silver- and copper-mine owners, Standard Oil, the Northern Pacific Railroad, various timber interests, electric companies, big banks, and so on—either owned or controlled most of the newspapers of the state, and dominated the legislature and—what was more important to me—the state board of education.

Higher education dated back to the creation of this board in 1893, when a state college was founded at Bozeman. The university at Missoula was created in 1896 and under its first president had struggled into a feeble life on a miniscule budget. In 1912 Edwin Boone

Craighead, a classicist possessing a wide and rich background of cultural and educational experience, was somehow persuaded to become president of the university, and increased the student enrollment from 230 to about 1,000 by 1916. He had formed a scheme for amalgamating four state institutions of higher learning into a single state system; but when he discovered that his scheme would put the whole system under the board of education at Helena, which was also to elect a chancellor to supervise the whole, with the chancellor remaining a member of the board, Craighead resigned in protest, since he foresaw that the board in Helena would be controlled by moneyed interests. The board had then chosen as its first chancellor Edward C. Elliott of the University of Wisconsin. The members of the board were not as well informed as they should have been for their own interests, though they soon learned. Apparently they did not realize that the University of Wisconsin was a hotbed of "radicalism," nor that La Follette's idea about the university in the service of the state and the Wisconsin Regents' policy of free discussion were part of Elliott's background, nor that his intellectual buddies were reformers and economists like E. R. Seligman and Arthur O. Lovejoy, one of the creators of the American Association of University Professors. For the new president at Missoula they had installed Dr. E. O. Sisson, a philosopher who, characteristically, retired to "experimental" Reed College when, a few years later, he resigned at Missoula.

Few members of the little English department were, as I remember, native Montanans. George Coffman, the chairman, had a Ph.D. from Chicago, had been at Washington University, and had studied the medieval period. Frances Corben was a gentle Americanist from somewhere east of the Mississippi. There were three instructors: R. A. Coleman; Helen Sard Hughes, who came from the University of Chicago and later joined the faculty at Wellesley; and Anders Orbeck, a Scandinavian who was to translate the early plays of Ibsen and have them published by the American-Scandinavian Foundation. I think none of them had any first-hand acquaintance with Montana and its eventful history. But the results of that history were to affect us all.

The University of Montana that I last saw in the sixties and that has since expanded even more bears little relation to the university I taught at in 1917–19. In that more primitive period the old red brick main building faced on the Oval, which was the center of the campus; and the little red brick library, scarcely larger than the public libraries in many New England towns, was far too small for what it was supposed to hold. Government documents were housed under the football bleachers. My own miniscule office was on the second floor of the library, where

George Coffman had only a slightly larger one; and the little hall leading to my office was formed on one side of unpainted wood, on which hung a preliminary sketch, presumably the original, of Paxon's painting *Custer's Last Fight*, every wound depicted with medical fidelity. I do not remember where I lived and where I took my meals when I first came to Missoula, but I remember occasionally dining "downtown" at the Florence Hotel, supposed to be the best hostelry between Bismarck and Spokane. The courses I taught were standard, and I remember that I was supposed to direct the university dramatic society, named The Maskers. The undergraduates made no special impression upon me, and I in turn, I fear, made no impression upon the university.

I was asked to teach an extension course in Butte, and I did so. It was a course in modern drama, mostly taken by high school teachers who, if they earned enough university credits to make up the requirements for a master's degree, would have their salaries increased. The interest in the course was at about that level. I went up by a train in the midafternoon, got a meal somewhere in Butte, taught my class, and came back by another train that reached Missoula, as I remember, about 11:00 P.M. But of the actual mining life of Butte I saw virtually nothing. The university and the extension course, so far as I could make out, were strictly eastern patterns in the humanities imposed upon a Western town. Of course I formed an impression of both Butte and Anaconda, but with the vast stretches of the Great Plains I had no contact whatsoever.

The truth was that university life in Missoula was overshadowed by two great problems—the war and the Louis Levine affair. The war was felt in a multitude of ways. Through some malfunction in Washington, the young men of the state had been overdrafted, a fact that made the university seem even emptier than it was. There was no faculty club and very little faculty life. The lone teacher had to seek what companionship or amusement he could find. There were rumors that the Germans were concentrating planes in hidden mountain valleys; these supposed planes were, by and by, to overwhelm us and fly off to bombard our national military and naval installations. There was a suspicion that a German name, a German background, or the speaking or the study of German was traitorous per se. Among other idiocies, the legislature had forbidden the teaching of German anywhere in the state, and as Mrs. Coffman (Bertha Reed) had taken her Ph.D. in German, she was inevitably embittered and restless. Research work in the little library was virtually impossible for an advanced scholar, and she had to be very careful in what she said.

Indeed, virtually any unorthodox utterance or appearance might lead to trouble. Returning one night from a bit of late study in my office, I was stopped by the police and questioned because I was not wearing a hat. The governor had appointed a somewhat illegal Defense Council and had given it police powers of instant arrest without much provision for trial, and the legislature, a little later, made this instrument of stupidity legal. When it is remembered that the war of the copper kings had ended only a few years before, that strikes and conflicts among unions were commonplace, that federal troops were patrolling the streets of Butte in 1917, that martial law was not lifted until 1918, and that one federal judge was impeached for insisting that a member of the IWW was entitled to a fair trial, something of the wartime atmosphere may be imagined even now. Anybody curious about this fantastic phase of Western life might turn to *Perch of the Devil*, Gertrude Atherton's novel of 1914, or to *I, Mary McLane* (1917; Mencken called her "The Butte Bashkirtseff"), or to Christopher P. Connolly's grim social history *The Devil Learns to Vote* (1938). For my part I wrote and later published "A Song of Butte," a poem in six stanzas. Here are two brief passages:

> I am the city demoniac! Desolate, mournful, infernal
> Dweller apart and alone upon the amazing hills;
> Seen of the poet of hell, I am she, the dark, the unvernal
> Cybele, wearing my crown of fantastic mines and mills!
>
> .   .   .   .
>
> I am likewise the challenge, the mixing of many in one:
> Lustful, reckless, I yield to the urge of life and the slack,
> A myriad races come and beneath my dispassionate sun
> I mix and change and remold and send them, a nation, back.

Butte is like that no longer, but I happened to teach my extension course just as the war of the copper kings was subsiding and World War I was going full blast. New modes of refining ore have since permitted grass and trees, flowers and shrubbery, to grow in the perch of the devil.

But as Emerson observed, action and reaction in human affairs are sometimes equal. Lawlessness, violence, and injustice, poverty, misery, and despair, engender or welcome movements of reform. Human life should not be lived under tyranny either covert or open. Another important thread, therefore, runs through Montana history—the thread of progressivism. Indeed, it sometimes took all the ingenuity of the company's legal staff and public relations men to stop the forces of enlightenment. Butte from time to time elected a Socialist mayor. Montana now and then chose a "progressive" governor, such as Joseph M. Dixon. It elected Jeannette Rankin to the House of Representatives, where she voted against our declaration of war against Germany, even though she immediately burst into tears. If the state produced Senator

W. A. Clark, it also produced Senator Thomas J. Walsh of Helena, who advocated woman suffrage, the child labor amendment, and the protection of farmers' unions and labor unions from the operation of the Sherman Anti-Trust law, and whose greatest public service occurred when, after eighteen months of almost single-handed study, he uncovered the Teapot Dome and Elk Hills oil scandals, thus revealing the inward rottenness of the Harding administration. Montana also elected to various public offices Burton K. Wheeler, and kept Mike Mansfield in the Senate until he was ready to retire. Likewise, it produces crusading historians, such as K. Ross Toole.

The constitution under which Montana lived in my years there was not necessarily representative of the plain people. (Fortunately a better one is now in force.) If one cut through the verbiage, one found that a huge corporation like the "company" was not to be taxed on its profits but mainly on what amounted to its surface holdings. In round numbers agriculture in 1916 had produced a little more than $81,000,000 in the state, whereas the gross proceeds of mining amounted to about $141,500,000. But an investigating committee set up by a Republican-Progressive legislature found that the distribution of taxation for that same year ran as follows:

Mining	8.79%
Farming	32.14%
Livestock	10.73%
Railroads	17.99%
Others	30.35%

The committee summarized its findings thus:

We believe that the large mining companies, the Hydro Electric Companies [Montana Power was closely allied with Anaconda] and the Pullman Car Companies are not paying their proportionate share of the State's taxes. We are also of the opinion that all these companies are abundantly able to respond to the needs of this state in the matter of revenue without injury to their business or in any manner jeopardizing the general welfare of the people of the state.

Lobbyists for Anaconda were alert and saw to it that all bills proposing to change this inequitable system, despite the pressures of eastern Montana and of dissatisfied progressives, were quietly smothered. The atmosphere was not precisely favorable to the humanities or to higher education in general.

Both Elliott, the chancellor of the university system, and Sisson, the president of the University of Montana, found themselves boxed in. None of the four institutions at Butte, Missoula, Dillon, or Bozeman could expand without money; more money could come only out of taxes; and taxes could not be levied on the greatest single outpouring of wealth in the state. This situation aroused the anger of the head of the Department of Economics at Missoula, a soft-spoken but determined man named J. H. Underwood; and Elliott, Sisson, and Underwood brought to Missoula Dr. Louis Levine, a brilliant young economist with a Ph.D. from Columbia, who had taught at various Eastern colleges and universities, studied in Russia, France, and Switzerland, and was producing a flow of able professional articles. He came to Missoula as an instructor, but in less than three years had been promoted to a full professorship. Elliott, it will be remembered, had come from the University of Wisconsin; and, believing that it was right and proper for an institution supported by the people to enlighten the public, he, Sisson, and Levine agreed upon the necessity of an impartial examination of the whole state tax system. Perhaps the idea had originated in a farmers' tax conference which Professor Levine had addressed. (My memory is that President Sisson had urged Levine to attend such a conference, his modest expenses to be paid by the university, and that he had done so, speaking there from notes. He was followed by L. C. Evans, chief legal counsellor for the Anaconda people and by "Con" Kelley, their public relations man, both of whom attacked Levine's statistics.) At any rate it was proposed that Levine should, under the auspices of the university, make a thorough study of the taxation of mines. When it was finished, President Sisson wrote that he knew nothing brought out in the American Northwest to equal it in balance, clarity, and judgment; and he and Elliott agreed that it should be printed by the university as a service to the state.

A member of the state board of education by the name of Kremer had attended the meeting Levine had addressed, and though he said nothing at the time, he informed fellow members of the board that Levine's ideas were "Socialistic" and that both he and Underwood were "radicals." The board held a succession of heated meetings. Levine, meanwhile, had briefly been called to Washington on some sort of research task for the War Labor Policies Board. When he returned to Missoula in January, 1919, he was summoned to the chancellor's office in Helena and informed that, as a result of various meetings of the state board of education, the university would not publish his monograph. Levine replied he would publish it elsewhere. Elliott, who had apparently yielded to the board's pressure despite his liberalism, forbade him to publish it anywhere. But it was printed through the interest of B. W. Huebsch, one of the predecessors of the Viking Press in New York, who brought out *The Taxation of Mines in Montana* (New York, 1919), factual in matter and temperate in tone. In February the chancellor suspended Levine for "insubordination." Levine demanded a hearing.

President Sisson appointed three members of the faculty of excellent reputation (a biologist, a historian, and a professor of law), who met, investigated, and in April, 1919, released a report which concluded, among other things, that Chancellor Elliott in suspending Levine (and stopping his pay) for publishing a valuable piece of research was a "horrible example of narrow mindedness, bigotry, and intolerance." Almost at the same time a committee of the state senate reported that they could find no evidence that either Underwood, Levine, or anybody else at Missoula taught "Socialism," "Bolshevism," or any doctrine of like kind.

The case had now attracted considerable public attention, the recently formed American Association of University Professors declaring in March that the chancellor's suspension of Levine and the board of education's support (instigation?) of this suspension were acts that could cause irreparable harm to higher education in the state by destroying popular confidence in the intellectual integrity of the university. Professor Levine demanded a hearing before the board of education, where the Anaconda people were represented by Con Kelley. Aroused public opinion compelled the board and the chancellor to back down; the board reinstated Levine and paid his back salary, after which he resigned to complete a distinguished career with the Brookings Institution, with the International Labor Office of the League of Nations, and as economic adviser to the American delegation to the General Assembly of the United Nations. Neither Elliott nor Sisson remained at the University of Montana.*

Robert Frost has a poem in which he expresses the wish to get the United States stated. My years in Missoula did little or nothing for me in the way of traditional scholarship. Yet one of the themes of this chronicle is the making of an Americanist, or how, out of the uncertainties of my earliest years, the conventional pattern of the Ph.D. program in the humanities, and my probable career as another professor of English, I gradually adopted an independent line of my own and became, however imperfectly, a historian of American cultural development. From this point of view my two years in Missoula were, I now think, invaluable, however digressive they proved to be from the conventional scholarly point of view. They have helped me get the United States stated, whatever imperfections the statement may contain or reveal.

* Memory being tricky, I have mainly followed the various studies by K. Ross Toole, especially *Twentieth Century Montana: A State of Extremes* (Norman, Oklahoma, 1972), and the detailed analysis by Arnon Guffield, "The Levine Affair: A Case Study in Academic Freedom," *Pacific Historical Review* 39 (February, 1970): 19–37. In a few details I have relied on my own recollections.

In truth, as Professor Toole points out, most of our historians are based on the East—on Eastern schools, Eastern libraries, Eastern conferences, Eastern foundations, and Eastern value patterns. The Pacific Coast, as it becomes "sophisticated," becomes Eastern rather than autonomous; and I think it significant that the American Historical Association has its principal office in Washington, D.C. Europe, wrote Emerson, extends to the Alleghenies. Suppose, as once seemed probable, that Chicago had become the cultural center of the burgeoning republic, or that St. Louis, formerly the headquarters of the fur trade and the starting point for scores of westward expeditions, had become, as once it threatened to be, the capital of the nation? Suppose that the great training schools for American history had been situated, not on the Atlantic seaboard or the Pacific Coast, but in the Mississippi Valley? Would the Pilgrim Fathers have retained their traditionary importance? Would the ecclesiastical vagaries of New England, running from Calvin to Mrs. Mary B. Eddy, have kept their national influence? Is it not possible our relations with Latin America might have been friendlier and more *simpatico*? Would publishing have been concentrated in New York? Would our painters have "Europeanized" as quickly as they did? These are but speculations, but speculations are the life of the historian.

Chapter XI

Back to Texas

MY SECOND YEAR in Missoula was not only to be darkened by the anxieties of war and repressive legislation and the shadow of the Levine affair; it was also to be troubled by personal anxieties, some of them in the long run insoluble. In my first winter there I had been conscious of discomfort amounting to pain in my abdomen, but as it seemed to be intermittent, I attributed it to the inferior food and irregular meals I had been eating. But some time late in the spring of 1918, I experienced such acute discomfort that I consulted a physician, who promptly sent me to a surgeon. This was Dr. Mills, kindliest of human beings, a man as tall and thin as Professor Law at Texas, but who, unlike Law, had a perpetual stoop, acquired, I suppose, from leaning over patients and operating tables. He possessed an inexhaustible wealth of sympathy that belied tales about physicians who were out to make as much money as they could as fast as possible. After a thorough examination he informed me that I had an infected gallbladder and probably other complications, so that an immediate operation was necessary. The leading hospital in Missoula was, and I think still is, St. Patrick's, a Roman Catholic institution run by an order of nursing nuns, an altogether admirable establishment.

The influenza was beginning to creep into the United States, even into the Far West. Moreover, St. Patrick's served the Blackfoot Indian Reservation a few miles north of Missoula. The hospital was therefore full, the only room available being one in that part of the building set aside for obstetrics. But Dr. Mills was a person of influence and got me into this room, the only male patient on an entire floor dedicated to motherhood. In those simpler years one "prepared" patients for a major operation by prolonged bed rest, followed by prolonged recuperation. I remained in isolation for two weeks before and two weeks after surgery.

Saint Patrick's had centered its entrance hall on a commanding statue of that great Irishman, the largest majolica figure, if it was majolica, I think I have ever seen. Perhaps my memory is influenced by my postoperational ether dreams. I am not skilled in the art of pottery and do not know whether it is possible to make a pottery figure ten or twelve feet high and coat it with enamel in all the primary colors—and more. Possible or not, the patron saint was superbly there, high on a pedestal, the largest human figure in all Missoula. He was red and green and gold and blue; and his skin, where it showed on his face, his hands, and his legs and feet, was of that off-white, eggshell color used in such cases to represent human flesh. In one hand he grasped an enormous crosier, and one powerful foot advanced to crush a writhing serpent of that excessively green hue one finds on the outside of metal window boxes intended to stay out of doors all year. The death agonies of the great snake had apparently been of peculiar interest to the potter, sculptor, workman, or whoever designed this gigantic figure. The serpent came to have a peculiar interest for me too, since, after my operation, he crawled and wriggled and squirmed his way night after night through my dreams, sometimes escaping from St. Patrick and coming after me with open jaws, sometimes pursued by the holy man with his crosier, and sometimes battling with the titanic saint, who, however, occasionally shrank to the size of an elf not much higher than the distended jaws of the serpent. I commonly woke just as the snake was about to devour either me or St. Patrick, or just before St. Patrick was about to flatten the snake into a green and bloody pancake.

So far as I knew, for most of the time Dr. Mills, an interne, and I were the only men left in a world of women except when, the door of my room being left ajar, I could now and then catch glimpses of an expectant father pacing up and down the hall. An occasional visitor came, but for the most part I led a solitary life. After other comforts failed, I got from the university library a set of the Valois romances by Alexandre Dumas of blessed memory, delighting in the skill and impudence of Chicot the Jester, the repartee, sometimes smart, sometimes foolish, of Dom Goremflot (the Falstaff of those glorious works), and satisfied that the history in the romances, such as it was, was quite good enough to support the stories. My notions of Henry of Navarre and his gallant queen, of the determined and unfortunate Catherine de'Medici, and of the weak and occasionally well-meaning Valois monarchs are to this day colored by Dumas's portraits of them. I recently reread the whole series and am again baffled to understand why French critics and literary historians commonly dismiss these imaginative triumphs and others like them (for examples, the *Musketeer* series and *The Count of Monte Cristo*) in a paragraph or a footnote, to spend pages on Dumas's second-rate melodramas, such as *Antony*. An imagination that could create D'Artagnan, Athos, Porthos, Aramis, Richelieu, Mazarin, young Louis XIV, Catherine de'Medici, and the rest—personages that, like Hamlet and Sherlock Holmes, have gone round the world—is a talent any culture should be proud of. What if he did have helpers? So did Shakespeare. I am reminded of a book purporting to be a scholarly study of American literary development which contains the immortal sentence: "Herman Melville also wrote novels."

I was successfully operated upon and learned later that Dr. Mills had drained my gallbladder, taken out my appendix, done something or other to the outer coating of my stomach, and rearranged my intestines. Recuperation therefore took a long time. Fortunately President Sisson of the university had a log cabin or beach house on the shore of Hood Canal, the extreme western arm of Puget Sound, and this he graciously offered at no cost at all. The little house faced the wide Canal, and beyond it rose the mighty dome of Mount Olympus and the green of the Olympic National Forest. The nearest neighbors were a couple of fishermen and their shy families and a small settlement, scarcely more than a general store and post office, called Seabeck. There was also a mighty weir, or salmon trap; and beyond its outer "fence" the blackfish, huge as whales, now and then came to play. There I settled down, a recuperating invalid and a married man. If the reader is surprised, so in some sense was I.

I now come to the most difficult part of my narrative. I had had various amatory adventures before coming to Montana, but like Kipling's young recruit I had been shy as a girl to begin. Up-to-date autobiographies are expected to be candid—"frank" is the fashionable term—about matrimonial and extramarital episodes in the life of the narrator. Although I was born when Victoria was on the throne, I doubt that I have any false modesty about my sexual successes or inadequacies. But my first wife is still alive, she hovers forever on the edge of a psychological collapse, she has from time to time had to be confined in institutions for the mentally ill or put under the supervision of those supposed to be skilled in the care of psychological disorders, and I have no desire either in what I write now or in anything else I may do or say to be the cause or the excuse for another breakup of whatever inner peace and harmony she may have achieved. Nor do I have any desire to

110

conceal the fact that I was an inexperienced and unskillful husband. I shall therefore not give her name but simply call her "W," an initial that is no part of it.

W is one of the many children of a Montana pioneer who came to that country in the sixties after an active beginning as a "freighter" to Denver, then as a cattle-drover, and finally as a prospector and miner in western Montana. He had had some luck in Confederate Gulch and more at Unionville, Butte, Philipsburg, and Granite; but he seems to have been more fascinated by speculating in mining stocks and organizing companies than in actually getting the ore out of the earth. As he died before my time there, I can only guess at his real interests, but I think he had lost most of his wealth either through stock speculation or by somebody's chicanery. At any rate the family, though living in one of the grander houses in Missoula, was always deploring its lack of money and dreaming of a future time, not very far off, when the courts or another discovery or something else would turn up to right its pecuniary wrongs. W's mother still lived, but I saw little of her, and some of W's brothers and sisters I never met.

W was an outdoor girl, lively, affectionate, and attractive, no university coed but eager to know what was going on on campus. She breathed a quality of freedom that I admired. Being with her was a great relief from the grey atmosphere of the university. I could find little or no companionship on the campus or off it, and to my uncritical eyes W bubbled over with a love of life. She liked riding a horse, and I, reviving my memories of the First Illinois Cavalry, took to riding with her. Looking back on these excursions, I now realize how often they led to an abandoned mine, an abandoned stamp-mill, a ghost town, or some other relic of get-rich-quick Montana. I fell in love with her, not realizing until much later the significance of these ghostly monuments of vanished wealth to her private and inward life. I now know that she was yearning after the vanished years when her family was rich and her father ranked as one of the millionaires of western Montana. I do not mean that she was avaricious or greedy, but she was bored with living on the fringes of wealth. I was "different," I came from the East; and to me she seemed the girl of the golden West, the only happy human being in all Missoula. Inevitably we fell in love. She was almost the only visitor I had had during my month in the hospital; and as the university had given me leave of absence for the semester of my illness, we agreed to marry in Seattle, and then I was to recuperate at Seabeck. We were married by a justice of the peace on July 13, 1918, went to Seabeck, and for a brief period were as happy as children of nature. I remember that we used to get salmon trout almost for the mere asking and that on one dangerous occasion, having rowed a boat too far from the protection of the fish weir, we found ourselves in the middle of a school of playful blackfish, whose game of tag threatened to upset our little rowboat.

Our return in the late summer by stage to Seattle and from thence by rail to Missoula was without incident, though a distance had already begun to grow between us and we had little to say to each other. Arriving at the university, I thought my first duties were to discover what my classes were about to be and, with W's help, to find a place to live. We settled on an apartment, not the most glamorous in the world, but sufficient, the only remarkable element in it being the large bed, which was in the dining room and slid like a huge bureau drawer into and under the built-in china-closet. If we rested on the bed during the day, we contemplated the family china, such as it was; and at night before the lights were put out, we glimpsed the same uninteresting panorama through the overornamented doors of the cabinet.

Our colleagues, who necessarily had seen little enough of the Joneses, tried to entertain us, but there was no ease in these formalities and very few common topics of conversation. Meanwhile, my mother arrived, and we had to house her as best we could, housing in Missoula in these years being a genuine headache. We finally got her an apartment in the same building as our own. I think W and my mother did the best they could, but dislike developed from the first, and I shortly found myself in the middle of the classic wife–mother-in-law situation. A few months after my mother's arrival, W announced that she was pregnant. False labor pains got her to St. Patrick's a week or so before the baby was born. The child, whom we called Eleanor, was healthy and happy and, as the phrase goes, "good." Her mother was devoted to her for a while, and my courses, the Levine case, and the general malfunctioning of the university system kept me perpetually busy. So, for a few months, we got along.

I could see no future for me in Missoula, since I had no doctoral degree and the welfare of the entire system of higher education lay in the hands of a remote board of education that was apparently controlled in Helena by the copper interests and of a chancellor who had not kept his word with Louis Levine and had suspended him for "insubordination." Suddenly, towards the close of the academic year 1918–19, I received a summons back to Texas as an associate professor at an increased salary. Ferguson had been impeached, the legislature had increased the university budget, as many professors as possible were being called back, and I was free at last, or so I thought, of the incubus of being a teacher of the humanities in a community far less developed than La Crosse. Meanwhile, however, W's family had begun to crumble as brothers and sisters found careers out of the state, and her mother was left more and more alone. When I came home with the Texas letter in my pocket, fairly shouting with joy, W announced her firm refusal to move to any such remote and barbarous region as the Lone Star State.

From many points of view her decision was rational enough. Texas was an unknown quantity hundreds and hundreds of miles away. She knew nobody there, and the academicians she had met in Missoula had not impressed her. She had a baby, and the long trip by railroad was more than she could face. Her family home was in Missoula, and though the family was disintegrating, her place was there. She was likewise put off, I think, by the anecdotes I had innocently told her about Texas and Jim Ferguson, and preferred the copper company in Montana, which she understood, to the Texas politicians, whom she did not. She thought of Montana, moreover, as potential income; if she could just hang on a little longer, her mines would miraculously reopen, or the bankrupt companies would somehow become solvent. In addition, the child would be healthier in the mountain air. As for me, I could commute from Austin to Missoula. I now surmise that her local allegiance was essentially divided between Missouri, from whence her father and mother had come, and Montana, where they had hoped for wealth. Beneath all this there was also the inevitable love-hate relationship between the two of us and between W and a good many members of her family, irresponsible as some of them seemed to be. As for me, I did not realize the vast potentialities latent in the story of Western development, or, for that matter, in American development as a whole. I was still in the grip of the conventional Ph.D. syndrome: I had somehow somewhere to write a dissertation on something, and since the library resources of Austin far surpassed those in Montana, I was determined to go back to a better established and more richly endowed institution, especially because it had cleansed itself of the same sort of ills that were still besetting Montana. W and I clashed, we quarreled, we argued, we sulked, we fought, we exchanged absurd accusations; but it was finally determined that I should go back to Texas, eventually sending for my mother, and that W and the baby would remain in Missoula at least for a time, although what that time was to be was never determined. I went to Texas.

Railways were still the principal means of communication in the United States of 1919. In my more bitter moments, when I contemplated the peculiarities of my marriage and the weary task of crossing and recrossing the whole United States north to south during each school year, I sometimes felt that railway surveys had purposely laid out their routes so as to make commuting as dreary as possible. This was of course nonsense, since it is obviously less expensive to put down trackage in flat country than through mountain passes and over mountain streams. Getting from Missoula to Billings was pleasant enough as the mountains slowly gave way to the plains; but at Billings you changed trains for a railroad that wound its monotonous way through our American Siberia to Alliance, Nebraska. The landscape was forever the same whether you looked out of the window in the morning or in the afternoon. Dusty railroad stations appeared along the route at irregular intervals, interrupting the ceaseless march of telegraph poles; and these, an occasional river-crossing, or a distant herd of ruminant cattle alone broke the eternal monotony. From Alliance, on you went over another extent of the Great Plains till you arrived at Denver, at the foot of the Rockies; and there you changed to still another line that shied away from the mountains, got slowly through southeastern Colorado into the wedge of Oklahoma that intervenes between Colorado and the Texas panhandle and then by slow degrees, stopping at every town or hamlet, reached Fort Worth and, by and by, Austin.

These long train trips from Texas to Montana gave me an opportunity for a good deal of reflection. I could see no future in my family life, nor, having returned to Texas gladly enough, could I on sober second thought see much future for me in Austin. I was the chairman of a phantom department, comparative literature, and the members of the Texas faculty in the liberal arts were, in my experience, conservative. Some members of the faculty in Germanic languages and literatures showed some mild interest in the theory of comparative literature, but that department was itself sore stricken by the anti-Germanism of our war psychology. The one possible exception was Lee M. Hollander, who by and by translated some excerpts from Kierkegaard in a pamphlet got out by the University of Texas Press; but Hollander, admirable scholar though he was, was of a retiring disposition and not likely to champion a cause. The romance language people had their hands full with French and Spanish, both tongues being in demand by the armed forces and our difficulties on the Mexican border having made Spanish popular among undergraduates. A. E. Trombly, E. J. Villavaso, and B. F. Woodbridge had, as I have indicated, helped me with my translation of Benelli's *Love of the Three Kings*, but that was a personal favor, not a professional move. The English department had not changed. I could find no ally except among the historians. But the department was fenced in by the divisional barriers I have earlier described, and a combination of history and literature such as I later found at Harvard had not been dreamed of at Austin.

Moreover, what had become of the regionalist enthusiasm with which I had begun my rather scanty writing career? I looked out of the car window as the Great Plains slid listlessly past me, and I could see no connection between these semiarid lands and either Wisconsin or the polite New England, New York, Pennsylvania, and Southern writers who, though they were in their own terms regional enough, now constituted the main corpus of American classical literature. Longfellow had in a way explored the Mississippi, but Banvard's panorama had little or nothing to do with eastern Colorado, and *Evangeline* made no sense on the Great Plains. Doubtless some one among the towns we passed through had a haunted house; but *The House of the Seven Gables* did not, to put it mildly, suggest the cow country, and I doubted that any of these farming communities could show a Jaffrey Pyncheon. Hepzibah, Clifford, Phoebe, and the rest. Even the "folk" stuff of *The Biglow Papers* and Whittier's *Snow-Bound* was totally alien to the Far West and scarcely at home in Texas. As for Howells and James—! These open spaces might be a proper setting for Owen Wister or even O. Henry, their virtues might even be Thoreauvian or Emersonian—"Trust thyself. Every heart vibrates to that iron string!"—but which was national and which was regional? The Great West could obviously produce realism in the raw, but I was forced back again and again on the problem of American origins and American qualities. It was too late for me to become a "Western" writer, but what was I doing as a professor of comparative literature? The Americanists in the English department at Austin were part of that slow, gentle tide which was imposing Eastern culture on frontier values, but that was not what I felt to be the key to the puzzle.

The Great Plains and the Rockies were a different country, a new world. Was it not as new to those engaged in taming it as the Caribbean had been to Columbus or New England's stern and rockbound coast to the Pilgrims and the Puritans? They came to the New World no better prepared for its surprises than the farmsteaders were prepared for the dry-land farming of the Dakotas; in each case the pioneers had had to adapt an Old World culture to a New World environment. And there began to shape itself in the back of my mind an uneasy feeling that Americanists, in striving for decades to get out from under the shadow of Europe, had perhaps overplayed their hands. They had insisted, as I had on occasion insisted, upon some unique quality in the American experience; if they had not called Emerson an American Bacon, they had declared with justice that Emerson's essays were quite as good as Bacon's. To hail Emerson's famous Phi Beta Kappa address on the

American scholar as our declaration of literary independence was all very well for propaganda purposes, and the Sage of Concord may well have been right in declaring we had listened too long to the courtly muses of Europe. But did that necessarily mean that the courtly muses of Europe somehow fell queerly silent within sight of Boston harbor? In the history of revolutions a crop of declarations of independence in all sorts of fields was commonplace, and it was well to declare in book after book that American writing was much more than a minor province of English literature, but such a doctrine was perhaps as one-sided as the doctrine it sought to replace. Europe, as Emerson said, extended to the foot of the Alleghenies. The root of the American cultural problem did not lie either in the fact that Columbus once thought he heard a nightingale, that thoroughly European bird, on one of his voyages, nor in the fact that Anne Bradstreet refers in her verses to crickets, grasshoppers, and other "local" creatures; it was revealed rather in that flash of insight that led Lowell to write in *The Biglow Papers*, "O strange New World, thet yit wast never young."

I do not conceive, even at this distance in time with all its mellowing influence, that my thoughts on these lonely railroad trips took on the coherent form I have just given them. But as I look back across the years and try to work out the process by which I passed from being a regionalist, however young and naive, to become—how shall I say it?—the cosmopolitan scholar of *America and French Culture: 1750–1848*, *O Strange New World*, *The Age of Energy*, and *Revolution and Romanticism*, I think I can trace the slow shifting of a point of view, a philosophy, a pattern of values backward across the decades to the time on which I am reporting. Grateful though I was for being recalled to Austin, I had no desire to become a Texan or even Texas-plated. I was, I confess, intellectually restless. I felt I had some sort of inborn ability I had not as yet operationally realized. I felt like a man who had committed a series of blunders, but one whose blunders were at least in the right direction. The great value of my duties as a professor of comparative literature was that, however superficially, I was required by the nature of the post to view the culture of the Western world as a single whole, particularly that great and fruitful period, the high culture of the eighteenth-century universe, out of which the theory of the American republic was born. It sounds commonplace enough nowadays, but in the distant twenties it was virtually revolutionary to believe that the American experiment in life and culture was not something dropped from the clouds but the observable results of the slow adaptation of Old World assumptions to a New World setting. Certainly there were uniqueness and originality in the theory and development of the United

116

States; but life in the United States was as it was because it represented the adaptation of European man to a new environment physical, emotional, and intellectual. It took me a long while to realize and act upon this obvious truth.

Put thus simply, the principle seems as obvious as A-B-C. The difficulty was in establishing it, since the force of American literary studies as such had been exerted in the direction of substantiating an opposite theory—namely, that American literature must be the mature utterance of a new nation, which, because it was based on primary principles of society and government, must of course instantly, or almost instantly, produce mature forms of expression. I had myself taken this position, and in fact, not until I gave the Messenger Lectures at Cornell in 1947 (published by the Cornell University Press in 1948 as *The Theory of American Literature*) did I indicate my dissent from current doctrine. The establishment of the American Studies Association in 1951, though its scope was by no means parochial, indicated how popular among scholars was the doctrine of the uniqueness of the American cultural experiment.

The effort to redefine the field of the department of which I was chairman, though philosophically laudable, was, I now think, a tactical blunder. Comparative literature implied a maturer approach to literary history than that common in the undergraduate world, but how could the Department of Comparative Literature confer advanced degrees when the chairman himself had no Ph.D.? Texas was a stickler for form, and what was here implied was something like legitimizing a break in the apostolic succession. And though, like the manservant in a British comedy, I continued to please (at least I think I did), my best friends in Austin began advising me to ask for a year's leave of absence, write a dissertation, and get the degree at last. After some domestic infighting I accordingly applied and after a decent interval of delay was informed that the leave had been granted.

Chapter XII

Domestic Rift

MY ATTEMPT to put together a coherent statement of my intellectual development as a scholar in the field of American letters and American culture has been at the expense of chronology. I must now go back to record some of the memorable incidents I recall from my final tour of duty in Austin, which concluded in the academic year 1924–25.

My most serious publication in this period was one on which I collaborated with Professor R. H. Griffith of the English department. We produced a solid bibliographical survey of the Byroniana in the university libraries, including the famous Wrenn Library, together with additional material loaned for the occasion by book collectors in Texas. The exhibit and the catalogue were intended to celebrate the centenary of Byron's death. This labor was the result of my long-standing interest in Byron and was also intended to mark the seriousness with which I took my duties as a professor of comparative literature, since it is hard to think of a greater international fame than that of Byron.

Meanwhile W had changed her mind and was resolved to come to Austin. I therefore went house-hunting, finally settling on a one-storey cottage on the Speedway, a road that owed its name to a time when the young bloods of Austin used to drive fast horses up and down its length. The automobile ended this sport, and the Speedway was now no more than any other long street except for the curious fact that there were virtually no sidewalks along it, gravel paths or footpaths with no stone at all serving in their stead. The house had about six rooms, a front veranda, and an ample back porch screened by a trellis, as I had good cause to remember; for, a year or so before leaving Austin, I came down with a case of dengue fever (also picturesquely known as break-bone fever) and slowly recuperated on a cot put up for me on this porch behind the trellis.

Although some members of the English department had thawed a bit, on the whole my relation with that group upon my return to Austin remained about what it had been. Most of my academic friends were outside the division—persons in history, romance languages, German, philosophy, even economics, a field in which A. B. Wolfe and Max Handman, a Rumanian, occupied leading places. And of course James Royster and his wife remained my closest and most trusted friends. They seemed to understand my queer matrimonial situation, and I think that my leave of absence, when it came, was mainly due to Jim Royster. As for my students, it is of course always difficult to know what real or lasting impression a professor makes, particularly upon large classes, and the history of tragedy continued to be a large lecture course. American students in the twenties, though the more "advanced" among them read H. L. Mencken, Sinclair Lewis, Carl Van Vechten, and James Branch Cabell, were still living in that atmosphere of acquiescence that characterized most colleges and universities before the great outbursts of the sixties. If I left any impression upon Texas as a whole, it was probably through The Curtain Club, for which I inherited responsibility as the successor of Stark Young.

The Curtain Club was organized and run entirely by the students save for the directorship, and we fell into the pattern of giving three productions a year. Membership was determined by a tryout and membership committee, composed of students save for me; and though my vote probably carried more weight than that of an undergraduate, it was but one vote, and the committee occasionally overruled me. So far as I know, no new member came in except as he or she exposed some sort of ability to the tryout committee.

Competitions for admission were held in the largest classroom we could find vacant at some set hour. Members of the committee scattered over it, some even sitting in the balcony if there was one, so that the carrying power of the applicant's voice could be fairly tested and his or her stage presence viewed from all possible angles and distances. Those who said they could paint or make costumes were of course not necessarily put to this test, but the committee tried to find out what sort of scenery they had made for what sort of plays, and so on. The vocal test was severe and even frightening, especially in the case of, say, a freshman.

One of my chief memories of these tryouts is the monotony of the

American voice. One could, of course, almost invariably spot a Louisianan, somebody from southwest Texas, a Midwesterner, or the rare New Englander who showed up. But regional variations aside, what troubled me was the lack of tonal variety, of musical range, of any sense that speech could be a beautiful instrument. Commonly the students could not even shift accent from one syllable to another if requested to do so, and the last half of the last phrase in any sentence almost invariably disappeared into the depths of the throat. I shall speak in a moment of two exceptions.

Tryouts being over, we fell into an easy routine. We produced no plays in the summer quarter; but in the fall quarter we put on a recent or contemporary play, commonly light in tone, in the winter some theatrical classic, and in the spring a bill of three one-act plays—this last for several reasons. One-act plays were very much in vogue among the colleges and highbrow drama societies and were supposed in some mysterious way to save the theater from ruin. In addition, three plays, even if they were short, gave more members of The Curtain Club a chance to perform, whether they had acting roles, were property men, designed and made scenery, or did some other humbler task. Finally, they cost us less to produce.

Our rehearsals were as regularly held as classes, and any absence from them, except for necessary causes, led to the substitution of the understudy for the member to whom the part had been assigned. In some matters we occasionally had great good luck. I remember a wandering painter by the name of Peter Vincent who turned up from nowhere just as we were discussing the possibility of producing Shaw's *Androcles and the Lion* and who made us a set for this comedy, a play that requires more scenic tricks and changes than one realizes until one tries to produce it. His sets were simple and movable, could be shifted into various necessary combinations, and, so far as theatrical illusion was concerned, gave something of a sense of Rome and a colosseum. We seldom had any trouble with lighting, for there were always plenty of engineering students on hand to solve almost any difficulty.

The "handsome captain" of the legion, as Lavinia terms him, was indeed as handsome a male figure as anyone could desire, with a fine voice, one of the two exceptions I spoke of. (Later on he was cast for the main role in a one-act play about Judas Iscariot; and I still can recall the mingled sorrow, bafflement, and bitterness in his voice as he spoke the curtain line: "Thirty pieces of silver, coined in the Roman mint at Jerusalem!") The part of Androcles was neatly done by an agile young man who managed just the right combination of servility, courage, sniveling, and dignity; and the Lion was enacted by Eyler N. Simpson, a favorite of us all. Eyler later published a fine book, *The Ejido: Mexico's Way Out* (Chapel Hill: University of North Carolina Press, 1937), a study of Mexico's faulty rural economy; accompanied Henry Allen Moe when Moe, then secretary-general of the Guggenheim Foundation, visited all the Latin American republics to devise schemes for Guggenheim fellowship applications that would be more or less free of political pull; married a beautiful ballet dancer named Keith Coppage; and died all too soon at the height of his powers as a member of the Princeton faculty. I still laugh affectionately at his attempts to be both leonine and loving in Shaw's amusing burlesque.

Androcles does not fill an entire evening; and since, what with Roman gladiators and legionnaires and Christian prisoners and zookeepers and the like, we had used up the whole male part of The Curtain Club, a girl named Selwyn Sage and I wrote a one-act comedy we called *The Fascinating Mr. Denby*, which to our joint astonishment somebody printed. This bit of froth is to this day occasionally put on by women's clubs and girls' schools and in church parlors.

Two other major productions of The Curtain Club especially stick in my memory. One is of Bayard Veiller's chiller-diller, *The Thirteenth Chair*, which we produced on three separate occasions. The first night of each run was accompanied by a terrific thunderstorm, which exploded over Austin just as the melodrama was about to begin in the Austin Opera House—for Austin too had one of these old-line, gilt-scrolled, moth-eaten relics. For the committing of the murder in Act One the entire house is supposed to be black, but when I turned off all the stage lights, I found that the exit lights and certain others not controlled by the master switch left action on the stage dimly discernible. What to do? The lights needed to be out only a minute, but the audience might think the thunderstorm had done something to the power plant; and of course it is illegal not to have the exit lights and certain others on. We had worked our way into the good graces of the union crew we were required to hire and into those of the solitary policeman detailed to be in the theater whenever the building was used. I explained to the latter that the lights would be out only sixty seconds, and he agreed to forget those sixty seconds. During that period the murderer, supposed to be expert with daggers, stabs the victim while the thirteen principals are all seated at a table, reverses the knife, and hurls it upwards to the ceiling, where it sticks. The weapon remains in plain view throughout the rest of the play, but what member of a theater audience absorbed in a mystery play ever thinks of looking at the ceiling, or supposed ceiling, of a set? At the climax, in the third act, an old Irishwoman, supposed to be gifted with second sight, suddenly half rises from her chair and screams: "The knife!

The knife! Glory be to God, the knife!" whereupon the dagger is supposed to fall and embed its point in the table below. In fact the knife is reversed and released by a trigger and slides down a greased piano wire invisible to the audience. We thought we had rigged everything correctly, but at the dress rehearsal the knife refused to fall. The cast was in despair. What if this same accident happened on the opening night? I was in despair also, but I would not admit it. "Don't worry," I said; "the knife will fall tomorrow night."

The solution was simple. We rigged up a duplicate knife on a second piano wire, the second one being behind the first and invisible from the house, and provided two triggers, the one on the visible knife so arranged that if it did not work, it would at least pull the offending instrument quickly out of sight while the second knife descended. At any rate the climax was not spoiled.

There were, as I have said, two exceptions to the flatness of American voices. The captain of the legion had one; the girl who played the old Irishwoman had the other. Her name was Kathleen Burnett. Though she came from West Texas, she was happily free of any noticeably southwestern intonations, and had a voice which for purity of tone, musicality, and power to convey emotion I have never heard equaled except occasionally by professional singers. She told me she had never had vocal training of any kind; yet her cry at the end of *The Thirteenth Chair* sent shivers down my spine. Kathleen is the only undergraduate I ever advised to take up acting as a profession, but she chose, rather, to go back to West Texas, marry, and produce twins, robbing the theater of one of its potentially fine actresses.

When the next year we produced Schiller's *Mary Stuart*, we did so because we all knew Kathleen could play the role of that emotional and ill-fated monarch. Our Elizabeth was adequate; most of the other roles were competently filled; and the disguised priest, who in the final act manages to give Mary the last sacrament, was enacted by a young Catholic who so fully entered into the spirit of the tragedy that he begged an unconsecrated wafer from his priest, found a philtre for some unconsecrated wine, and gave the scene a dignity that was deeply impressive. I could find no Cecil, Lord Burleigh, in the club and took the part myself, adding a slight humpback and a limping foot to my getup in order to emphasize Burleigh's subtle intent—evil, consistent, and thoroughly of the Renaissance. We used the Coleridge translation (there are now better ones), which I cut and modified into something resembling modernity, and the play was advertised as a new translation, for which I was rightly reproached: I should have used the word "revised." There are two large towns near Austin many of whose citizens are descendants of the numerous German settlers from the days of the Republic of Texas; the elders among these families drove over to Austin to see the astonishing spectacle of a play by Schiller produced in the state capital.

I have chosen to dwell upon these continuing elements in my Texas life rather than attempt to describe the vagaries of my domestic existence. Sometimes I had a wife. Sometimes I had none. Sometimes she was in Montana and sometimes somewhere else. We did not have enough money, and she wanted a job, but what sort of job? There was nothing in the South to suit her. Besides, there was the baby. In Montana, Eleanor developed an ear infection and had to be sent South and kept there, my mother maintaining our establishment. We had moments of peace, but paranoia is unpredictable. I did not then understand what was the matter with W, and I prefer to remember her as in a poem I wrote in one of our more peaceful weeks:

> You that were beautiful,
>   Why did you go?
> Breast of moonlight,
>   Body of snow?
>
> O white wonder
>   Fled like a tune,
> You were a fountain that
>   Swayed to the moon!
>
> Marble and silver
>   Slip away
> Over the edge of time
>   Past night and day.
>
> You that were wonderful,
>   Where have you gone,
> Whose breast of ivory
>   Like silver shone?

Chapter XIII

Hull House

WHEN I TRY to sort out what I was doing and feeling during the long, unhappy months that elapsed before I found myself living at Hull House in Chicago, my recollections are as jumbled as things are in an old attic. The one regular pattern from year to year was of course my classes, but as I traveled, intellectually speaking, back and forth like a suburban train from Aeschylus to Shaw in my principal course, these journeys melt into one journey and these classes into one class, out of which now and then a face, a figure, a scrap of conversation, a problem about grades, and similar academic trivia emerge and vanish. Odd things take the place of regular order. Thus, for no good reason I recall the voice and face, both unctuous, of a minister in a small town in Central Texas. I remember a camp-out on the banks of the Texan Colorado River, the campfire, and the sleeping bags, when, after being informed of the marriage of a rather effeminate member of the faculty to a coed, we had fallen silent, and Dean Benedict suddenly asked in a drowsy voice, "Do you suppose they do?" and we howled with ribald laughter. I can remember walking in the middle of the Speedway during a downpour, the paths on either side of the road having turned into ditches of muddy water, and, on looking over my shoulder, seeing in the far distance a small black car. I thought no more about it and splashed on in the rain, leaving plenty of room for two cars abreast to pass me. Suddenly I was gently bumped in the rear. I turned, and saw that I had been hit by this same car. It was driven by a middle-aged woman, who glared at me, her mouth like an *O*, through the rain-beaded windshield. I stopped, thinking she would get out; on the contrary she backed away and drove furiously off to my left, just missing the ditch. I was not hurt, but to this day I wonder how so curious an episode could have happened.

I could draw, were I gifted that way, a picture of the monument to the Volunteer Firemen of Texas—a squat little man held up by a sort of chamber pot. I can still hear the slow drawl of Frank Dobie's voice as he read aloud with increasing distaste some far from authentic cowboy story in a popular magazine. I remember going with my assistant in her car to the shores of Lake Austin above the dam, taking a rowboat, tying up to an anchored houseboat, and climbing up to the roof of it. My assistant called my attention to a peculiar rock formation in the riverbank, which I could not make out; as I stared at it, I heard a plop in the river and turned to find a heap of female garments behind me and my girl friend swimming off in the curiously colored water of the Colorado. She shouted to me to follow, but I thought it better to decline. Conformity ranks high among the seven deadly virtues.

I traveled to various parts of the vast Texas empire giving lectures or commencement addresses—to Denton, Fort Worth, Dallas, San Antonio, Houston, Corpus Christi, Amarillo, and to hamlets whose names I have forgotten, though some of them were enchanting. I was sometimes asked to add to the glories of a high school by giving the commencement address and sometimes to the culture of a city or village by addressing the women's club. I do not know that, as a professor of comparative literature, I was ever asked to address a men's club.

The women's club circuit developed a well-worn pattern. Because I was that mysterious creature, a Humanist, anything I was likely to say was bound to be Improving; and as those who knew anything about me (they were few) knew I was a modernist, perhaps the only modernist on the University of Texas faculty, I was usually asked to address myself to such topics as "Trends in Modern Fiction," "The Meaning of Imagism," "H. L. Mencken as a Literary Critic," and "Is the South the Sahara of the Bozarts?" I had the experience in one small town of having the head of the program committee steal up to me and ask in a sweet voice if I would be good enough to explain where the Bozarts are, as she felt sure that some of the ladies might not know. I resisted the impulse to tell her the Bozarts were just north of the Ozarks and also a desire to include Edith Wharton's mischievous story "Xingu" in my remarks. (If you do not know that wonderful tale, you should read it forthwith.)

On such occasions I was met by the president or the secretary of the club in an impressive car, brought to the president's home, ushered into an immaculate guest room, invited to rest, and informed that there would be a simple family dinner at 6:30. The evening repast was never in my experience accompanied by preprandial, prandial, or post-prandial liquor. I was a professor, a university professor. I was an Example to the Young. After dinner there developed the virtually insoluble problem of Conversation. Had I been a professor of economics or government, the host would have seized upon me and carried me off to his library, den, or study, where we would, I assume, have engaged in brisk but friendly combat, the practical man against the theorist. But I was that terrifying thing, a scholar. My host therefore said that he wished he had more time to read and that he heartily approved teaching Good Books, and then, inevitably, the conversation veered to the problem, Why didn't the colleges teach better English? He had hired graduates so ignorant of grammar that they would spell God with a small *j*. My best move was to inquire how the problem was being met at the local school, and I soon discovered that Henry had made the basketball team and that Gertrude, his younger sister, was one of the sweetest girls in town. As soon as I decently could, I begged to be excused, pleading the fatigue of a long journey and thanking my host and hostess for a delightful evening. Breakfast would be at seven or whenever I came down.

The lecture was always in the afternoon and was always followed by Questions, and ice cream, cake, and coffee. The questions seldom touched upon the topic I had discussed; but when there had been enough of them, whatever their character, the president would announce, "We mustn't tire Doctor Jones," and invite the assembly to the dining room. The ice cream soothed my throat, but the cake was more icing than substance. By and by I was rescued as the company began to break up— the club members had to be home to prepare or supervise the evening meal—and then came the delicate question of the check. Up to now everything had been on a high plane, but vulgar commercialism now raised its ugly head. Did I want a check now or could it be sent? I came to prefer commercialism to culture, since in my experience club treasurers are not necessarily punctual. Having fulfilled my obligations and received my pay, I sometimes got back to Austin the best I could and was sometimes taken to the railway depot by a member of the club in her car.

I had during my Texas years occasionally taught in the summer quarter of the University of Chicago, for I remember our living in one of those long, dark vestibule apartments that used to be available near the Midway. I can remember being so tired towards the end of one of these summer quarters that, noting a puzzled expression on the students' faces in my class in Romantic poetry, and coming back to the sense of what I

126

was saying, I found with a shock that I had been comparing the qualities of lyric poetry in two bards named Kelly and Sheets.

After I received my leave of absence from the University of Texas, however, W and I lived in an apartment in Hull House while Jane Addams was still alive and while Halsted Street kept its traditional flavor. I think W did her unpredictable best to adjust to this novel situation, which at any rate was in a big city, but our marriage broke up during 1924–25. She found somebody more to her liking, and I, to my great good fortune, found a wife who, ever since we married in 1927 in New York, has been true and courageous, a remarkable stepmother, and an amazing writer of books in her own name, with other authors, and with me. But let me sort out my memories of this year into some sort of coherent pattern.

In the course of a varied life I have met many persons of talent, but only a few of genius. I am not a mystic, and I cannot explain the psychic process that tells me that the individual I am confronting belongs to the rare and few elect; but I had no sooner met Jane Addams than I knew I was confronting genius. Born in 1860 in central Illinois, she, together with Ellen Gates Starr, created Hull House in 1889 at the corner of Polk and Halsted streets in the midst of a notorious Chicago slum inhabited by five or six thousand Greeks, Italians, Russians, Germans, gypsies, and other strange peoples, who had come to the Promised Land but did not quite know what to do next. Miss Addams knew, and she gently led the other inhabitants of Hull House to share her knowledge. These were human beings, not statistical units, criminals, or hopeless derelicts. *Twenty Years at Hull House*, her most famous book, which she published in 1910, tells only half the story. At some time or another Hull House sheltered the homeless, university professors, hopeful young talent in all the arts, serious students of sociology, and both the overprivileged and the underprivileged. Although she made many trips over the United States and in foreign countries, Hull House was her base, her home, her invention. She headed, it seems to me, every lost cause in the tumultuous life of the early twentieth century. She was opposed to war, wherefore the Daughters of the American Revolution expelled her from their midst; Jane Addams's quiet comment on this action was that she had supposed she was by birth a life member, but that this was apparently only during good behavior. I sometimes think the only professional men who thoroughly understood her were the ward politicians of Chicago, who respected her command over people and situations. Whether her visitor was the Russian radical Prince Kropotkin, a convict just out of jail, a vague and puzzled philanthropist, a graduate student, or Mr. Bimbo, king of the gypsies, who lived across the way at Polk Street in an apartment magnificently furnished with clean newspapers, she was always serene, gracious, and helpful. She shared the Nobel Peace Prize and helped to found the American Civil Liberties Union, and just before her death was an international figure to whom statesmen listened with care. But her heart was always at Hull House, which, alas, no longer exists save for the ancient main building that bears a plaque containing her name. Just to be in the same room with her brought peace to the soul and tranquillity to the troubled. She was to me and I think to thousands of others a Protestant saint, and I have never seen her like and do not expect ever to see her like again.

I read recently in an issue of the *Times Literary Supplement* a review of a novel in which the critic says that the book under scrutiny is a persuasive study of the dark storm that can settle over a man in the middle of his life—a phrase that has haunted me ever since I began writing this chapter. If in 1925 I was not precisely at the midpoint of my journey according to Scripture, I was close enough to it to make this year the dark night of my soul. W was clearly unbalanced; yet she had her moments of humor and of generosity of spirit, nor did she fail in her duties as a mother, notably when Eleanor contracted whooping cough and had to be confined to our floor in Hull House for some weeks. Periods of generosity, however, were likely to be followed by periods of withdrawal, especially withdrawal from me, so that I never knew on what plane we were going to meet. I fear neither of us contributed much to the avowed purpose of Hull House. W had disliked the academic life in Missoula and resented it in Austin; now she resented being confined to Hull House—an understandable resentment, but not one that bred peace and harmony. W got a job in a bookstore and by and by found some sort of acquaintance I knew nothing about; and so did I, of necessity, since I spent a great part of my day in the Harper Library of the University of Chicago and, for some weeks, a great part of my late afternoons and evenings as dramatic director of the North Shore Players, who put on their productions regularly from Evanston northward.

In such hours as I could find, I tried to reason sanely about both my domestic and my professional situation. For my family I could see no future; and my central duty, as I saw it, was to insure that the life of our daughter should not be too greatly marred by these rapid shocks. As a scholar I felt that I was in honor bound to continue that research for which the University of Texas had given me leave; and since there was slowly forming in my mind a new concept of the interpretation of the American experience—a matter to which I shall recur—I conceived that, come what might, my duty was to spend the year in profitable study. This I continued to do, diving into the bowels of the Harper Library to

128

come up at noon for a lunch, usually of a hot dog, a bun, and a cup of coffee from a street vendor on the Midway, and then diving back again. I read and read and read—oh, how I read!—histories, biographies, autobiographies, travelers' accounts of the New World, "literary" works, anything and everything that had to do with the New World from 1492 to 1848, slowly shaping a thesis that would be acceptable to the Department of Comparative Literature. My thesis was accepted so far as the department was concerned. I then applied to the dean of the graduate school for permission to be examined for the Ph.D., only to be turned down on the ground that I had not taken enough courses. In vain I pointed out that, according to the university catalogue, a Ph.D. was not awarded on course work alone and that I had in successive summers been paid by the University of Chicago for teaching courses of the caliber I was now unexpectedly called upon to take. Nothing shook him. I withdrew from the graduate school at the University of Chicago, and I have never entered it or any other graduate school as a student from that time. Years later the University of Chicago made a sort of amends: in 1974 the Alumni Association voted me a medal "pro singulari eius merito."

One day, in the spring of 1925, W and I faced reality. She was in one of her better moods. She agreed that she was not a right person to be the wife of a literary scholar; she proposed a divorce (I think I had previously said to her that a breaking-up of this sort was inevitable); she wished to retain the custody of our child (something to which I consented with a heavy heart, yet betting it would not last); and she was determined not to accept alimony but only a monthly sum sufficient to take care of Eleanor. I agreed and faithfully fulfilled my part of the contract. She left Hull House, later established herself somehow in New York, and eventually turned up at the Gurdjieff Institute near Paris. Of her later years I shall not speak.

I was sustained through some part—no, indeed, through all—of this dark year by the intelligent compassion of the woman who in 1927 became my second wife. This is Bessie Judith Zaban, born in Atlanta, youngest daughter of David and Anne (Springer) Zaban, who with other members of their families had emigrated from the old Austro-Hungarian Empire in 1895 or earlier and had come by way of Boston to Atlanta. I never met either Bessie's father or her mother—the father because, after an honorable business career in Atlanta, he died in 1921; and the mother, I think, because she disapproved of her daughter's marriage with a *goy*. Bessie turned up in a class I was teaching at the University of Chicago in the summer of 1922. She was then a short, merry-faced girl with wonderful dark curly hair and a sense both of subdued mockery in her eyes and of a spirit that demanded something more solid of life than mere entertainment. She was graduated from the University of Chicago in 1923 and on her own initiative got a job in the advertising department of Marshall Field and Company and an apartment with a girl friend, where Carl Sandburg occasionally turned up. Bessie was, and is, musical; she demanded and usually secured the best in books, in painting, in companionship, in fun; and even before our marriage she introduced me to the glorious and generous-hearted Jewish community that in the twenties occupied apartment houses in the Hyde Park district of Chicago. For me, at least, the life of this community was a revelation of what civilized behavior could demand and be. The group took me in without a shadow of discrimination; and I particularly remember the warm and affectionate welcomes I used to receive in the Abt family's home. The elder Abt was a labor arbitrator for Hart, Schaffner & Marx; and his two gifted children, Marion and John, were later under attack in the gloomy years dominated by Senator McCarthy. After our marriage the Abts were also responsible for introducing Bessie and me to Vermont; and one of my vivid memories of Vermont as I knew it in the late twenties is an image of Closson Gilbert, on whose land we were permitted to be squatters before we purchased our own summer place near the village of Peacham, walking down the road with a hayfork in one hand and a copy of the current *New Republic* in the hip-pocket of his overalls.

I think I am not the brooding type, or at least I do not commonly carry my anger in my bosom to keep it warm; but in the late spring of 1925 I received a letter from the University of Texas I cannot forget and find it hard to forgive. That institution now had a new president, a new dean of the faculty of arts and sciences, and a Board of Regents essentially new to their jobs. Nobody in Austin save for a handful of teachers knew me or my work or the reason I was on leave of absence. In my absence, therefore, they abolished my department, my job, and my salary. I was given no opportunity to show that I had faithfully fulfilled my contract as arranged by Acting President Battle. I curtly acknowledged the reception of this letter and wrote to Professor E. C. Barker, head of the Texas chapter of the American Association of University Professors, saying I had been discharged without cause and without a hearing. Ought I not lay my case before the association? He replied, saying the authorities had grossly violated the code of the AAUP. I started preparing a statement of my grievances.

As the blows of Fate fell one by one on my defenseless head, I began to feel like a character in some novel by Thomas Hardy. I had put together an unusual dissertation—this verdict was not mine alone but that of members of the faculty who had read it—yet my doctoral career had ended in total failure. My family life, irregular at best, had collapsed. I might or might not see my daughter again. I had never lacked employment before, but I was utterly inexperienced in the matter of landing an academic job, and my small experience on a couple of small newspapers scarcely qualified me for journalism. And then, as if to prove the ancient saw that it is never darkest than just before dawn, I received from Jim Royster, now at the University of North Carolina in Chapel Hill, an offer of a place there as associate professor of English at a salary that, for those days, was excellent. Jim had been called to his native state as Kenan Professor of English Philology in 1921 and had immediately accepted, feeling that to modernize the department at Austin was a hopeless task. From 1922 to 1925 he had been dean of the College of Liberal Arts; and when Edwin Greenlaw, the great patriarchal figure of enlightened southern scholarship, had gone to The Johns Hopkins University in 1925, the president of North Carolina, Harry Woodburn Chase, promptly moved Royster into the post that Greenlaw had vacated, that of dean of the graduate school.

I saw no reason now to advertise, either to Texas or to the world, the injury Texas had done. I wrote at once to Royster gratefully accepting his offer, and l wrote a curt resignation to the president of the University of Texas. I resolved to throw off as much as I could of the burden of the past, and with two jolly young companions take a brief vacation in the late summer before reporting for duty at Chapel Hill. My comrades were Eyler Simpson and John Abt, and we traversed North Carolina from Asheville to the sea by foot, by accepting rides, by any honest device. I was determined this time not to move into a commonwealth I knew nothing about. We ended by going through the Great Dismal Swamp Canal and landing at Norfolk, Virginia. I made my solitary way from Norfolk to Durham by an ancient railroad, the Norfolk & Southern, whence I took a bus to Chapel Hill, twelve or thirteen miles away.

BOOK FOUR

THREE GREAT UNIVERSITIES

Chapter XIV

Chapel Hill

MY EXCURSIONS out of the Middle West into Montana and Texas had not on the whole brought me either happiness or content. I had of course known nothing about life in the Far West or the Deep South, and I dare say that my initial ignorance had been as much to blame as any hostile force lurking in the commonwealths in question. Now I was about to become a citizen of another state, one I knew slightly more about, brief though our excursion from Asheville to Cape Hatteras and Norfolk had been.

The ever thoughtful James Royster had arranged for me to have a room in the house of C. Addison Hibbard, a Wisconsin graduate and the genial dean of the College of Arts and Sciences, and to take my meals with Mrs. Wilson, whose small dining club was jocularly known as the Old Soldiers' Home. The reason for this descriptive term was that Major Kane, a veteran of the Confederate army and a retired professor of mathematics, took his meals there, as did a select group of faculty members. The major was a gallant of the old school and, despite being deaf, a genial companion. He embodied all that was admirable in the Lost Cause.

I count my years at Chapel Hill among the more blessed ones of my life. I came there in the ripe afternoon of the intellectual and cultural renaissance of the university and of the state. This rebirth had begun with Governor Aycock at the opening of the century and had continued; and as noted in a report by Frederic A. Ogg, published in 1928 by the American Council of Learned Societies, "the leadership in the new research movement in the South is traceable to one institution, and to certain men and women in it, namely, the University of North Carolina." When Aycock had taken office as governor in 1901, North Carolina was sometimes humorously referred to as a valley of humiliation lying between two mountains of conceit, the mountains being Virginia and South Carolina, with their traditions of the old plantation South. Aycock's inaugural address in January, 1901, rang like a trumpet call:

On a hundred platforms, to half the voters of the State, in the late campaign, I pledged the State, its strength, its heart, its wealth, to universal education. I promised the illiterate poor man, bound to a life of toil and struggle and poverty, that life should be brighter for his boy and girl than it had been for him and the partner of his sorrows and joys. I pledged the wealth of the State to the education of his children. Men of wealth, representatives of great corporations, applauded eagerly my declaration. I then realized that the strong desire which dominated me for the uplifting of the whole people moved not only my heart, but was likewise the hope and aspiration of those upon whom Fortune had smiled . . . our wealth increases, our industries multiply, our commerce extends, and among the owners of this wealth, this multiplying industry, this extending commerce, I have found no man who is unwilling to make the State stronger and better by liberal aid to the cause of education.

Edgar W. Knight, the historian of education in North Carolina, reminds us that in 1900–1901 the platforms of all the political parties favored educational reform and that by 1903 seventy-eight of the ninety-seven counties had planned educational rallies. Between 1907 and 1911 more than two hundred rural schools had been established. Dedicated members of an older generation were in these same years rescuing the University of North Carolina from the doldrums of Reconstruction; and under a succession of able presidents—Francis P. Venable, Edward Kidder Graham, and Harry Woodburn Chase—the institution at Chapel Hill had been changed from a ghost town to what E. K. Graham had envisioned in April, 1915:

The state university is an instrument of democracy for realizing all these high and healthful aspirations of the state. . . . The whole function of education is to make straight and clear the way for the liberation of the spirit of man from the tyranny of place and time, not by running away from the world, but by mastering it.

When I was called there, the president was Harry Woodburn Chase, one of the most remarkable educational administrators the South has ever known. By birth a New Englander, he was better informed about southern affairs than most southern businessmen; and he had that most wonderful of administrative gifts, the appearance of not ordering anybody about when as a matter of fact he was in full and equable control of any situation. He left with reluctance in 1929–30, the year when Addison Hibbard transferred to Northwestern; when James Royster, broken in health by the death of his beloved wife and by overwork, died of self-inflicted burns in Richmond, Virginia; and when I left for the University of Michigan. Chase could not have accomplished all he did without the help of a great generation of faculty members, among them Howard W. Odum, Rupert Vance, Paul Green, and Frederick Koch of Playmakers fame. The founding of the University of North Carolina Press (incorporated in 1922) was intended to create another organ of information for the South, and it shortly took its place among the leading university presses of the republic. Among the influential branches of the university, the Graduate School of Arts and Sciences was not least. To it came scholars and scientists not merely from North Carolina but from other states; and from it, and from the School of Commerce after September, 1919, went out a remarkable procession of graduates not merely into the state but into the nation also—so many, indeed, that humorists took to making jokes about the Tarheel conquest of New York City. The Great Depression interrupted but fortunately did not quench this expansiveness, this geniality, this fine combination of higher education and the desire to benefit the state, the region, and the country. I think it not without meaning that many who helped to reshape the University of North Carolina were also students of the work of the University of Wisconsin "in the service of the state."

I found the members of the English department a congenial group; and since as a result of World War I the university had gone on the quarter system, I fell back into a familiar routine. I regularly taught in successive quarters of the academic year a course in the literature of the Restoration, followed by one in the literature of the eighteenth century, and that by the literature of the romantic movement, and of course others besides. But this triple-quarter instruction of mine was, I hope, good for the students, and I found it was especially good for me, since, in revising my doctoral dissertation, it gave me a surer basis and a wider understanding of what I wanted to do.

What I wanted to do took shape as *America and French Culture: 1750–1848*, published by the University of North Carolina Press in 1927 and long kept in print. In 1932 this volume received from the American Historical Association the Jusserand Medal as "a distinguished contribution to the history of intellectual relations among nations"—an award that should have interested those of the University of Chicago Graduate School who had rejected me as an applicant for the doctorate.

In the twenties, of course, social history was much in vogue; and I think one element in this study that gave it special interest was the opening analysis of three great forces in American history—the cosmopolitan spirit, the frontier spirit, and the spirit of the middle class. As I remarked in the conclusion of the book, "There are varying levels of American life; there are varying aspects of French culture, and in the relation between the two lies the fascination and complexity of the problem." But I noted also that one continuing obstacle to a sympathetic reception during these years of things French by the Americans has been "a sense of religious difference," whereas an element that worked in the opposite direction was the social prestige of Frenchmen and things French among the Americans. And I found that "on the whole it is in the departments of manners and fashions that the French have exerted their most notable influence in shaping American culture. In intellectual matters they have had vogue rather than influence." I stated too ambitiously in the preface of this volume (which runs to 615 pages!) that I hoped some day to write a sequel to it, but alas, I have never again found the opportunity to do so. Other scholars have, fortunately, carried on where I broke off.

America and French Culture was not the only book I was able to produce, at least in part, during these years at Chapel Hill. In 1928 the Press brought out *The Romanesque Lyric: Studies in its Background and Development from Petronius to the Cambridge Songs, 50–1050* by Philip Schuyler Allen and me. The prose of this volume was Allen's; the verse translations, almost seventy-five in all, were mine. Many of these date back to long afternoons in Phil Allen's office in Chicago, when— equipped with quantities of chalk, an eraser, Migne's dictionary of medieval Latin and other reference books, a typewriter, and one or more dusty volumes from the Harper Library—I struggled with the an- fractuosities of an alien tongue. I got into this particular job by reason of my affection for Allen and through the urging of friends of his, who said that unless some external stimulus (meaning me) was applied to Allen, he would never produce the volume to which most of his learned life had been dedicated. He did produce it; and a little later, the University of Chicago Press brought out his *Medieval Latin Lyrics* (1931), with which I had much less to do. I have no Gaelic, and I had to depend upon literal translations and the help of Tom Peete Cross for a handful of lyrics from the ancient Irish; yet it was precisely from these that Samuel Barber chose for part of his musical sequence *Hermit Songs* (1958). These two books had, in the nature of things, no great popular success, and the reader may not care about the problems a translator faces. Inasmuch as the stanzaic forms of the originals were greatly varied, and Latin verse slowly lost its quantitative character in the Christian era, I felt free to choose whatever stanzaic form seemed to me likeliest to convey in English the effects, as I understood them, of the Latin originals. I remember what a struggle it was to turn some of the Latin hymns into English, the reason being that the vocabulary of English hymnody is frayed and tired beyond belief, but I hope I may be pardoned for thinking that

> Thou splendid giver of our light,
>   O luminous serenity

is not bad for

> Lucis largitor splendide
> Cuius sereno lumine,

and that

> Fate to beauty still must give
> Shortened life and fugitive;
> All that's noble, all that's fair
> Suddenly to death repair,

is something like what Claudian meant when he wrote:

> Pulchris stare diu Parcarum lege negatur.
> Magna repente ruunt; summa cadunt subito.

Nor were these the only products of my North Carolina years. I brought out an edition of the lyrics of Edgar Allan Poe for Joseph Blumenthal's Spiral Press in 1929; and in 1930 I joined Dougald MacMillan of the English department there in editing a volume for Henry Holt and Company called *Plays of the Restoration and the Eighteenth Century*, long a textbook in college courses. I took on the plays of the Restoration and Dougald those of the eighteenth century, but we shared responsibility for the whole volume equally, and each of us was amused to try writing the introductory essays and other commentaries in a style that would at least suggest the period we were talking about. I think neither editor has complained about the vogue of this collection. It was widely used and generously received.

Nor were these all of my extracurricular activities during these golden years. Addison Hibbard had invented a syndicated weekly literary column subscribed to by a dozen or fourteen newspapers distributed over the South; but finding the burden of reading, criticizing, and writing a weekly column more than he could meet and yet carry out his duties as dean, he sold me the column, and I found myself obligated to watch the advertisements in *Publishers Weekly* of books about the South or by southerners and write for review copies. It kept me busy merely reading new publications as they reached me. Sometimes I literally read a new book a day, although the more important works required a longer time for an estimate of their quality as a contribution to literature or as an analytical approach to the problem of the "New South." I think I strove my best to be fair, but in the nature of the case "The Literary Lantern" dealt with problems of new southern industrial and commercial order rather than the nostalgic backward glances of the "Fugitives," whose intellectual capital was Vanderbilt University. I recognized the charm of the plantation order and the dangers of the new industrial one, but I could not for the life of me see how the South could ward off industrialization. As I was but one of the many at Chapel Hill striving at once to welcome industry to the late Confederacy and also fend off some of its more depressing consequences, I suppose I was regarded as an enemy of the Neo-Confederates at Nashville.

The second of my extracurricular activities at Chapel Hill would probably have been possible nowhere else and under no other president than Harry Woodburn Chase. The town of Chapel Hill existed for the sake of the university, and, contrariwise, the university had to take on many of the municipal duties of a small community. Thus the university ran the only hotel in the place, an excellent hostelry called The Carolina Inn. It maintained the only medical service in the village, made itself responsible in greater or lesser degree for such chores as street-sweeping and road-building, and from an unfavorable point of view was in fact paternalistic rather than democratic in its interpretation of civic responsibility. About halfway through my time at Chapel Hill I grew more and more uneasy at the lack of any general bookstore in the little village. There was, of course, the student Book Exchange, another aspect of academic paternalism, but this dealt only in student supplies and textbooks; yet Chapel Hill was more and more becoming a literary center to which writers like Wilbur Daniel Steele and James Boyd were coming by reason of the intellectual stir on its campus. But neither their books nor books reviewed in "The Literary Lantern" were anywhere available.

Finally I went to Harry Chase with my problem and my special solution. I sketched out a plan for a beginning: I would secure copies of books likely to appeal to the increasing student body and those who came to Chapel Hill because of its intellectual stimulation, and with the sympathetic cooperation of the manager of the Book Exchange, which I thought I could be sure of, and with the help of interested colleagues and graduate students, run a nonprofit bookstore in my office. Chase thought a bit. Then he consented to try it on an experimental basis and authorized me to negotiate my business relations with the manager of the Book Exchange. I accordingly equipped my office with a few tables and some comfortable chairs, distributed ash trays (North Carolina was, after all, the tobacco center of the New World), and got some books from the University of North Carolina Press and afterwards from general publishers. Students were welcome to come in and browse or buy. At the end of each quarter I held an auction of any shelf-worn volumes, auctions that were among the more amusing episodes of this rather unusual business enterprise.

But what to call it? I do not now recall how we arrived at the name The Bull's Head Bookshop, except that we wanted something vigorously masculine for a title and, I suppose, took over the idea of "bull" from the then celebrated tobacco Bull Durham. At any rate we had a sign painted resembling vaguely an Elizabethan tavern sign—a portrait of a blue-eyed bull (something of a rarity in nature), which amused the sophisticated and reassured the timid undergraduates. Slowly but surely we began to increase our business. Colleagues were most obliging at spelling me when I could not preside over the shop; and as all our transactions were on a cash-and-carry basis, we had but small bookkeeping problems. I am to this day profoundly grateful to the Book Exchange administration for their sympathetic support of my invention, which, after I left Chapel Hill, was for a time made a branch of that institution, and when the new library was erected, was housed in the basement of that building. I can find no history of the University of North Carolina that rehearses the humble beginnings of the first general bookstore in Chapel Hill.

Nor did I entirely give up the production of plays. I was responsible for a production of A. A. Milne's amusing *The Dover Road*, the cast including graduate students and members of the faculty. The sentimental solution, if it be a solution, of this drama did not obliterate its quirky good humor and was in a sense a relief from the determined seriousness of the folk plays it was the business of Professor Frederick Koch and the Carolina Playmakers to produce for the benefit of the state at large.

A small fleet of buses took the actors to the remotest corners of the commonwealth; their tours included towns in which the stage crew had to use the utmost ingenuity to fit the portable scenery into some local auditorium or, if necessary, on an outdoor platform. Koch and I had met, as it were, indirectly, when I was at the state university at Missoula and he had sent an associate to Montana from North Dakota to produce a pageant of Montana history, the one which ended in a wind storm. I had occasionally made fun of folk plays, but, I hope, in an entirely good-natured fashion, and Koch's total dedication to his version of drama for the state was too admirable for anybody to try to laugh off. He was in large degree responsible for Paul Green's beginnings as a dramatist and pageant-writer. (*The Lost Colony*, it will be remembered, has played each summer for years.) Some of the folk plays dealt with tradition; some of them showed the impact of contemporary research through the increasing opportunity offered the younger generation to attend modern schools and to avoid the worser aspects of nineteenth-century industrial society.

One of the more notable elements in the far-flung influence of this statewide renaissance was its effect upon the younger generation in nearby commonwealths. Young citizens of South Carolina, for example, came to Chapel Hill, absorbed such skills and outlooks as suited them, and went forth—sometimes, to be sure, in a northerly direction—to apply what they had learned in Appalachia generally or even in Northern cities. South Carolina has since shaken off its lethargy.

Harry Chase was so closely identified with the vigorous life of the Upper South that I never once heard the epithet "damyankee" applied to him. As for me, as I pondered the cultural development of the South, particularly the Upper South—and my book-review column compelled me to think about it constantly—the conviction was more and more borne in upon me that the bases of American culture were not colonialism and independence per se but a rich amalgam, that its roots were deep in Europe, in the peculiar varieties of Old World culture transported into the transatlantic world. But I was not yet prepared to launch on scholarly excursions substantiating this theory. American literature at Chapel Hill was taught mainly by Norman Foerster, who carried thither his special brand of neohumanism, and by Gregory Paine, a bluff, stout-hearted representative of the current orthodox opinion. Paine was a notable representative of the first commandment for the scholar: first get your facts straight and then sort them out.

Bessie and I were married in New York on June 11, 1927, and in the fall we were installed in the Dan Grant house some distance from the village proper in an environment so rural that when George Coffman came to Chapel Hill from Montana one summer to teach and roomed with us, the outdoor noises of birds and insects would not let him sleep and he therefore found a room in the village. The Grant house was but a temporary shelter; by and by we came to rest—Bessie, Eleanor, who now lived with us, and I—in one of a group of cottages erected by the university as faculty personnel expanded in a locality in town popularly known as Baby Hollow. Our house and grounds abutted on the grounds of the house occupied by D. D. Carroll, dean of the new College of Commerce, and was close to that of Francis Bradshaw, philosopher and administrator.

Not especially with reference to these colleagues but having in mind the University of North Carolina generally, I may remark that one of the great virtues of Chapel Hill was its tolerance for individualistic peculiarities, a tolerance developed, I suppose, as a consequence of an institutional life that had seen endless generations of students and teachers come and go. The dean of the School of Pharmacy, for example, was of course an excellent pharmacist, but he also liked to collect Confederate postage stamps, baby caps, and herbals—that is, books describing herbs' curative properties. Horace Williams, virtually the oldest member of the faculty, a man whom somebody described as the last Hegelian in the United States, had a profound distrust of all modern publishing, and when he finally got around to printing two small volumes containing, as he thought, the garnered wisdom of a long philosophic career, he had them done by a local printer and seemed surprised when they attracted no professional attention. I wish I still possessed either or both of these volumes, for they contained such sentences as "Apples are not photographs," and "The multiplication table has no birthdays"—dogmatic assertions that are not only profoundly true but had something to do with Professor Williams's philosophy.

I can never forget the warm companionship that Bessie and I enjoyed with Russell and Dean Potter, midwesterners both, who had come to Chapel Hill some years before our arrival. Russell taught in the Department of English and in the University Extension Division. Dean was a skilled secretary and took a position in Jim Royster's office when Royster was dean of the graduate school. What between "Dean" as the Christian name of the secretary and "dean" as the title of the post, the resulting mix-up among unwary students was sometimes wonderful to behold. Dean was a gentle soul, rather more placid than Russell, who was by birth and training inclined to be somber, the darkness of his spirit having been increased by his experience in World War I. He never imposed stories of that brutalizing period on his friends; and on the surface he was amiable, whimsical, and, for the benefit of his children, the creator of a private cartoon strip about the adventures of Mousefoot and his friends. He was also a serious worker; and once, when he was ill and could not go to an extension class in a town some distance from Chapel Hill, we discovered that he spent three hours in each class meeting and that it took three of us at an hour each to replace the ailing Russell when we were called upon to substitute for him. When Ellen Glasgow published *They Stooped to Folly*, we could not help identifying Russell, at least so far as spirit is concerned, with Martin Welding in that fine novel. When the general exodus from the Chapel Hill English department occurred and the president left, Russ accepted a post at

Columbia as the man in charge of their public lecture series, an onerous task, since he had to prepare for any sudden whimsicality or balkiness in his row of celebrities. He recuperated from these tensions by buying a farm near West Cornwall, Connecticut, itself a small center attracting literary worthies like Mark Van Doren; and when he was finally retired from the Columbia staff, he stuck with his farm, taking a cheerful part in the town meetings and raising the vegetables that that part of Connecticut with its peculiar soil permitted to grow. He could talk with the local blacksmith or neighboring farmers with the same ease he displayed in his dealings with celebrities. Alack, that Dean and he are no longer among the living!

I must record one amusing memory of the last commencement ceremony I attended at Chapel Hill. Addison Hibbard had proposed, and I had enthusiastically seconded, that Ellen Glasgow be awarded an honorary degree. This degree was to be awarded at the first outdoor commencement to be attempted at Chapel Hill in this century, for the holding of the ceremony in the awkwardly shaped wooden auditorium had proved more and more difficult as the years drifted by. A platform was accordingly erected for the dignitaries, and chairs by the hundreds were put on the lawn. Miss Glasgow was extremely deaf and, this being her first honorary degree, also extremely nervous. Hibbard tried to assure her: "Miss Ellen," he said into the little box she used as a hearing aid, "all you have to do is to march in a short procession from the president's office to the platform, take a chair you will find with your name on it, and then, when the time comes, Howard will tap you on the shoulder. All you have to do then is to stand up, step forward two paces, then somebody will put a hood over your shoulders and the president will give you a diploma, and then you sit down again."

Miss Glasgow obeyed her instructions. Her seat on the platform was at the end of the front row of chairs. Unfortunately, when the commencement procession reached the platform, some small accident in arrangement prevented me from sitting immediately behind Miss Ellen. Unfortunately also, as the ceremonies went forward, a small breeze, cooling and grateful, sprang up, but the platform had been built in the shade of one of the fine trees on the campus, a branch of which began to wave, coming closer and closer to Ellen Glasgow's right shoulder. I was at the wrong end of the second row of chairs to do anything about it, and I had not the time to write a note and have it passed from hand to hand down a row of stately colleagues telling the man behind Ellen to stop a branch from hitting her head or shoulder. I watched with anxiety, but I could not prevent the small catastrophe. The branch finally touched her, and, obedient to her instructions, she jumped up, took two paces forward, and waited for the hood to descend upon her. Hibbard, however, came gallantly to the rescue, led her gently backward to her seat, and when the time came, saw to it that she arose to receive her diploma and her hood.

Chapel Hill was a sunny interval in our lives, the more alluring in that, when we revisited the village a couple of years ago, we found it had grown, indeed, but not changed its character. Bessie had been happy as advertising manager and copy editor for the University of North Carolina Press. Eleanor had done well in the local school, and I was content. But in 1929 the Great Depression began to show its ugly face to the state legislature, and the state was not prepared for all that this catastrophe implied. Our salaries were cut at Chapel Hill, as was the general budget for higher education, and a second cut was imminent. Jim Royster, as I have indicated, had left to be a visiting professor in Great Britain, but had broken down and died in Richmond, Virginia. He had made me acting head of the Department of English during his proposed absence, and had also given me certain confidential in-structions about other members of the department that I was to carry out if I could. Meantime, O. J. Campbell had left Wisconsin to go to the University of Michigan as a person of certain importance; and I owe to him, I am sure, an offer to me in the spring of 1929 of an excellent post in the English department at Ann Arbor. Although I asked for a year in which to give Michigan a decision, a request which the university graciously allowed, too many persons of importance were leaving Chapel Hill for me to feel easy, and no prediction for the future seemed, at the time, sound. I therefore resigned in 1930. I later discovered that members of the department, or most of them, had been holding meetings without me, the reason alleged being that I was somehow plotting to have a favorite friend of mine appointed chairman in Royster's place. I went to Harry Chase with my problem. He, too, was leaving, but he made it clear to my erring colleagues that departmental meetings without the chairman were scarcely ethical and in fact illegal. Somewhat hurt by this disclosure, I was later amused to discover that the English department had agreed to call George Raleigh Coffman to the vacant post. He was the chairman I had worked with in Missoula and the man to whom I had dedicated *America and French Culture* in 1927.

Chapter XV

You Can't
Go Home Again

WE LEFT Chapel Hill with regret but of necessity. The first reduction in salaries at Chapel Hill we thought we could manage, but when the second cut threatened (it was soon carried through) only a few months later, I could not see, nor could Bessie see, how we could live in Chapel Hill even on our combined modest incomes, nor why we should stay when Michigan offered an attractive post at more money and what looked like financial stability. I therefore sent my letter of resignation to Harry Chase, who was about to become president of the University of Illinois, and I also published an open letter in the *Chapel Hill Weekly* imploring the governor not to damage the university further by more cuts in its appropriation—an eloquent but futile performance. The fall of 1930 found us in Ann Arbor.

The University of Michigan requires a touch of historical explanation. The state came into the union in 1837 under a constitution drafted in 1835 and accepted two years later. The university, legally created by this document, was given a unique place among state universities, one that makes it, in the opinion of some historians, a fourth arm of the government. The constitution enumerates an executive, a legislative, a judicial, and an educational function for the commonwealth; that is to say, a governor (with appropriate subordinates), a bicameral legislature, a state supreme court and power to create lower courts, and a body of eight regents, who, together with the state superintendent of schools and the president of the university, are to create and govern a University of Michigan. The terms of the regents run for eight years, two expiring

146

biennially, and the regents are elected as independent officers by the whole body of the voters. With understandable pride many alumni have declared that their alma mater is not a state university but a university supported by the state. The duty of the legislature is to provide funds for the university, but beyond that it cannot go. Because of the semiprivate character this gives the school, and for other reasons, the University of Michigan has acquired a large private endowment; and though it is a member of the midwestern Big Ten Conference, it frequently goes its own way. Perhaps for this reason the legislature created in 1857 a State College of Agriculture and Applied Science at East Lansing, which it later retitled Michigan State University. In Michigan, all moneys for the support of education flow into a unit called the Literary Fund, which wholly or in part supports the public schools of the state, the former normal schools which are now branches of one or another university, Michigan State University, and the University of Michigan. Some decades back, furthermore, a canny superintendent of schools in Detroit studied the Literary Fund. That city then had a modest College of the City of Detroit, which he parlayed into Wayne State University. This institution, of course, inherited its predecessor's right to a slice of the financial pie. The state of Michigan has a peculiar shape, as a glance at a map will show. Most of its population is found in the lower tiers of counties in the Lower Peninsula; yet in a state whose land mass is about 58,000 square miles, it is remarkable that all three of its leading institutions of higher learning are concentrated in about one hundred square miles in the southeast corner of the state.

The original campus of the University of Michigan, the one I knew, was forty acres on the east side of Ann Arbor, together with sundry contiguous or neighboring plots of ground. Thus the famous University of Michigan Hospital, run by the Medical School (although the counties may send patients to it), is only a few blocks from the main campus. Since my years in Ann Arbor the campus holdings have doubled in area by the creation of a new or North Campus across the little Huron River, the university providing bus service for connection between the two. The old campus, my campus, was rather crowded with buildings, the cluster being increased by structures not on the forty acres but close to it; yet in 1930 this relatively small plot of ground included almost all the major components of a great institution.

This was so in part because of the farsightedness of one of the great educators of the nineteenth century, Henry Philip Tappan of Rhinebeck, New York, trained in German philosophy and familiar with the Prussian theory of academic learning. He came to Ann Arbor in 1852 when the university was struggling to keep alive, and he was dismissed by the

147

regents in 1863, a shameful act for which, repentant, they later issued a public apology. Tappan knew what a university should be, and he was determined that the infant school at Ann Arbor should achieve his vision.

The University of Michigan was going to be, he said, dedicated to scholarship, science, and research. In 1852-53, he issued a catalog like a summons: "An institution cannot deserve the name of a University which does not aim, in all the material of learning, in the professorships which it establishes, and in the whole scope of its provisions, to make it possible for every student to study what he pleases and to any extent he pleases." The last clause may be excessive, but the development of the University of Michigan has in general been the practical working-out of Tappan's idea. In the beginning a faculty in the arts and sciences; then a medical school (1850); a law school (1859); a college of dental surgery (1875); a school of pharmacy (1876); a college of engineering (1895); a college of architecture (1913); a school of education (1921); a school of business administration (1924); the William L. Clements Library of American History (1924); and a school of forestry and conservation (1927). This was up to my time; the North Campus reveals what has been added since.

The greater presidents of the University of Michigan after Tappan— men of the caliber of James Burrill Angell (1871-1909) and Harry Burns Hutchins, twice acting president and then president (1910-20)—have simply followed where Tappan had told them they must go. The president in my day was Alexander Grant Ruthven (1929-51), who faced the necessary but unglamorous job of holding the university together during the Great Depression and World War II. Such, in brief, was the formidable institution of which I was now going to be a part.

Bessie, always the practical one, disposed of some of our meager furniture, saw to it that the books, which to a scholar are more valuable than Hepplewhite chairs, were properly packed and sent off, and went as an advance agent to find a place for us to live. She was welcomed by Oscar James Campbell, my loved instructor from Wisconsin, and by his good wife Emily. They canvassed the housing situation, and Bessie rented for the next year, furnished, the house of Professor Samuel Moore, who was to be on leave of absence. I remembered him from my days at Madison, an old-line philologist who always observed the proprieties. I never studied under him, but I remember vividly that at the University of Wisconsin he had a class with one student in it, a woman. Professor Moore conducted this tiny class as ceremoniously as if the enrollment had been hundreds. He would enter the classroom, seat himself at the desk, wait for the solitary girl (I hope she was amused) to take her place immediately in front of him in the first row of chairs, and then begin lecturing as sonorously as if he were addressing the Modern Language Association of America. His Michigan house was big, old-fashioned, and comfortably furnished, and the year gave us plenty of time to look around for a permanent abode.

Before the lease was out, we bought a brick house on Brockman Boulevard, which was then on the edge of town, though nowadays, since Ann Arbor and Ypsilanti are virtually one city, it no longer enjoys the wide prospect it formerly had. This house stood on a gently sloping hillside, part of an old apple orchard, some of whose trees were still flowery in the spring. There was a two-car garage with a wide, unfinished room above it. The living room on the ground floor, set among the trees, had insufficient fenestration, and the kitchen was at the road side of the house and got the best view. In between was a dining room ingeniously contrived to prevent the giving of large dinner parties. There were bedrooms on the second floor and a maid's room on the third. The house had been recently built, but we found that the water-softener (a necessity in Ann Arbor) wouldn't work and had to be replaced, and that the plumbing and heating systems left something to be desired. Nevertheless I loved the house, especially when the big room over the garage was fitted out with shelves and I luxuriated in a large, well-lighted study, where Bessie and Eleanor also spent as much time as they could.

Universities create their peculiar characteristics almost in spite of themselves, and Ann Arbor was no exception. I can understand why its alumni are a devoted body; and we developed strong affection for many members of the faculty—Jack Dawson of the Law School and his wife Emma, Henry and Marian Hutchins, Guy Maier the pianist and his wife Lois, who commonly played ingenue roles in the Nell Gwynne Players, to which I shall come, and a long list of others, usually from the younger faculty. Many, alas, now are dead. But I never felt professionally comfortable in Ann Arbor. There was too much pride of place, self-assurance, and emphasis on money and rank, too little connection with the problems of a state as complex as Michigan, Detroit excepted, too much looking to the ivy universities with envy, too much looking down on other state universities in the Middle West and the South and of course on those mushroom growths, most of the trans-Mississippi institutions. When the chairmanship of a department was about to fall vacant, virtual political campaigns began to boost Professor X or Professor Y for the coming vacancy—a curious reversal of the Harvard formula, wherein, it seems to me, everybody of any consequence dodges being made chairman of a department as long as he decently can. I had of course a natural pride in being at the University of Michigan, a pride justified by the international repute of its medical school and its law school, to name but two branches of a major institution, and in the renowned scientists and scholars who had been or were members of its faculty.

Having come from Chapel Hill, where the economic and cultural condition of the state was everybody's problem, I found myself somewhat baffled by the low temperature of any such concern at the University of Michigan. In 1934, I published in the *Michigan Alumnus* an article on the need for a study of the intellectual history of the state, called "Local Literature and the State of Michigan," applying my favored doctrine of regionalism to this commonwealth; but the essay produced not a single response. "Culture" was apparently something that came from the east coast or from Europe. One could, of course, get into one's car and in little more than an hour be seated in readiness for a concert by the Detroit Symphony Orchestra, which occasionally visited Ann Arbor and filled Hill Auditorium with listeners; but the orchestra was then conducted by Ossip Gabrilowitsch, Mark Twain's son-in-law, a conductor with a timid beat and utterly conventional tastes. At Ann Arbor we had a yearly musical festival principally given by imported artists. There was as part of the campus the Lydia Mendelssohn Theatre, which lacked proper contemporary theater equipment; here, each spring, a man named Robert Henderson managed our spring drama festival, invariably importing Broadway hits, internationally known actors, and satisfying, as he thought, the campus taste for cosmopolitanism. In 1928 Avery Hopwood, a Michigan alumnus, author of *Getting Gertie's Garter, Why Men Leave Home*, and *The Bat*, had died; in 1931 it appeared he had left a considerable sum of money for the Hopwood Literary Awards; and the English department (which included some veterans from the former Department of Rhetoric) hastily organized courses in original composition ("creative writing"), principally under the directon of Roy W. Cowden. I gave one such course without developing any students of professional caliber; and though a careful search of the annals of American writing since, say, 1940 will reveal four or five well-known names associated with the Hopwood awards, I doubt that the fund has dramatically reshaped American literature.

My courses at Ann Arbor did not differ markedly in subject from those I had been teaching at Chapel Hill. My standard offerings included a course in American literature and one in British literature, usually of the romantic period or some associated era, and I gave the usual seminars. I now have a feeling that I was insensibly getting a firmer grasp on the nature and problems of writing in America, notably after the success of *America and French Culture*. Moreover, being approached by a representative of Harcourt, Brace and Company, who asked if I would join with Ernest E. Leisy, an Americanist at Southern Methodist University in Dallas, in getting out a first-class anthology of American literature for the use of college courses, I consented; for a good deal of cordial correspondence with Leisy had revealed that he was as disturbed by the superficial quality of most of the books in the field as I was. The project eventuated as *Major American Writers* in 1935. It was precisely that: we confined ourselves to selections from major writers, each as carefully edited and annotated as if we were dealing with Shakespeare. The book went through three editions, Richard M. Ludwig joining as a third editor during and after Leisy's sickness and death. I cannot say that this work revolutionized the textbook field, but I do claim that it was one of the books that forced a more careful consideration of text and meaning on American studies. And in 1935 I deepened my own and, I hope, my readers' understanding of the relation between the culture of the Old World and that of the New by an article in the professional journal *American Literature*, "The Influence of European Ideas in Nineteenth-Century America." Undoubtedly I was being influenced by the vogue of social history and of the history of ideas, approaches to the past which were slowly reinforcing the political history that had hitherto virtually monopolized the American field. I cannot claim to be the only one who was so affected. But the relative success of my book and articles seemed to indicate I was on the right track. By and by, at Harvard, I was to summon up courage to invade the fields of art history and of the history of music when these contained anything that seemed relevant or illuminating to my central themes.

Books may be born out of books, as somebody has said, but I have known few writers, professional or otherwise, whose circle of friends was confined to the book world only. I was voted into a club of professors in various fields, the club being called the Azazels, I know not why, and also into the Research Club. The Azazels was something of a burden on Ann Arbor housewives, since it was a dining club, and the wife of the member who was to give the paper of the evening was supposed to tender dinner to the members, who, fortunately, seldom numbered more than twelve or fourteen at a meeting. In the thirties food was, from the point of view of 1977, relatively cheap in Ann Arbor; but a dinner of that size puts a strain on the professor who has no other income than his salary, and a greater strain on his wife.

We employed during our stay in Ann Arbor a succession of "help," each of whom was odd. One, for example, noisily drew a chest of drawers across her bedroom door every night as she went to bed and also hoarded glass milk-bottles, which she washed and stood around the baseboard, the idea being that anybody attempting to rape her would undoubtedly knock over some bottles and make a crash. Another rubbed her stomach affectionately against anyone seated at the table when she served a meal. It was not until we found the faithful Christa Landgraf, a student, highly reliable as a cook, a confidante, and a companion to our daughter, that domestic matters really settled down. We parted from her with regret.

Once dinner had been served, the Azazels adjourned to the host's study if he had one. The host read the paper of the evening, observations were made, and I think, after the twentieth amendment was passed, there were nightcaps. The Research Club was a much larger organization and commonly met in a large room in a university building. It was dominated by scientists, who had developed an admirable custom: on the centennials of the birthdates of preeminent scientists a member was delegated to write a memoir of the life and work of the deceased genius. Nothing gave one a better sense of the continuity of learning.

Bessie, meanwhile, had got a sort of editorial job in an Ann Arbor firm, Edwards Brothers, which did a good business in producing books, particularly dissertations, by a photolithographing process that preceded microfilm and microfiche; and she there met Eugene Power, who later rose to fame and fortune in the microfilm world. He was requested by the British government to photostat virtually all the rare books in British libraries when the Battle of Britain threatened to destroy them; he was elected a regent of the University of Michigan; and he has been a notable public figure in the state. Eleanor, meanwhile, had entered the Angell School, and after a year there, enrolled in the University High School, supposed to be superior to the public school in Ann Arbor, though in what its superiority lay I could never find out. The University High School had fits and starts of applying some new or experimental device to this or that part of its curriculum, to the harm of the subject and the bewilderment of the pupil. It took my daughter a long time to overcome the defects of "new" and "experimental" teaching.

An unexpected and important event occurred in 1932, my second year at Ann Arbor. One day there appeared at my desk side a roly-poly, jolly sort of man, the fatness of whose cheeks did not conceal the keenness of his eyes. He introduced himself as Henry Allen Moe and suggested that we go out to lunch. I was not at that time familiar with the names of important personages among the capital foundations, and I fear I put him down as another traveling textbook salesman. Lunch was lunch, however, and after informing home that I would not be there, we met at

12:30 at some downtown restaurant. He was, it appeared, the secretary-general of the Guggenheim Foundation, and he was scouting the country for talent. We talked generally about scholarship, the state of Michigan, and the present level of the humanities, when all of a sudden he asked me, "Haven't you got something you'd like to do?"

"Well," I said hesitantly, "I have always wanted to make a study of Byron as a satirist of Regency society, but 1924 being the centenary of his death, so many books have appeared in the last decade that I don't see much room for another one."

I thought I saw a gleam of respect for me in his eye. "That's true," he said, "but that needn't throw you out. Isn't there anything about Byron you would like to investigate?"

"Well," I said, "I can't find in print anywhere a competent study of Tom Moore, one of Byron's closest friends, his biographer, and one who had a very great influence upon him." I warmed to the subject of Tommy Moore, but, looking back on this crucial interview, it seemed to me that Moe already knew a great deal more about Tommy Moore than I knew; in fact he seemed to know a great deal more about most topics than most applicants for fellowships seemed to know. We concluded lunch with his suggestion: "Why don't you put in an application for a Guggenheim Foundation Fellowship for next year? I can't guarantee that they will grant it, but there is a board meeting about six weeks from now, and you will lose nothing by applying." We rose; he paid the check; and we parted, I somewhat dazed, at the restaurant door. Within six weeks or so I was a member of the next crop of Guggenheim Fellows, but I shall reserve the events of that unusual year for the next chapter.

I did, however, write another biography while I was a member of the University of Michigan faculty. This was *The Life of Moses Coit Tyler*, and the subtitle explains how it came into being: "Based upon an unpublished dissertation from original sources." Fred Casady, a brilliant student in history, had died before quite finishing his doctoral thesis; and my recollection is that the then director of the University of Michigan Press, some of the historians, and Mrs. Casady joined in appealing to me to put the book into presentable form. The dissertation was well done and lacked, or so it seemed to me, only a proper setting for Tyler's youth and a conclusion setting forth his influence on American historical writing. He had been one of the founders of the American Historical Association, and nobody else has had the courage he displayed in hunting down the remotest fragment of American writing between 1607 and 1789. His two classic works, *A History of American Literature, 1607 to 1765* and *The Literary History of the American Revolution*, each in two volumes, are still authorities in their field, however Victorian their style may be. His biography of Patrick Henry is consulted by the modern writer, and his scholarly papers in general are still worth reading. The job attracted me for two or three reasons. One was that the paucity of Casady's information about Tyler's early years offered an opportunity for me to learn more about regional history. I did not expect when I began my task that this would lead me into the history of gymnastics in America or send me abroad. Tyler was something of a popular preacher and organizer; and these and other by-products of his industry had to be dealt with. The book finally ran to over 350 pages, was illustrated by various stately photographs, and seemed to me, at least, to throw a good deal of light on that group of historians I called "The Bearded Generation." The volume came out in 1933, and since nobody else has ventured to write Tyler's life, it remains the standard biography.

A less arduous and far more amusing aspect of our life in Ann Arbor was the Nell Gwynne Players, an informal group of citizens, faculty members, and graduate students which put on plays for the fun of it. As most of the productions we saw at the university were either undergraduate performances of Shakespeare's plays or those Broadway successes Robert Henderson lured to the Lydia Mendelssohn for our brief spring drama festival, this left a wide gap in the history of the British theater. I do not now remember at whose dinner table the idea was born that there was possibly something presentable between the death of the Bard of Avon and the successes of Oscar Wilde, but somebody suggested: "It would be fun to get out some of these neglected plays and see how they read." From reading to acting was but a step. We called ourselves the Nell Gwynne Players (we sometimes referred to ourselves as the Bitches and Bastards of Nell Gwynne), and we resolved that our peculiar province would be anything originally produced between the Restoration and our own Civil War. We found, as might have been expected, that heroic dramas and tragedies from this long period are, most of them, unactable, but we found also a world of merriment in the comedies and farces. We put on plays wherever we could—in somebody's large living room, if it had enough doors and windows and especially if it had double doors; in the Lydia Mendelssohn Theatre; in the downtown "Op'ry House"; or in fraternal organization halls having a platform or a stage. We reduced scenery, painted by Paul Slusser, to the simplest possible number of items and proportion, so that I do not to this day know how many elopements were carried on through the same set of windows; and we got around the difficulty of outdoor scenes by placing two large potted plants or indoor shrubbery at either end of the footlights, if there were any, and printing on the program that the scene took place in St. James's Park.

After a little experience we rediscovered two truisms. First, a willing audience will accept any scenic deficiency if the plot be good and the conversation clear. The second should have been self-evident. Since Restoration and eighteenth-century comedies were written for standard companies of players, we required only some twenty types of persons to fill our ranks and be fully prepared, provided the actor or actress was anywise competent, to stage virtually any play within the temporal limits we had staked out for our own. Indeed, on one or two occasions, we ventured to revive some once-vaunted masterpiece because time had made it silly, and on most of these occasions the audience seemed to enjoy itself as much as at a revival of *The Beaux' Stratagem*. Some costumes we made, some we rented from Detroit, and some we resurrected from old trunks, closets, and attics. If there were anachronisms in our stage sets, once the play got started, nobody seemed to mind. We had, of course, our failures, one of which was George Lillo's *The London Merchant*, which formerly drew tears from the entire house, but which, I suspect, will never make anybody weep again. On the other hand, *The Relapse* by Sir John Vanbrugh was, in our terms, a great success, partly because of the excellence of the actor who played Lord Foppington and partly because of the rumor that an internationally known historian of the law, whose whole part consisted of the line, "My Lord, these shoes become you very well indeed," forgot his entire role at the first performance. Every production was followed by a party of some sort, and I think the general hilarity produced by our mingling of expertise and awkwardness helped to reduce the general gloom of the 1930s.

Chapter XVI

The Humors
of Research

AS I HINTED in the previous chapter, my experience as a Guggenheim
Fellow was so enchanting that it deserves a discussion to itself. Any
college or university is honored when one of its faculty members becomes
a Guggenheim Fellow, and though I had been at Michigan only two
years, the university gave me leave and also gave me a research grant
towards a biography of Thomas Moore. (I still think some persons
thought I was going to investigate the life and works of Sir Thomas
More, statesman and saint.) Blessings come not single spies but in bat-
talions, for I also now received an appointment as an associate, if that be
the right term, of the Henry E. Huntington Library in San Marino,
California, an institution which, as someone has said, is not a library but
a library of libraries, for the Huntingtons bought whole collections of
books, pamphlets, and manuscripts and did not forage item by item. I
was the more interested in San Marino when I learned that Maurice
Block, my comrade of Hitchcock Hall days, was on the staff of the art
museum, a part of the library, and that Louis Booker Wright, formerly
of Chapel Hill and the future director of the Folger Library in
Washington, was also at the Huntington. In my spare time at Michigan I
began looking into possible sources of a new biography of my Thomas
Moore and found they were scattered over the Atlantic world from the
Huntington to the British Isles, not forgetting Bermuda and Paris.

We rented our Ann Arbor home for a sum we thought sufficient to pay
the taxes and the upkeep, through our tenants moved out before our return and never did pay the last few months' rent—a catastrophe that led

me to meditate on the wisdom of the California custom of demanding in advance from a tenant the first and last month's rent. How best to get to California? Henry Allen Moe had suggested the desirability of some sort of brief vacation before I plunged from one task into another, and so had several Ann Arbor friends; and we learned we could get to the California coast by boat through the Panama Canal. Accordingly we booked passage, tourist, for the three of us on the S.S. *Panama*, now, alas! outmoded by the airplane, and made our way to New York to pick up the necessary documents and the money at the Guggenheim office. Moe greeted me with the affability that seemed never to leave him; and when I had secured a statement that I was a bona fide Guggenheim Fellow, and he had examined my passport and found it in order, he gave me a letter of credit.

"Have a good trip," he then said cordially and shook my hand.

"But," said I, "don't I make some sort of regular report to you?"

He now seemed a little bewildered. "When your job is done," he said, "send us a copy of the book. When we appoint a Guggenheim Fellow, we appoint him, and after that he's on his own. If you get into trouble anywhere, let me know, and I'll try to get you out of it, but," he added, "what would I do with a lot of reports?" This being contrary to the conduct of most universities, I gasped and expressed my admiration, and we parted on a note of mutual trust and affection.

The boat on which we sailed to San Diego was crowded, both first-class and tourist; but as this was the first ocean voyage for any of the Jones family, we were not critical and settled down to the routine of ship life without much grumbling. We had a calm sea and a prosperous voyage. The ship stopped for most of a day at Havana, and we went ashore with our swarming fellow passengers. Except for occasional dips into Canada, this was my first visit to a foreign land, and I was duly impressed by the tropicality of the atmosphere (which I did not like), the crowds of blacks, and the fact that everybody seemed to live in the open air. We found a restaurant and had lunch, for which I suspect we were overcharged, and returned to the *Panama*. Going through the Canal was to me more interesting than the day in Havana; for, though I have not a vestige of engineering training, I could not but admire the straight, clean lines of everything; the quiet, ease, and orderliness with which we passed through locks and cuts and lakes; and the virtual invisibility of human beings except those on shipboard. We paused for a while at Panama City, where I could find little of interest except gambling—and I have neither the knowledge of, nor interest in, gambling necessary to a full-rounded life. Finally we disembarked without incident at a wharf in San Diego and got by train and interurban trolley to Pasadena. San

Marino, the Huntington estate on which the library and museum stand, is adjacent to this city, and we had found a small comfortable, thoroughly Californian furnished house on Rose Villa Avenue, which we rented and which was a pleasant walk from the library. By 1932 the depression had hit southern California so hard that the owner of the house, a real estate dealer, had decided she could do better by renting her own home and living elsewhere than by staying home and finding houses for others.

The living room had a fireplace in one corner, an open hearth affair in a toy medieval round tower, which was supposed to heat the room. The kitchen was adequate, the beds were good enough, and a slight earthquake shortly after our arrival reminded us, if we had forgotten it, that we were no longer in the Middle West. Outside were two struggling orange trees in the back yard, a front lawn the size of a large carpet, and a graveled driveway for a car. But we looked in vain for a garbage can. In a day or two there was a knock at the door, and Bessie opened it to a smiling and attractive black man, who said that he had been collecting garbage for the owner on a regular basis for such-and-such a sum and would like to do the same for us. "But doesn't the city collect garbage?" Bessie asked in some bewilderment. "No'm," said our visitor, "they's a garbage trus', and I do it for less than they do." It appeared that, through some error in platting, four blocks, in one of which our house stood, were no part of Pasadena but were still legally part of the county of Los Angeles, and that we had to depend on the sheriff, not the police, for protection and on our black friend for the disposal of waste. I forebore to inquire on whom to call in case of fire. This odd situation did not interfere with Eleanor's enrollment in the Pasadena public schools. We found that the Pasadena schools were suffering from an attack of that form of educational measles called progressive, or experimental, education, so that she was required to enroll in a six-week course entitled "Broadening and Finding Course in Languages," two weeks of which consisted of Latin, two weeks of French, and two weeks of Spanish. There was no German. If she failed the whole course or any third of it, she was "not adapted" to foreign languages or to the language she had flunked in the Pasadena school system. We argued in vain that we were going to Europe shortly and that French, at least, would seem desirable. We got nowhere. Theory is implacable. Naturally, most pupils found it easier to flunk.

The Huntington Library was, as we had anticipated, immense. Bessie and I were greeted by Carey Bliss, the librarian, and eventually by the formidable Max Farrand, whose *Records of the Federal Convention of*

1787 remains a monument of historical accuracy. The rules of the library were simple: Bessie and I were given chairs side by side and a table to ourselves, and pages brought us books and bound periodicals as we needed them. No book ever left the library except under guard. The books were on one level, the manuscripts on another, and this sometimes produced amusing incidents. Tom Moore wrote a forgotten novel, *The Epicurean*, which he metamorphosed out of an unfinished poem, *Alciphron*. The item is of some interest to collectors, since its frontispiece is by no less a personage than J. M. W. Turner. I discovered that the Huntington had not only the novel, copies of which are by no means rare, but also the first half of Moore's manuscript, and I conceived it my duty to collate the text with the manuscript. But the book was on the first floor of the library, the manuscript on the second: how get the two side by side? This grave managerial problem was finally referred to a council of the library staff, who solved it by appointing a page to bring the book to me on level two and restore it to its proper place on level one each day when I went home. This was done ceremoniously. The little red volume was laid on a salver covered with a soft cloth, placed carefully before me when I went to work upstairs, and as ceremoniously removed when I left in the late afternoon. The Huntington has the first half of the manuscript, the Pierpont Morgan Library in New York for some curious reason possesses the second half, and I therefore had to wait a long time before I finished with the book.

Since Maurice Block was, as I said, more or less in charge of the picture gallery, he gave us a guided tour, and introduced us to C. H. Collins Baker and his wife. Baker, erstwhile Keeper of the King's Pictures in Buckingham Palace and other royal residences, was a jolly Englishman, so near-sighted that when he inspected a painting, he almost brushed it with his eyelashes. Nevertheless, his books on painting are impeccably written out of an enormous fund of scholarly lore. Once, the genuineness of a canvas being questionable, the painting was brought to Baker to determine its authenticity. He inspected it in his usual fashion, just barely missing every square inch of it with his nose, and handed it back. "Raphael?" was his verdict; "I should call it good commercial Raphael." When, later, we met again in England, he gave us a tour of Buckingham Palace and also, as I remember, of Windsor, where I noticed with amusement that, art being of no interest to the king, the queen was its real patron, and that Baker and the staff always referred to their mistress as "she."

Bessie and I worked hard at the Huntington, reading books by Moore we had never before seen and coming across scores of his contributions to the periodicals of the age—for in the Regency period and the days of the First Reform Bill, satiric verse performed the function which the newspaper cartoonist has today. Moore, a patriotic Irishman by birth and, except for a brief Tory period, an important Whig journalist, wrote hundreds of lines of this sort, most of which appear in his collected works but, to my interest, only after careful revision, a fact that doubled our task and our respect for Moore. We had also, of course, to read widely in the literature of the great Whig group of which, according to tradition, he was the delight. Bessie's notes were a pleasure to have, for she has a faculty of getting to the point rather faster than some of the writers she toiled through, and except for the fact that the fellowship had been granted to me, *The Harp That Once*, as we called our book when it appeared in 1937, should have said, "By Bessie Z. and Howard Mumford Jones."

But we of course could not labor at the library or anywhere else all week, and besides, there was Eleanor to look after. So we bought a second-hand car and began touring the vicinity, getting as far north as Santa Barbara, having picnics at Laguna Beach, trying to find something interesting in Hollywood, or driving to the top of the coastal sierra to a house Paul Green had rented, which had among other features a portable wishing well; a refectory table too long and heavy to be moved, so that the Greens and their guests commonly dined at one end of it; and a short walk along the mountain top leading to a pirates' cave containing sacks spilling out fake gold coins behind iron bars. Most of the residences of the "stars" we visited had some such fakery. Our weekend wanderings were often cut short because Eleanor was devoted to a radio serial, "Chandu the Magician," which always opened with a great boom on a Chinese gong; and if we got back too late for this program, life around her fell to ruin and desolation.

The Louis Wrights, of course, were hospitable—were they not southerners?—Maurice Block and others did what they could, and there was a memorable dinner and reception for Robert Frost given by Dr. and Mrs. Millikan. (He was the head of the California Institute of Technology.) Mrs. Millikan drove about in her limousine personally delivering invitations; when she reached our modest abode, only Eleanor was home to answer the bell. In response to the grande dame's explanation, "To meet Robert Frost," Eleanor responded innocently and in entire truth, "But we already know Robert Frost." After the dinner, which was large, Frost offered to "say some of his poems" (his phrase), and did well enough until he got to one he said he had just written, "A Record Stride." It so happened that Robert Frost, Garland Greever, and we had had lunch together the previous day, when he had recited this same poem, a passage from which had stuck in Bessie's memory. Frost started out:

> In a Vermont bedroom closet
> With a door of two broad boards,

and then, for the only time in my long acquaintance with him, got stuck at the end of a stanza and looked extraordinarily embarrassed. To my astonishment, Bessie called out:

> Two entirely different grandchildren
> Got me into my double adventure.

Frost shot her a grateful look, picked up the rest of stanza five, and went on to the triumphal end:

> And I ask all to try to forgive me
> For being as over-elated
> As I had measured the country
> And got the United States stated.

He afterwards sent Bessie a manuscript copy of the poem and a charming letter.*

The automobile had emphatically come in, so that when I walked to the library of a bright morning alone or with Bessie, dogs barked at this strange sight, and gardeners stopped watering flowers to stare at us. These walks gave me opportunity to think over the significance of our research generally. I did not feel that a biography of Tom Moore was necessarily at cross-purposes with my general wish to become as good an Americanist as I could. On the contrary it enriched that purpose. Moore had spent some time in America and had delivered himself of some furious denunciations of the United States in general and of Jeffersonianism in particular. It also became more and more evident that no book about my Anglo-Irishman would put him in his true light as an important literary and political figure if it failed to create around him, not merely as background but as conditioning and motive, a feeling for the framework of the political and social history of the Atlantic world from the years of the American Revolution, during which he was born, to the Compromise of 1850, shortly after which he died.

* This is the same poem with which Frost tried to bluff T. S. Eliot at a dinner at the St. Botolph Club in Boston in December, 1932. For an account of this amusing performance (which is also in Bessie's letter) see Lawrance Thompson, ed., *Selected Letters of Robert Frost* (New York, 1964), pp. 389–90.

Among its other immense resources the Huntington Library contained a vast collection of materials, mostly in pamphlet form, relating to the later seventeenth and the entire eighteenth century in North America and beyond; and as our joint industry had done well by the Moore biography, I began to extend my curiosity to these documents, which I would have difficulty getting in Michigan. I began reading and taking careful notes on sermons, orations addressed to the colonials, defenses of and attacks upon British policy, or on the French, or on Roman Catholicism, on problems of education, art, ethics, and science in the American colonies and, less often, in Ireland, London, and Edinburgh. It was work that required considerable attention to detail, since I put my notes (which I took at the typewriter before the time of Xerox) on cards and had to copy out with great care the hundreds of bibliographical items that identified the originals I was summarizing or copying. I stuck doggedly to it, filled two and a half boxes with my cards (I still have them), and instructed myself about early colonialism, the Americans as provincials, and the Americans as patriots or loyalists in a way I had never anticipated. Later on, as a result of this labor, I contributed a paper to *The Huntington Library Bulletin* in 1934 on American theories of style; and in 1936 I wrote "The Drift to Liberalism in the American Eighteenth Century" for *Authority and the Individual,* one of the Tercentenary Publications brought out by Harvard in 1937. It also unconsciously prepared me to deal with such of my future Harvard colleagues as Kenneth Ballard Murdock, F. O. Matthiessen, and Perry Miller, who, like the Cratchit children, were steeped to their very eyebrows in New England writing.

The time came (and in midwinter, too!) to bid farewell to our friends in California, recross the continent, and take ship for the Old World. We had passage on one of the smaller, one-class vessels of the Red Star Line, the *Pennland,* now at the bottom of the Atlantic, sunk by a German torpedo. The *Pennland* was not a fast boat, the passenger list was small, the officers and crew friendly, and aside from one small storm, the voyage was pleasant enough. We landed at Portsmouth March 6, 1933, the day FDR closed all the American banks; and but for the friendliness of British bankers, there would have been difficulty in turning traveler's checks into pounds, shillings, and pence. The cashier agreed to take the check at what had been the current rate with the proviso that when American banks reopened (which they did after a week) if I owed the bank money, I should pay it, and if the bank owed me money, they would reimburse me. Thus equipped with funds, we went to Hastings, where Eleanor was to enter a typical (and excellent) private school taught by some excellent and typical British ladies administering an

The Humors of Research

excellent traditional curriculum. Not to our surprise, we were told by the headmistress that our daughter was "veddy, veddy backward" on the monarchs of England; to her classmates she was equally backward because she could not tell them all about the stars of Hollywood. Another grievance was the school uniform, which included long black cotton stockings. These, when the school filed off to church two by two on a Sunday morning, made the pupils look like a huge worm with a blue body and innumerable black legs. But these little matters wore down after the passage of time. Eleanor won respect by her swiftness in running matches, and my guess is that the prospect of a trip to the Continent at the end of the school year helped to comfort her for the strangeness of her setting.

Bessie and I went on to London, where we had reserved a room at the Whitehall Hotel in Bloomsbury Square, a favorite hotel of many American professors, about seven minutes walk from the British Museum. For proper tipping and handling of our luggage we put ourselves in the capable hands of Body, the doorman, who became our guide, philosopher, and friend during our whole stay in London. Body registered us; guided us into the unmistakably British lift, all over grillwork and operated by a stout cable; and brought us to an upper floor, where he showed us into a neat, comfortable room with lavatory facilities and genuinely efficient central heating. One of the good features in this modest English hotel was the use of exposed hot water pipes to provide racks for the towels, which were always kept warm and dry.

Body, as I later discovered, had been a member of the Black and Tans in Dublin and had no use for the Irish, nor, I take it, did the Irish have any use for him; but he was the most bookish doorman I have ever known. He knew all the proper bookshops, he knew what books ought to cost, and when he found that our problem was Tommy Moore (even though Irish), he began keeping an eye out for Moore items, and frequently brought me some work he had found in a bookstall and borrowed or offered for inspection toward possible purchase. By and by we thus acquired almost a complete collection of original or interesting editions of our author. These, when my Cambridge bookshelves became too crowded, I later gave to the library at Clark University in Worcester, which bestowed an honorary degree on me in 1952.

Aside from the foreign, mostly American scholars, the clientele of the Whitehall was thoroughly and traditionally British. The patrons ate their breakfast in silence and in style, they had their tea in the lounge in silence, each face secure behind a newspaper, and the dining room held about as little clatter as a large, well-run American bank. Only once in our stay was the barrier broken. Katharine Garvin, daughter of the editor of the London *Observer* (I had known her from a summer session at Western Reserve in Cleveland), dropped in on us one afternoon, pulling an enormous, unwashed sheep dog on a leash. Instantly every paper went down. "Is it a sheep dog?" asked one bald-headed Briton as the dog went by him. "And what other kind of dog would it be?" she responded. Every paper went up again, and Katharine, Bessie, and I murmured over our tea while the dog lay composedly at our feet.

The British Museum, that most wonderful of democratic libraries, requires only proper credentials to issue you a reader's card renewable for the rest of your life. The American Embassy put the official stamp on the proper documents for Bessie and me, and we were admitted, after which the universe of books was ours for the reading. Books were brought to you as soon as they could be located on the shelves, and could be held for you day after day if you made the proper arrangements. For relief from too much bibliography you could refresh your spirit with the Egyptian Room or the Greek Room, the Elgin Marbles miraculously preserved from war, pillage, and shipwreck, or you could leave your desk and explore some part of ancient London. For lunch we frequently went to a nearby pub, feasted on bread, cheese, beer, and tomatoes, and struggled not to appear to listen to wonderful conversations.

By and by it appeared useful for me to take the tube out to Hendon, where the bound volumes of the great British newspapers were kept, and where I recovered more and more of Tommy Moore in his character as Whig columnist and verbal cartoonist. We went to Holland House, which was then still standing, and were courteously received by its owner, who gave us access to what Moore memorials he had. Bertrand Russell, later Lord Russell, sent me, carelessly wrapped, original letters between Tommy Moore and the Reverend William Lisle Bowles. By bus or local train we visited all the country seats we could find where Moore had been a guest, and the various castles and cottages associated with him—Bowood and Donington, Ashbourne and Sloperton. We also went to Bromham churchyard, a Protestant cemetery where this fighter for Catholic Emancipation lies buried beneath an ornamented Irish cross cut in stone, on which appears one of his own verses about "light, freedom, and song," together with Byron's pithy statement, "The poet of all circles and the idol of his own."

Ireland was still to do, but we needed a vacation. So, before quite finishing in London, we took ten days off to visit the Lake Country. We left the train at Windermere, found all the inns full, but began to notice a series of hand-lettered signs on trees and walls labeled "Brookside Inn."

Following these, we reached both brook and inn, each, so to say, in excellent repair. We went in and asked if we could have lodging for the night. We could. They showed us to a large bedroom, very plainly furnished, but spotless. I explained that we had left our luggage at the station and that I would fetch it at once, but as we had had almost nothing to eat since breakfast, we hoped we could have some supper. When I returned with the bags, we found that the bed had been refurbished with linen sheets and a luxurious looking quilt, and we were served a delicious supper of cold salmon, watercress, sliced cucumbers, and bread and butter, tea, and little cakes. It was like fairyland. The fact was that we were the first guests. The place was an old pub that had run down after it was sold outside the family, and had been repurchased and restored by two members of it (brother and sister, I think), who thought that in the depths of the depression they could do better in a Cumberland pub than in London. We stayed on night after night. We encountered few other Americans in our Lake Country wanderings. One early afternoon the large and masculine form of Raymond Dexter Havens, author of that standard study of Wordsworth, *The Mind of a Poet*, loomed in a doorway, announced sonorously

> I wandered lonely as a cloud
> That floats on high o'er vales and hills,

and invited us to break into his solitude. On another occasion we were joined by Howard F. Lowry, enjoying a Sterling Fellowship from Yale (later, president of Wooster College), who was working on Arnold and who wheedled Bessie and me to join him in retracing part at least of the walk Matthew Arnold and "Fausta" had taken in "Resignation." We ended at Keswick for rest and tea, but I am still puzzled by the disjointed topography of that poem, which ends with the Wanderers bathing their weary feet in the sea. If they did all this in one day, starting from where they are supposed to have begun their walk, they surpassed Robert Frost's famous stride in his effort to get the United States stated.

After our return to London, the head of the British Museum gave me a cordial note to the director of the National Library in Dublin. I left Bessie to make her solitary way to Paris, got off the boat at Dunleary (Dun Laoghaire), left the train at Westmoreland Station, and walked to a busy street I now know is O'Connell. I had a reservation at the Hotel MacDermott, but where was it? And there I was, alone in Ireland.

Chapter XVII

In Dublin's Fair City

WELL, I STOOD THERE like a man befuddled, my two bags beside me, wondering what to do next. In London I would have gone to the nearest bobby and asked for directions; but this street was not in England, and moreover, there was not a bobby or anybody remotely resembling a policeman in sight. I must have radiated bewilderment, for presently at my right ear I heard in the most soothing tones and the gentlest of baritone Irish voices the question "Can I help ye?" I turned. There was standing next to me a round-faced, well-shaven priest, clad in a black cassock, the front of it all over snuff, of which the wind from time to time blew little pinches in my direction. "Can I help ye, me boy?" he repeated. I recognized the confessional manner and thought I might as well succumb at once.

"Father," I said, "I am an American. I have never been in Ireland before, and I want to go to the Hotel MacDermott, where I have a reservation, but I don't know how to get there."

"Faith," he said, "and what have you come to Ireland for?"

I thought I might as well break down and tell all. "I have come here," I said, "because I am working on a biography of your fine poet Moore, who wrote *The Irish Melodies*, and I thought of course that—"

"The songs of Thomas Moore!" he exclaimed. "Faith! The songs of Thomas Moore! Me father and me mother used to sing them together, and very well they sang them, too. Ach," he continued, "there was a time when a man couldn't step into a pub anywheres, before it was time to close up, but you would hear a song by Tommy Moore sung, five or six of them of an evening," he added, "and sometimes they sang the same one three or four times over." He seemed to forget the traffic of O'Connell Street and the roofless stranger at his side, and broke into "The Harp That Once Through Tara's Halls" in a voice that, though it suggested snuff and whiskey, was true and penetrating.

But I interrupted. "Yes," I agreed, "that's Tom Moore's own song all right—it's in the first number of *The Irish Melodies*, and I am glad you know it."

"Know it!" he said. "Know it! Why, my poor mother used to sing me to sleep with that song hundreds of times. But," he said, suddenly realizing that he could not tell me the whole story of his life, "touching on Mr. MacDermott's Hotel—you'll cross the pavement here, and take the bus that's labeled so-and-so, and go to the top of the hill there, and there near the stopping place is MacDermott's Hotel you want on a cross street, and they'll let you off, and there it will be, almost staring you in the face like. And a very good hotel it is, too. And now, good-bye, my boy," he said as I picked up my bags, "and treat yourself well, and we'll treat you well, and you'll find us a dacent people and a homely one."

I followed his directions, found the hotel, a quiet place mainly frequented, I thought, by priests from the west country, and all over lace curtains. And they were indeed a dacent people and a homely one. I was given a chamber on an upper floor, informed of the hour for meals, and left to my own devices.

The next morning I repaired to the National Library of Ireland and presented my note of introduction to the librarian. The red-haired functionary behind the desk said he would send it in, but meanwhile was there anything he could do for me? "Well," I said, "I came here to look at any original letters and documents you may have about your Thomas Moore, the great writer and singer."

"Well, then, why don't you have a seat somewhere, and I'll see what we have."

The reading room was not large. I sat down within easy reach of his eye while a sort of page went off on some mysterious errand. By and by the lad returned bringing me a great sheaf of manuscripts and newspaper clippings in a parcel tied with a string. "Here y'are, sir," he said, and departed. I opened the bundle expectantly and with care only to be disappointed: these manuscripts belonged to another Thomas Moore, an Irish member of parliament in the nineteenth century. I brought them back to my red-headed mentor at the desk.

"I'm afraid there's some mistake, sir," I told him. "These are not the papers I want to see. They belong to another Thomas Moore"—I gave him the dates—"a member of parliament, but not the writer and singer."

He stared at me in amazement. "Now, how did ye know that?" he asked.

I explained that I had seen a great many sheets of my Thomas Moore's handwriting in the course of my travels and was familiar with his penmanship.

He stared at me; then a smile broke over his face, and he said, "You're American, now?"

I answered, "Yes."

"Well, then," he continued, "you must be all right," though the logic of this escaped me, "and I'll have another look around. Sit down again, if you please."

I went back to my seat and waited. Presently the page came to tell me that the librarian was not in town that week, but would I please make myself at home in the library. After another lapse of time he brought me a smaller container holding some inconsequential letters of Moore's and some verses. These were at least the genuine articles, but it took me no time to ascertain they contained little to my purpose. Nor was this surprising. When Moore visited his native land, he commonly stayed with his parents, and letters were unnecessary. As for any collateral descendants, Heaven alone knows where they might be, and if I may amend the famous lines by Yeats:

> Romantic Ireland's dead and gone,
> It's with O'Leary and Thomas Moore in the grave.

This was indeed the truth. As a matter of fact Moore is buried in Protestant England.

There seemed to be an agreeable amateurishness about the National Library, and an agreeable lack of overall direction. It was not until my third day that I discovered the card catalogue, and not until the fourth that I went up to my red-haired friend and said, "I'm sorry to have broken the rules, but I have just discovered that visitors are supposed to sign in and sign out in that book in the hall."

"Ah, that's where they put down their names and their numbers," he said.

"Numbers?" I inquired.

"Yes, the number on the little visitor's card they give you."

"But I've never had a visitor's card," I said. "You will remember that when I first came here, you took the note I gave you to the chief librarian, and he was away."

"So he was," agreed my friendly Cerberus. "Now," he asked after a brief pause, "how long is it now you are going to be in Dublin?"

I said that I supposed I'd be there for two more weeks.

"And you're at the Hotel MacDermott?"

"Yes."

"Ah, well, now," said he, "that's a nice place to be, and, sure, you won't be needing a card for the few more days you'll spend in Dublin."

So I neither recorded my name nor took out a card for my whole scholarly stay. I never did meet the National Librarian.

When Moore died in 1852, there had been an unseemly rush to secure some memento (Longfellow was given an inkwell), yet a single coach contained all the mourners, and the dispersal of his effects was left to a Mr. and Mrs. S. C. Hall, literary worthies long forgotten, I fear. Ireland, I also fear, remembered the songs and forgot the poet. Then I recalled how, as an undergraduate, Moore had haunted Marsh's Library while he acquired the antiquarian lore that supported at the bottom of the page the translations at the top of his *Anacreon*, and I inquired my way to the library, if, indeed, it still existed. Exist it does in the shadow of St. Patrick's Cathedral, to which it has been attached since 1707. After some little difficulty about a key, I got access to this neglected collection of learning. Though the little building was scrupulously kept, I sometimes fancied that nobody had blown the dust off the tops of the volumes since Moore was a student there in the nineties of the eighteenth century. Attending one day a service in the cathedral, I looked down, found I was sitting on the grave of Swift's Stella, and hastily shifted my seat.

The Hotel MacDermott was not precisely a house of merriment, and lonely mornings poring over ecclesiastical volumes, looking for I knew not what, constituted a rather depressing life. Fortunately, in England I had been given two letters of introduction, one to James Montgomery and one to Oliver St. John Gogarty. I shall come to Montgomery presently, but my introduction to Gogarty I shall never forget. I had sent him my note of introduction and my present hotel address by post, which I understood was the proper thing to do, and Gogarty appointed a particular afternoon to meet him at his home library. The Irish Dail (Parliament) was then composed of two houses, the lower house and the senate, then of sixty members, of whom Gogarty was one. Whether land or repute or partisan politics was the basis of membership I never knew. I do remember that my favorite title among the senators was Senator The McGillicuddy of the Reeks, which looked to me like a long, long inherited rank.

At any rate, at the appointed hour I presented myself at the appointed address and was sent upstairs by the neat and efficient maid, who said that Mr. Gogarty was delayed by a prolonged meeting of the senate. Would I please make myself at home? The library was rich in volumes, most of them books I had never heard of, and at proper spacings on the wall were paintings by the leading Irish artists of the day, such as Jack Yeats. I was absorbed in contemplating an abstract canvas opposite the principal doorway when there was a sound of a small whirlwind outside. It subsided; it grew; then it seemed to be making its way upstairs. The door burst open as if under extraordinary pressure, and Senator Gogarty rushed at me, exclaiming, "The Irish peyple have a gaynius for destruc-thion! The Irish peyple have a gaynius for destructhion," and only when he had whirled me into a chair and sat down in another did he bang a silver bell and order tea. As this was during the period when the Dail was turning itself from a bicameral to a unicameral house, I assumed that it was the tempest about the change that had hurled him into his own library.

By and by our pulses slowed, we breathed more regularly, and our voices resumed their normal cadence.

"And what brings ye to Ireland?" he asked. "Sure, I'm just back from New York myself." This was true. He had just finished a tour of the American east coast, where his lectures and readings from the (as yet) unpublished *As I Was Going Down Sackville Street* had convulsed American audiences. "What's brought ye here?"

I explained that I was at work on a biography of Tom Moore. "Sure, and one is needed," he said. "That one by Stephen Gwynn is no good at all, at all. It's long out of date, and it has no sparkle."

I agreed.

"Now, how can I help you?" he asked. "With a name like Jones you can't be Irish."

I said I was partly Irish, partly Welsh, and the rest of me a mixture of English, Scottish, and Heaven knows what else.

"Well, ye'll do," he said judiciously, "since you've come to Dublin to do it. And how can we help you?"

"Well," I said, "I have about all of Tom Moore's books except his second one—the one that created the scandal. I have never found in any bookshop a copy of *The Poems of Thomas Little* I could afford to buy. That was the book, you will remember, that got him a reputation as an erotic poet. It came out in 1801."

"Ah, yes," responded Mr. Gogarty; "my father had a copy, which he used to hide from us, so we all read it, and it's somewhere in this room. Come, let's find it. You look, too."

For the next half hour an observer, had there been one, would have been either amused or amazed at the antics of two men, the one a senator of the Irish Free State, and the other a Guggenheim Fellow from Michigan, as they pulled out books and put them back again, looked for hidden shelves and secret drawers, paused from time to time to dust themselves off, and issued or followed directions: "You try that section— I'll take this one." About two-thirds of the way through this curious session Gogarty suddenly jumped to his feet, unhooked a picture, and commanded, "Here, take this."

"Why?" I asked.

It appeared that he had been so regally entertained in America he wanted somehow to repay the debt he felt he had immensely incurred. "This" proved to be a pale green Irish landscape in watercolors with a pale green Irish lake and two or three cows that escaped being pale green also only because they had retreated a respectful distance up a slope of pale green Irish grass. "But—but—but—" I sputtered.

"Take it, I say; take it. You can easily put it in your bag. It's all the peace and harmony of rural landscape. Put it on the chair over there. Now let's try the wall over there for Little's *Poems.*" The wall over there proved productive, for, from behind a tall row of sporting books tumbled a small, black, dusty copy of *The Poems of Thomas Little.* "Now," said he, "take it. We need a drink."

He jangled a bell. The maid came in, gave a look at the room, and was about to flee, when she received orders from her disheveled employer. "Bring us two whiskies at once," he told her, "then see if you can find enough newspapers to wrap up this picture in."

The whiskey was no problem, nor were the newspapers, but we could find no ball of twine; and while the maid went out on furtive expeditions after pieces of string, Gogarty and I refreshed ourselves with the whiskey (Irish whiskey is the best in the world), folded copies of the *Irish Times* around the framed watercolor, and then sat patiently tying odds and ends of butcher's cord, grocer's twine, shoebox string, and any other handy kinds until we could get a line long enough to hold the picture safely and create a sort of rainbow handle from which it could be dangled by a couple of fingers.

"Well, we did it," said Gogarty triumphantly from the middle of the chaos of the room.

"We did!" I echoed fervently. "But how am I going to repay you for all the time and energy you have spent, not to speak of the book and the picture?"

"Nonsense! my dear boy," he cut me short. "Now I'd ask you to stay for dinner," but there was some important engagement, political or otherwise, that stood in the way.

I did not especially care for the picture; and as I scarcely knew how to manage the wrapped-up watercolor with its scores of knots, I was a bit less enthusiastic about a gift of art than I might have been. But if a man takes a picture off his wall with a "Here, take this," and gets himself all dusty crawling about the carpet looking for a book of dubious morality, what can one do except express feelings of gratitude? The watercolor was just too large to fit into my bag, so that I carried it aboard the boat for Holyhead on a Saturday afternoon, literally the last in line of hundreds of passengers. I drew up at an endless inspection table.

"Sure, and what's that ye've got?" asked the weary inspector, who had gone through my two bags and found nothing illegal.

"It's a picture—a work of art," I answered. "Do you want to see it?"

"Who wrapped it up?" he asked.

"Senator Oliver St. John Gogarty," I replied as impressively as I could. "He took it off the wall and gave it to me."

"It must be a work of art," he decided. "No decent shopman would send out anything wrapped like that. Go on."

I went on. The steamer was crowded. I could find no place to sit down and no place to store my two bags and the green Irish lake except alongside a lifeboat swung athwart the deck. At Holyhead I was again the last person in line, and almost the last person to board the train. Holyhead was no more interested in unwrapping my work of art than was Ireland, but a trainman helped me to get comfortable, picture, bags, and all, on the express for London. At present, so far as I know, the cows are staring across a pale green lake at the Green Mountains of Vermont, where I left them when we sold our house there.

While still in Dublin, I had also used my letter of introduction to James Montgomery. He had played an important part in the "throubles" that followed upon the uprising of 1916, and during the subsequent English-Irish civil wars he had at one time or another hidden Irish fugitives of considerable notoriety from the Black and Tans. His house was never searched. "How did you get away with it?" I naturally asked.

"Faith now," he said, "did you ever know of an Irishman named James Montgomery? I'd open the door and I'd say, 'My name is Montgomery—James Montgomery. What do you want of me?' and they always asked pardon and went away."

Montgomery held down some permanent post in the government, in the equivalent of the Civil Service, if I am right, since changes in political parties seemed never to affect him. He was good enough to introduce me to the proper social circles, including the literary group composed of Yeats, "A. E." and others, men and women who seemed capable of drinking strong tea at midnight and sleeping the rest of the night. Since conversation at any level is an art in Ireland, but in the upper set one of the fine arts, my education was enormously advanced.

172

I remember that Yeats turned up at someone's evening salon—we had met casually many years before in Texas—and naturally inquired what I was doing in Dublin.

"Writing a biography of Tom Moore," I promptly replied.

He fell silent, retreated into himself, and then brought forth the oracular command, "Write it in Regency brick, my boy, write it in Regency brick." I endeavored to follow this engimatic utterance by making Moore a citizen of his age and not a mere poet, and I hope I succeeded. Since my volume appeared in 1937, Professor Dowden of Rice University, with a finer detective instinct than mine, has discovered that the originals of Moore's letters and journals still exist, though as the preface to my book truthfully asserts, I was solemnly assured that they had long ago been destroyed. He is trying to repair the damage that Lord John Russell's rough pen and careless editing have done to these now fragile pages and promises a genuine transcription of the poet of all circles and the idol of his own. Moore was as indefatigable a diarist as Pepys was, and the work, when and if it appears, may prove to be one of the most distinguished contributions to the social history of the first half of the last century.

The rest of my time in Dublin had to be brief, since, aside from familiarizing myself as well as I could with the physical conditions of Moore's native city—not merely such prominent objects as Phoenix Park and the Liffey, the part of the city he had been born in, and the homes of the wealthy and the aristocratic who had entertained him, but also the slums and the immediate environment of the capital—I needed the exposure to Irish ways and Irish speech. Moore was, like Shaw and Oscar Wilde, an Anglo-Irishman; and though he was in his lifetime regarded as a champion of Irish freedom no less than as a reviver of Irish song, he was also, except for a few years in Bermuda and North America, a staunch member of the Whig party. Intricate as the history of Anglo-Irish relations has been, I found the view from the other side of St. George's channel a useful counterweight to the emphasis that today recognizes him only as a lyric poet and forgets his tremendous labor as a satirist and writer of half a dozen prose works, including a well-intentioned *History of Ireland*. All biographers have to translate themselves and their readers backward in time to the age and country, the problems and people of another period; and this, I found, was peculiarly necessary if one were to understand the endless labor of Thomas Moore in trying to maintain harmony between Protestant England and Catholic Ireland. I returned to London not much richer in documentation but wiser, I hope, as a writer and a historian.

Our research labors came to an end, and the three Joneses—joined by Karl and Marjorie Litzenberg, friends from the Ann Arbor faculty—met in Paris, got to Switzerland, and traveled on a wonderful Swiss train to Buchs, on the River Rhine. We crossed that famous stream by bus, and in Vaduz, Liechtenstein, put up at the Gasthof zum Löwen, which had not changed, I think, since the Austro-Prussian War. In the early thirties, before the Nazis took over and long before the tourist rush began, Liechtenstein was a country out of a nineteenth-century German *Dorfroman*. Its total area is 62 square miles. It is bordered on the west by the Rhine, and elsewhere by Austria and Switzerland. Switzerland manages its diplomatic affairs, but it is nonetheless an autonomous principality, governed by a reigning monarch and a *Landstag* of 15. I think the police force was about ten, and there were no army, no taxes, and no tariff. The capital is Vaduz, which, when we were there, had more cows than human beings. Our Gasthof was on the bank of the Rhine, and I am under the impression that trout from that noble stream, at the call of the cook, leaped from the water, put their tails in their mouths, landed in proper pans on the stove, and died to make the most delicious breakfast in the world.

During our stay the principality celebrated the seventy-fifth birthday of the founding of the Vaduzer *Saengerverein*, and once the cows were put out to pasture, we gave the day over to festivity. A pretty blonde in an open carriage headed a procession from the top of the main street to the bottom, where the municipal park was laid out. The procession consisted of the police, the Liechtenstein band, the Saengerverein, and all the bands and singing societies from nearby Swiss or Austrian towns. We had music all day long. The light poles on the main street were, moreover, hung with bannerets of blue and purple, the prince's own colors, and in the afternoon the prince and princess appeared in a large black car, scattering chocolate candies as they slowly rolled towards the park. Everyone thereupon burst into the national anthem:

> O du mein Liechtenstein,
> Du stehts am deutschen Rhein
> Du schönes Land

We sang too, to the immense gratification of all the nearby Vaduzers, for the air is that of our own "America" and the British "God Save the King." Beer and sausages were served all day long at pine tables in the park, and when darkness came there were fireworks and, on an elevated platform, a trick bicycle act. A voice came out of the crowd obviously for our benefit: "So was hab'n Sie nicht in Amerika!" Whereupon a younger voice replied: "Nein, nein, in Amerika hab'n Sie viel besser."

I shall not pause on ghostly Vienna, that magnificent capital without an empire. Here Karl got into an amusing medical difficulty. He had been drinking a good deal of beer for a resident of the dry states of Minnesota and Michigan, and he went to a Viennese doctor recommended by Karl's father, who prescribed less beer and the regular imbibition of a drink called, I think, a *Weinchaudeau*. We repaired regularly every day to the same café, where Karl as regularly drank his Weinchaudeau, and I noticed he was treated with growing respect by the waiters. I later learned that a Weinchaudeau is what elderly gentlemen drink just before going to a bordello to show off their sexual prowess.

Chapter XVIII

The Harvard
Tercentenary

OUR RETURN to Ann Arbor was without incident, and the three Joneses settled down, as we thought, to a calm life as members of the University of Michigan community. I took up my courses in American and Victorian literature, plus the usual work with graduate students, and I kept on directing the Nell Gwynne Players. Eleanor returned to school and Bessie to her post at the Ann Arbor printing establishment. During the thirties, in addition to the titles already mentioned, I brought out a book mainly of sonnets in various experimental forms entitled *They Say the Forties*, and published in 1937 *The Harp That Once: A Chronicle of the Life of Thomas Moore*. The biography was received with a curious mixture of reviews, the tone depending on whether the reviewer was of Irish descent and, if Irish, what sort of politics he held.

The principal office of the English department was on the second floor of Angell Hall, where a secretary in the outer room attended to routine matters, and in an inner office Louis Strauss, the lovable and much-enduring chairman, had his desk. A group of English teachers casually gathered in the outer office about mail time. I was one of such a group on a spring morning in 1936. The secretary had already received the mail and was engaged in sorting it into the various pigeonholes, when, noting that a group of four or five of the faculty was right at hand, she gave each of us his own letters. My portion was two large envelopes, one bigger than the other and both looking official. I opened the smaller one first and almost fell to the floor in astonishment, for the envelope contained an official invitation from James Bryant Conant, president of

Harvard University, asking me to become a professor of English in that institution on tenure at a salary of $10,000 a year. The other members of the group stopped talking and looked at me with some astonishment as I turned pale and then red. As we were about to suffer a salary cut at Michigan, the offer was more than welcome and totally unexpected. I then opened the second, larger envelope, the contents of which were even more bewildering. I was invited to be one of a group of about one hundred scholars and scientists from all parts of the world to come to Harvard and discuss either the woes of the world or the future of the sciences, and, if they had not already been honored by Harvard, to receive an appropriate honorary degree. The section of this formidable regiment I was invited to join concerned "Authority and the Individual," to which I was supposed to contribute a paper. If I had been invited to lecture on the planet Mars, I could not have been more amazed. Midwestern newspapers were filled with news of the Midwest and with stories about the woes of the world, but they had had no place for stories about Harvard University; and I had not, in my wildest dreams, ever thought of going there as a member of the faculty or as a member of a distinguished group of learned men from all over the globe. I could not speak. I silently handed the paper to O. J. Campbell, whose Ph.D. came from Harvard, and tried to regain my self-control. When he had read the paper, he dropped to the floor like a Buddhist monk and held up his hands in an attitude of prayer and admiration. The others looked at the two of us in profound bewilderment, and it was only after I told O. J. to get up and he handed the papers around that I was heartily congratulated by my colleagues on these unexpected honors.

Too late I reread the two communications and noted they were both marked "Confidential," but my friends agreed to keep quiet on the matter, though decency required that I inform Louis Strauss of my resignation to go east. In a vague sort of way I had of course known that Harvard was founded in 1636, but I was not a graduate of that institution and had had no inkling of the great Tercentenary preparations. Harvard, I discovered, does things with its right hand but sometimes forgets to inform the left hand of what it has done; and I had been chosen as a member of the English department at a time when the English department as a whole knew little more about the Tercentenary program than I did. As it had been resolved from the beginning that no Harvard faculty man was to be included in the hundred notables, whenever my name appeared on one of the Tercentenary programs, it was accompanied by an asterisk and a footnote explaining that the program had been made up and the degree conferred before Professor Jones joined the Harvard faculty.

All this entailed another move. After I had taught in the summer quarter at the University of Colorado, we sold our house in Ann Arbor, disposed of as much of the furniture as we decently could, yanked poor Eleanor out of another school, and on a fine early September day in 1936 set out for Cambridge. Our route took us through Detroit, not one of our loveliest American cities, across the Detroit River into Canada, then traversed endless miles of flat landscape until we escaped via Niagara Falls, which Oscar Wilde once characterized as the first disappointment of married life. We crossed New York state by a road paralleling the Erie Canal, worked our way past Albany, noted that the landscape was becoming hillier, and by and by entered Vermont, thus retracing the trail my ancestors had taken many years before. I cannot say I had any sense of an exile's return, but the three of us, I think, quietly rejoiced in the mountains of Vermont, New Hampshire, and Massachusetts. By and by we reached Worcester and followed route 9 into Cambridge, where Bessie had engaged a small suite of rooms for us at the Hotel Commander just off Harvard Square. This was to be our home for some weeks.

As one of many participants in it, I shall describe the celebration of the Harvard Tercentenary at length and in detail for a reason that will become manifest at the very end of this chapter. Thoughts about celebrating the three hundredth birthday of the oldest American institution of higher learning went back to the opening of the decade. On September 30, 1930, the Board of Overseers proposed a joint committee with the Corporation to plan a celebration; the Corporation agreed on October 13; and the Directors of the Harvard Alumni Association were stirred to set up an associate committee. These committees were shortly fused into a single body; and Jerome D. Greene, a directing genius if ever there was one, then the secretary to the Corporation, was on May 14, 1934, made Director of the Tercentenary, to take up his duties in September. Three general governing ideas were evolved from various high-level discussions, which can be followed in Greene's *The Tercentenary of Harvard College*, published by Harvard University Press in 1937. The first was that emphasis should be laid on the university of today rather than on its history. The second was a succession of festival occasions in 1936—summer schools, special institutes, conferences, and notable gatherings of distinguished scholars and scientists from all over the world to announce the results of their work and to suggest plans for the future. The third was a three-day climax (September 16, 17, and 18). On the first of these three days representatives of universities and learned societies from all countries were officially received by the president; the second day was dedicated to thanksgiving and remembrance; and the third day was a formal convocation, including the conferring of sixty-two honorary degrees upon the scholars who had participated (there were seventy-one participants, but nine already held honorary degrees from Harvard). The last days included other glamorous events: special concerts by the Boston Symphony Orchestra under the direction of Sergei Koussevitzky; an illumination of the Charles River especially managed by undergraduates; special exhibits in the Boston Museum of Fine Arts, the Gardner Museum, the Fogg Museum, and the Busch-Reisinger Museum, which began as the Germanic Museum. The Congress of the United States appointed a committee to attend, headed by President Franklin D. Roosevelt, himself a Harvard alumnus, and including members of both houses and representatives of the naval, military, and civil establishments. Invitations had also been sent to representatives of foreign governments, to governors and mayors, and to the masters of secondary schools and preachers.

The great open space bounded by the Memorial Church, Sever Hall, the Widener Library with its vast steps, and University Hall was turned into an enormous outdoor theater, seating an audience variously estimated at 17,000 or 18,000; and the south portico of the Memorial Church was made a central element, on which was built a large platform seating 840 persons in eight tiers of seats. There was a special platform or stand for the Tercentenary chorus, another for the band, a "tribune" for the speaker in the center of the platform and slightly in advance of it, and platforms hidden in trees for moving picture men and photographers.

The general committee divided all learning into four quadrants, and I must confess that to this day I am not quite clear as to what these quadrants were. I am but following the authority of Harvard University Press, which published the papers delivered by the participants, in saying that the three quadrants of most concern to me are exemplified in the titles of three printed volumes: *Independence, Convergence, and Borrowing in Institutions, Thought, and Art*, largely concerned with international cultural influences; *Factors Determining Human Behavior*, principally concerned with psychology, custom, and law; and *Authority and the Individual*, which might, by an unfavorable reviewer, be regarded as a potpourri of pronouncements about politics, law, and the arts, but which was itself split into four "quadrants": "The State and Economic Enterprise," "Stability and Social Change," "The Place and Functions of Authority," and "Classicism and Romanticism," which included my own modest contribution. The other papers in this last section were by Friedrich Meinecke, Paul Hazard, and Edward Joseph Dent, the musicologist; and their general drift, with the possible exception of Dent's, was to assume that romanticism was a liberating force and classicism a conservative one. After a good deal of work, I had been unable to discover any agreement among scholars in American literary history either that we have experienced a romantic age or, if we had, what its temporal boundaries (or, for that matter, its topographical locations) might be. I fell back upon what is perhaps a rash generalization:

In the sphere of political action a romantic revolution in European terms was at once tautological and irrelevant [in the United States]; tautological, since, by the terms of its own 'democratic' revolution, America *was*, politically speaking, the romantic revolt; irrelevant, because the return to throne and altar, which is the romantic phase of the European reaction, was meaningless in a Protestant and democratic republic with no medieval past.

Were I rewriting the paper nowadays, I think I should stick to my principal proposition, but I am less certain about the absence of medievalism in American history. I think I overlooked many medieval elements in the earlier decades of American political and economic history, and that I also minimized some important medieval elements in American thought and art. Perhaps I should have said more about the importation or revival of scholasticism by the Roman Catholic Church in nineteenth- and twentieth-century America. Amidst the symphonic richness of most of these papers, mine now appears to me not much more than a minor piping in an immense orchestra—to paraphrase Meredith, a performance on a penny whistle.

The memorable concluding ceremonies were as thoroughly organized as a great military review. The various gates into the Harvard Yard were guarded by policemen; and the entrances into the Centennial Theater itself were decorated with heraldry after designs by Pierre de la Rose, who, once past the official arms of the United States, the seal of its president, and the great seal of the Commonwealth of Massachusetts, turned to history for other suggestions. The Law School, for example, used the arms of Isaac Royall, who created the first professorship of law. For the Medical School de la Rose used the arms of Professor John Warren as shown on his bookplate. Each of the several Harvard "houses" had its special gonfalon, that of Leverett House, for example, of which I became an Associate, being three leverets sable (a leveret is a small hare) on a silver field. And of course the arms of Harvard with "Veritas" and its three open books were everywhere. The language of heraldry is perhaps needlessly arcane, but Pierre de la Rose faithfully observed all the rules.

180

The audience had virtually filled the theater by nine o'clock on the morning of September 18. The various segments of the great procession, except those stationed in the Widener Library, assembled in the Old Yard; at 9:40 the bugles blew "Ready," and at 9:45 they commanded "March." An endless and orderly procession poured through the central aisle of the theater; and, headed by the Chief Marshal, Charles Francis Adams '88, and his deputy, Joseph R. Hamlen '04, it began its majestic way. The oldest living alumni of Harvard College, John T. Morse, Jr., of the class of 1860 and Henry M. Rogers of the class of 1862, came first. There was no living survivor of the class of 1861, but after Messrs. Morse and Rogers representatives of class after class filed by, each preceded by a class marshal carrying a banner indicating its year. When it was time, the President and Fellows, the members of the Board of Overseers, and an enormous number of dignitaries also fell into pairs and, emerging from the doors of Widener, sedately descended the steps and joined the procession. The various marshals, each bearing his flag, had meanwhile lined the central aisle from the door of Widener to the platform, each pair falling into place as the particular part of the procession that was their concern passed them, and some eighty-six flags were at length evenly stacked in clusters on either side of the speaker's tribune. Mr. Roosevelt came in at the back of the platform, escorted by his military and naval aides. At 10:28 the entire procession was seated, each in his proper place, and at precisely 10:30 the bells of Southwark Cathedral in far-off London (the church where John Harvard was baptized) came through great amplifiers on the platform and among the audience. In spite of occasional rain the variegated colors of the gowns and uniforms on the platform shone, I am told by observers, with extraordinary brilliance. When the bells fell silent, the Chief Marshal called upon the Sheriff of Middlesex County, who, in a ceremony as old as Harvard itself, advanced to the front of the platform, struck the wooden floor three times with his sword (in its scabbard) and announced: "The meeting will be in order."

The University Marshal then announced that the invocation would be spoken by Willard L. Sperry, the chairman of the Board of Preachers, who had a fine voice and a fine ear for noble English; and he was followed by Professor Edward K. Rand, whose voice rivaled Sperry's and who delivered in Latin the salutatory oration. Then Professor Samuel Eliot Morison, the official historian, spoke clearly and well about the founding of Harvard, quoting, as he was bound to quote, from the original charter, which says that Harvard College had been created for "the advancement and education of youth in all manner of good literature, arts, and sciences." The Tercentenary chorus sang briefly from the music of Gabrielli. The governor of the commonwealth spoke, stressing the peril of the times. The president of the university then called forward representatives of the Universities of Paris, Oxford, and Cambridge, the far-off intellectual ancestors of Harvard, and gave to each, beautifully printed, a message of thanks; and then the slight figure of John Masefield, England's Poet Laureate, appeared, and he read his "Lines Suggested by the Tercentenary of Harvard College." The chorus sang, this time something by Bach; and President Conant, apparently unexhausted by all the addresses he had had to make during the summer, uttered a noble oration on the need for continuing the search for truth. The Tercentenary chorus sang after he concluded, this time a selection from Handel.

The reading desk on the tribune was now removed so that everyone in the huge audience could see the recipients of honorary degrees. President Conant moved forward a step or two, flanked by two aides, and pronounced the ancient formula: "By virtue of authority delegated to me by the two Governing Boards, I now confer the following honorary degrees." In many other institutions the candidate at this point is escorted to the president and presented to him, and a summary, often too long, of his life and achievement is then read. By tradition, however, the conferring of an honorary degree by Harvard is Spartan in its simplicity. There is no hood to throw over the candidate's shoulders and no extensive biography. On this occasion sixty-two biographies would have been too much for the audience to take, especially as the threat of rain and finally the rain itself were discouraging. At Harvard the president, taking in his hands the large, beautiful leather case that contains the diploma, finds, lightly fastened to the outside of the case, a square of cardboard on which is printed in large capitals the full name of the candidate, the nature of the degree, and a short statement, commonly of not more than two sentences and usually only one, of his achievement. The president calls the name, the recipient rises where he stands, and doffs his mortarboard if he has one on; the president again reads his name, the nature of the degree is pronounced, and the sentence of achievement is read. On this day an aide then brought the diploma to the right or left as the candidate was seated. The candidate received the degree, bowed to the president, and sat down, resuming his mortarboard or his hat.

I do not know who determined the order in which the sixty-two degrees were conferred. It was certainly not alphabetically by names of candidates nor was there any attempt to keep to the chronological order of the founding of the candidate's institution, which had played an important part in the reception of delegates, when the representative of the University of Cairo came first and the representative of the University of Panama, founded only in 1933, came last. I was eleventh on the list, between Sir Arthur Stanley Eddington and John Harold Clapham; my degree was that of Doctor of Letters; and the citation read: "An American writer and scholar whose critical study of our literature assists the country to appraise justly its own culture." This simple statement pleased, and pleases, me immensely, for it puts into the fewest possible words exactly what I have been all my life trying to do in my professional work. I shall come later on to an estimate of what I think American writers in 1976 are doing with regard to the ideals of either 1636 or those of 1776.

The scholars and scientists who gathered at Harvard in the autumn of 1936 were far more uneasy about the future of mankind than the newspapers were. As an example I quote part of the conclusion reached by William Emanuel Rappard, who spoke on "Economic Nationalism" on September 8. Dr. Rappard, Professor of Public Finance at the University of Geneva, a post as nearly neutral as can be imagined, concluded his address:

The qualitative and quantitative progress in the arts of destruction has been such in the course of the last century, and more particularly since the [First] World War, that the civilization which has developed since the Middle Ages could probably not survive the shock to which it would be exposed tomorrow if economic nationalism were to engender the same political consequences to which it has ever given rise in the past. Our imagination shrinks before the vision of universal devastation, suffering, and death which the thorough application of modern physics and chemistry to the task of mutual annihilation must evoke.

But that, of course, is no sure protection. Men and nations have gone mad in the past, and previous civilizations, no less ambitious than our own, have been engulfed in dark ages in centuries and millenaries gone by.

Such a tragedy may be in store for our generation. It is, however, not inevitable. Men may yet recoil before the fatal consequences of their criminal folly. They may yet allow reason to triumph over the promptings of inflamed and misguided nationalism.

Men did not. Three years and a week, almost to a day, after Dr. Rappard's solemn peroration, on September 1, 1939, Hitler invaded Poland.

The curse laid on Cassandra was of course that nobody would believe her. The role of Cassandra was not played by Dr. Rappard alone at the Harvard Tercentenary. Speaker after speaker, scientist upon scientist, scholar after scholar warned their audiences that research for its own sake is not a good in itself, but must be estimated in terms of its social, its economic, its political, and above all its moral consequences—a warning that has almost been forgotten. The great Harvard Tercentenary, planned for years and conducted with incredible skill by Jerome D. Greene, Director, looked admiringly at the past but apprehensively at the future; and the same James Bryant Conant who presided so graciously over most of the general exercises of the commemoration within less than a decade was called to Washington and Los Alamos, leaving Harvard to the guidance of a substitute, while he and other scientists created an atom bomb that, dropped without warning upon Hiroshima, killed or injured more than 400,000 human beings. I sometimes think the true moral of the Cassandra myth is never to celebrate anything; you may be totally wrong.

But judgments of course differ with perspective, time, space, and viewer or auditor. A graduate of Christ Church, Oxford, wrote in to say that in his opinion the Tercentenary proceedings vied with the Declaration of Independence. Bernard Faÿ, the French scholar, declared that the Harvard celebration was the one bright and encouraging thing in the dark days of 1936. In one of his finest columns, under date of September 17, 1936, Walter Lippmann noted how little the Tercentenary proceedings glorified Harvard and how much was devoted to men everywhere and to advancing knowledge. The character of the ceremonies, he said, "reflects . . . the knowledge which only the wise are able to believe, that things endure in human affairs where they are made not of pride and power, but of humility and the love of truth." Harvard, he continued, is great, not because of great wealth, since it has often been desperately poor. It has outlasted all the governments there were when it was founded, and he commanded his readers not to ask whether universities have "served the contemporary purposes of states and of the partisans within them" but whether "states have been loyal to that great tradition of order actuated by the love of truth of which the universities are the appointed guardians."

One may reasonably doubt whether such another pageantry of learning and brilliance, worldwide in its significance, will be again seen in the United States of America, supposing our nation survives that long and clings to its original principles.

Chapter XIX

Places
and Persons

WE STAYED in the Hotel Commander during the Tercentenary ceremonies; then, while I tried to learn how I was to fit into the English
department, Bessie found us a vacant apartment at the top of 983
Memorial Drive, one of three tall apartment buildings that face the
Charles River. Various persons of almost legendary importance lived in
them, including the world-famous Alfred North Whitehead, who was
that same year retiring as a professor of philosophy at Harvard, a simple
man with a mind so profound that in the words of a reference book he
passed from a knowledge of the higher mathematics to a knowledge of
the absolute in God. The owner of the apartment that Bessie had in mind
was extremely anxious in this Depression year to secure tenants and
readily agreed to repaint and redecorate as she suggested as well as to
tear down the wall between the living room and the dining room,
replacing it by a half-wall lined with bookshelves. This not only gave us
space for books but also flooded both rooms with light in the morning
and in the evening. The building next door was the monastery, if that is
the right word, of the Cowley Fathers, an Episcopal order, who were as
quiet as mice; but unfortunately, the large corner next to them was
the terminal of the MBTA—the Massachusetts Bay Transportation
Authority, which operates subways and trolley cars, most of which, it
sometimes seemed to me, came to Memorial Drive to reverse their
direction. Inside, the apartment was pleasant, but it was without air
conditioning; and since we had to leave most of the windows open on hot
summer nights, we were plagued by the noises of the terminal and of the

automobile traffic on the Drive. We stood this for three or four years and then in 1940 resolved to seek quieter quarters.

The dauntless Bessie again sallied forth alone against whole regiments of realtors, discovering among other things that older houses in Cambridge were content with soapstone sinks, dirty grey paint, and one electric bulb dangling from the middle of the kitchen ceiling. We thought for a time of retreating to the suburbs as many of the Harvard faculty had already done, but she finally discovered a house on Francis Avenue, which, after some necessary structural changes were made, she decided we should rent. Francis Avenue is off Kirkland Street, a busy thoroughfare, and the original Francis mansion, all white with a fine lawn and an immaculate picket fence, was still standing. The house she lighted upon was number 12–14, a large, irregular dwelling vaguely like an enormous Cape Cod cottage, shingled, and cut irregularly into two parts, the one half (number 12) being the residence of Ralph H. Wetmore and his family. The edifice had been at one time the home of the Turner family and the Crothers clan, including the widow and daughter of the famous Reverend Samuel McChord Crothers, the American rival of the Reverend Sydney Smith, the Anglican clergyman and wit. (In the decades when literature was supposed to exhibit a certain degree of refinement, he had written an essay, "Every Man's Natural Desire To Be Somebody Else," which anticipated by several decades the solemn identity-crises of the contemporary world.) The Cambridge Historical Society attributes the plans for this house to the firm of Ware and Van Brunt, architects of Memorial Hall, about a block and a half away and well-planned or hideous, all depending on one's taste for "Gothic" architecture.

From the moment we moved into 14 Francis Avenue, the Wetmores proved to be the most agreeable and thoughtful of neighbors, an important point since the grounds and the cellar were in common, as was the outside of the house. Ralph is a distinguished botanist, a fact wonderful in itself but the more wonderful in that he is color-blind and confines his research work to cellular botany. He was a widower with two daughters when he met his second wife, Olive, who was associated with Radcliffe College and later with the New England Conservatory of Music. Our friendship with the Wetmores is now so old we cannot remember when we did not know them. In a few years the owner of the house wanted to sell, and we two couples bought the estate, holding it together or, as the legal phrase goes, each party owning an undivided half of the whole. This contract drives lawyers up the wall, but it has worked.

186

Eleanor had been present for the Tercentenary, but she finished her secondary education at a small private school in Worcester and went from there to Swarthmore College. She found Swarthmore either too permissive or not permissive enough, I never knew which, and transferred for her junior year to the University of North Carolina in order to do playmaking to her heart's desire. In 1936–37 Paul Green's "pageant," *The Lost Colony*, was being played nightly near Hatteras, North Carolina, and at half-past ten for a long series of nights Eleanor had to appear on stage, half-demented, imploring somebody to tell her where her baby was. In a later summer she worked with some summer stock companies on the Massachusetts coast. My chief memory of this epoch is that she was in a company that supported the aging Mrs. Patrick Campbell. But Eleanor—who now preferred to be called "Elex"—had met at Swarthmore a young engineer, Raymond C. Ingersoll, son of the former borough president of Brooklyn; and in 1941, a year after we had moved to Francis Avenue, the two were married in the Appleton Chapel in the Harvard Yard. There followed a wedding reception, for which the Wetmores and the Joneses threw everything open that could be opened. There are two children by this marriage—a daughter, Carolyn, now a trained nurse, and a son, Raymond V., now an assistant professor of geology at the University of New Mexico. Carolyn also married, it proved disastrously, but out of the wreckage she saved her life, her sanity, a profession, and a charming little girl, so that I am now a great-grandfather.

When my mother was compelled to give up her Ann Arbor lodgings, we got her a large front room in the rest home on Kirkland Street, half a block from our own home. She gradually grew senile and had to be taken to a state nursing establishment a good many miles from 14 Francis Avenue, where she died while I was engaged in war work. But Bessie arranged with Willard Sperry, the dean of the Divinity School, for a simple and memorable funeral service.

We brought with us from Memorial Drive to our present home the most wonderful Irishwoman we ever knew, the indomitable, the unconquerable Mary Myers. She had married a young German who, unfortunately, became mentally deranged and had to be confined in a state institution at Worcester, so that when she asked for a day off to visit "him," we knew where she went; and she had produced a daughter, Grace, now a trained nurse. She usually came with a small cocker spaniel named Honey, who seemed to be immortal until I one day discovered that when one Honey died, a second was immediately procured to take his place.

Mary had gradually worked her way from scullery maid to cook, maid, housekeeper, and similar posts. She had been a servant to the rich, or at least to the well-to-do, where, as she said, we were "eight on help," and concerning whom she had many anecdotes to tell in a brogue not affected by her years in America. I believe her first earnings were $1.50 a week, with, of course, "keep." Out of this pittance she managed to save enough money to help the rest of her family to leave Ireland, including a brother who rose to fame and wealth in the liquor business. At first Mary would take no help from any of them, but in her later years she did allow her rich brother to help with the rent and the groceries.

Tales about Mary have become legendary. If we proposed to have a small dinner party and informed Mary in advance, her immediate response was invariably, "Be they Haavahd people?" and being assured they were, she would say philosophically, "Ah, well, they'll be late," and automatically change the dinner from 7:30 to 8:00. She subscribed to the Boston *Post*, a paper now defunct, that specialized in crime; and pushing open the swinging door between the kitchen and the dining room while carrying a tray in both hands to the table, she would begin with a Vergilian *in medias res*—"Ain't it a shame now, the way they found that poor girl's body in the quarry?"—and we got the beginning and the ending of the tale only by degrees as she brought more dishes to the table.

In those simpler times before chain stores, while grocers and meat-markets delivered orders as a matter of course, one could hear Mary talking to the butcher at, let us say, S. S. Peirce or Sage's. Her conversations invariably began, "This is Mrs. Jones's house spakin'," and if the order concerned a fowl, her last sentence was inevitably, "And mind now, young man, no pin feathers." Some friends of ours had gone through the divorce mill, and we tried to explain to Mary that some old, familiar guests now had new names. She worked diligently to straighten out this marital tangle, and at length concluded philosophically, "Well, well, what can ye expect nowadays, what with all these wars and rumors of wars?"

Mary was of course a Roman Catholic, but being Irish she had towards the church that queer combination of irony and awe that Ed O'Connor has caught in his wonderful novels *The Last Hurrah* and *The Edge of Sadness*. She used to invite some of the local clergy to her apartment for dinner, an invitation that was, I think, never refused, for her dinners were fabulous. One evening she invited four young priests. They came in the neatest of clerical array and were greeted warmly by Mary as she came out of the door to the little kitchen. She got them comfortably seated in her immaculate living room and then said, "Now, boys, I know ye all. Take off them stiff collars, and hang your coats in

188

the closet over there, and if you like, take off your shoes, too, and we'll all have a drink and a good time."

One powerful Irish personage inevitably leads me to another: John Shea, who never got beyond the sixth grade and who had helped carry books from the old Gore Hall, since demolished, to the new Widener Library when the Widener building was dedicated in July, 1915. He was made a member of the staff with some such title as "Superintendent of Books." Of this he was justly proud. He opened the library every weekday at twenty minutes to eight and closed it each evening at ten. The interval he mainly spent in prowling about the stacks, the professors' studies, and the carrels—that is, the desks set along the outer walls of the building, each desk having a shelf for books reserved by the occupant or occupants of the carrel. I never caught him reading anything but the morning papers, but he had been so long associated with the Harvard collections that, when I first got to know him in 1936, I used to wonder where he picked up his knowledge. It was intuitive. Any faculty member or graduate student unable to locate a book he badly needed appealed at once to John Shea, who would inquire the title of the book, its probable size, whether it had illustrations or no, and what the general topic might be—this last helping John to eliminate a good many places where he need not look. He would shamble off at his bearlike, strolling pace, and by and by return either with the missing volume or a statement of who had it, where it was, and how the petitioner could best get hold of it. Whatever the great merits of the faculty of arts and sciences, I think John Shea got more doctoral theses finished and more learned papers done than any member of the academic staff.

He had an office in the bowels of the building, but one usually saw him at the front entrance, the Boston *Post* spread out before him, a fact that did not lessen his sharp, immediate glance at everyone who entered. He was, unless put out by someone's stupidity, one who would roar at you as gently as any sucking dove. I was in those days an early riser, and John and I had many a morning chat, John using a vocabulary of his own. He once informed Professor Munn that the material he was looking for was on Floor A in a "vanilla" envelope. Mrs. Shea, another wonderful cook, once suffered a small traffic accident in Harvard Square, and on the following morning I of course inquired into the cause of it. I drew the characteristic reply: "I dunno, professor, but I think she stepped on the exhilarator." On another morning, when John and I for some reason had strolled into the room containing the union card catalog, he paused, looked up at the huge windows, and said earnestly, "Professor, them venereal blinds need dusting."

Keyes Metcalf, a remarkable and skilled professional librarian, came into office a year or so after I had come to Harvard. He had a professional's interest in rank, order, and titles, and it struck him that so sonorous a title as "Superintendent of Books" ought to be borne by a trained librarian, not by John Shea. His secretary telephoned John in the cave downstairs where he hung his overcoat and said that Mr. Metcalf wanted to see him. John said he would be right up, but when he reached Mr. Metcalf's office, Mr. Metcalf was occupied by an overloquacious visitor, and John had to wait. John naturally inquired of the secretary what Mr. Metcalf wanted of him, and the secretary incautiously let slip the information that a change in John's title was in the air. John's pride was touched to the quick. When the visitor at length departed from the librarian's office, Mr. Metcalf apologized for the delay, asked John to come in, and offered him a seat. John briefly replied, "Mr. Metcalf, I prefer to stand," and stand he did while Mr. Metcalf explained as tactfully as he could that the library was under new management and he wanted to alter John's title to "Superintendent of the Building" or something of that sort. Mr. Metcalf is a kindly man and grew more and more embarrassed as the sentinel-like figure before him made no comment. Finally, he said, "Well, what do you think of it, John?"

The silent listener uttered a laconic sentence: "Mr. Metcalf, I resign."

Shocked, the librarian said, "Well, I didn't expect this from you, John."

To this Shea replied, "You don't give me an appetite, Mr. Metcalf," and departed.

He went back to his den of an office and after some thought telephoned Paul Buck, the historian, who was substituting for President Conant during the construction of the atom bomb. Paul heard the story sympathetically and asked only, "Have you put anything in writing, John?"

"Not yet," answered John Shea.

"Then," said Paul Buck, "do me a favor, John. Don't write anything and don't talk to anybody about your resignation until after I telephone you on Tuesday morning."

John promised. The fateful interview with Keyes Metcalf had occurred late in the week. The Corporation always met on a Monday, and Paul Buck, as provost, was taking President Conant's place. The secretary had prepared the usual agenda for this meeting. But Paul said he would like the privilege of interpolating a piece of business ahead of the agenda, and he told the story of John Shea's long service to the Harvard College Library, indicating that Mr. Metcalf had had no evil intent. The Corporation listened in silence and then unanimously voted John a "Corporation" appointment. Such an appointment can be terminated by the Corporation only, not by one of its officers, and on Tuesday morning Paul telephoned both Metcalf and Shea. There the matter rested until the legal time of John's retirement loomed on the horizon.

A group of Harvard professors, users of the library, had meanwhile got together and recommended John for an honorary degree, which was granted by the Corporation and the Board of Overseers. Who is to receive an honorary degree is one secret that Harvard never discloses until the day such degrees are granted, and any recipient is of course sworn to secrecy. When the commencement procession formed, Professor Munn escorted John to the platform, where he sat with ambassadors and others of like prominence. I ought to add that the evening before the commencement, the president gives a dinner for all the candidates for honorary degrees, and some of us worried about John's behavior in this august assembly. We need not have done so. Before the dinner concluded, most of the other candidates were gathered around the end of the table where John Shea sat while, in his inimitable English, he told them stories of the Harvard faculty. At the commencement the following day, John's name was the first to be announced. He rose and stepped forward to become an honorary Master of Arts, when such a yell went up from the students—both the graduate students and alumni who had profited by John's kindly ministrations—as I never have heard, even in the Harvard Yard.

Before he died, a year or so after his retirement, John turned up in my study one day with a bundle of papers in his hand. It was the story of his life, written out on pads of half-sheet paper such as are commonly used in the grade schools. He had used up one entire tablet with rosebuds at the top of each sheet, and had gone on to a second, plainer tablet of the same dimensions. "I want," he said briefly, "to give this to you to keep." I was deeply touched by the confidence he reposed in me, and promised to guard the document. When John left my study, I began reading with a sinking heart, since it is my observation that many excellent conversationalists become commonplace when they try writing about themselves. Not so in this case. John wrote as he talked; and he had filled his pages with, among other data, pen sketches in prose of the famous Harvard professors he had known. I could not publish the manuscript because there were too many home truths about too many members of the living faculty, but I turned it over for safekeeping to the Harvard Archives.

Arthur Darby Nock was a distinguished scholar, notably in the

Pauline epistles and the early history of the church, who had risen from what I may gently call a humble background in Great Britain to become a member of the Harvard Divinity School. The dean of the Divinity School, Willard Sperry, in those days lived across the street from us with his extremely English wife, and Arthur Nock was accustomed to spend weekends with the Sperrys. Mrs. Sperry, I may note parenthetically, had Strong Views on almost everything. She was a gifted writer too, but she never finished the book she had begun, to be entitled *Dear Dead Women*, the phrase coming from Browning's moving poem, "A Toccata of Galuppi's":

> Dear dead women . . . what's become of all the gold
> Used to hang and brush their bosoms? I feel chilly and grown old.

I read the two or three sketches she had accumulated towards the proposed volume and found them moving and accurate. ("What of soul was left, I wonder, when the kissing had to stop?") Arthur Nock, in addition to being a profound scholar in Greek, Hebrew, and Heaven knows what related tongues, had also his little peculiarities, one of which was the fear of falling. One frosty autumn morning— one of those mornings when sounds carry farther than they ordinarily do—I went out to pick up the morning paper. Two telephone linesmen were working on a pole across the street from my front door, when Arthur, a worn black cape over his shoulder, an ancient hat on his head, and a heavy cane in his hand, came out of the Sperry front door, crept cautiously down the steps (it had snowed lightly the night before), hobbled along towards the sidewalk as if he were walking on glass, turned to the right, and made his way with equal caution to the end of the block, where he again turned right and disappeared, clinging with his right hand to a long picket fence that encloses the former Francis house. The two linesmen stopped working to watch him in his slow progress.

"Sure, and what's that?" one of them inquired.

"Ah," said the other, spitting, "it's nawthin' at all. It's jist one of them at Haavahd."

Another one of them at Harvard was Professor Harry A. Wolfson, possibly the most erudite Hebraist of his generation. He was a bachelor, whose only relief from incessant toil was, so far as I could make out, going to the movies. He lunched at the faculty club every noon with the same set of cronies year after year, and he occasionally dined out at the invitation of hostesses who were not too awed by his enormous learning to invite him. For a good many years he had had a study in the basement of Widener, ill-lighted and dusty, but no maid and no janitor were allowed to touch his notes or his books. During one of my earlier years at Harvard a study was vacated on the top floor, larger, sunnier, and in every way more desirable than the cellar-hole where Dr. Wolfson had lived. It occurred to Paul Buck, who was then director of the libraries, that so distinguished a scholar deserved better housing than his basement den. Long conferences followed. Professor Wolfson was shown the proposed new quarters and was visibly shaken in his determination to spend the rest of his life underground. Finally a solemn agreement was entered into: Professor Wolfson would move, provided that the movers replaced everything—books, filing cases, manuscripts, notes, desk, and chairs— in the new study precisely as they had been before. This was done after a good deal of drill-work on the part of whoever superintended this delicate operation, and Wolfson moved upstairs. I met him two days after this momentous transaction and asked, of course, how he had endured his ordeal. "Oh, my dear Chones," he replied, "it was fine, fine. Everything was where it should be. But you know, Chones," he added confidentially, "do you know something?" I did not. "Well, Chones, I found a pile of offprints I had never sent out!"

Wolfson was a perfectionist, at once the glory and the terror of Harvard University Press, which, I think, published almost all his books, at considerable expense. He would send in a manuscript he had toiled over for years, a manuscript involving any and every language in the Middle East; Harvard Press would toil over it meticulously and eventually return galley proofs to the great Hebraist. But weeks or months might have gone by since the original manuscript was "completed," and in this period it was entirely possible that some other learned Hebraist in some other part of the world had stumbled on some point, had corrected some trifling error, had referred to some distant manuscript source that Wolfson had not seen. He *was* a perfectionist, and he would not release the galleys until such a point had been settled to his satisfaction. The result was that the type on Wolfson's books was kept standing for months and sometimes for years before the composition room could get a final approval from the great scholar. His special interest was, as I understand it, the relation of Greek thought to Hebrew philosophy during the centuries immediately before and after the beginning of the Christian era; and if perfect scholarship means that the investigation being made never need be made over again, Wolfson was that kind of scholar. Immensely learned, he concentrated his powerful mind on a smaller sector of time than do most of the rest of us, and the result was, however disastrous to the finances of the Press, as near perfection as human frailty can ever come.

A near neighbor of ours, a member of the faculty of the Business School, had lost his wife. He knew Harry and liked him, and finally mustered up courage to ask Dr. Wolfson to come and share with him his fine house, now desolate. After a long inward debate with himself, Wolfson consented; and the two met at breakfast, I think, and at dinner and in the evening. Their conversations must have been choice, though I never overheard any of them. One evening after dinner, Mr. Wolfson's host, himself Jewish, asked some question about a passage in the book of Job. "I cannot tell you that;" said Wolfson briefly; "Chobe is not my field." Soon after that, they parted, Harry discovering that living with another human being was beyond his social capacity. Professor Wolfson was nevertheless warmhearted, a man who, despite his erudition, could not overcome a temperamental shyness that made him at once lovable and exasperating.

I do not know how many Ph.D. orals I have attended in my time, but one stands out with peculiar vividness. Harvard has a program at least, a department at best, in comparative literature; and when I first came to Cambridge, the chairman of that department was the renowned and learned Fernand Baldensperger (1871–1958), author of a small library of books and articles in the field. He subsequently resigned from Harvard, and, Heaven itself knows why, I was picked out as a *locum tenens* while a search committee looked around for a proper successor to this learned Frenchman, who remained in Cambridge finishing out the academic year. There was this spring but one candidate for the Ph.D. in comparative literature, who had written, as I understood it, a very learned dissertation linking early Italian music and Arabian poetry. My duty was, not to read the thesis, but to put together an examining committee of sufficient knowledge and dignity to impress the young scholar. As the dissertation had been written under M. Baldensperger's direction, there seemed to be no good reason why he should not be on the committee, which was to consist of five, with me as chairman. The problem involved Arabic, and I feared my Arabic was not equal to the occasion. Accordingly, after a good deal of negotiation I persuaded Professor Thomson, our professor of Arabic, to join our ranks. Music formed no small part of the candidate's offering; and after a long diplomatic struggle I persuaded Dr. Hugo Leichtentritt—a renowned musicologist, a refugee from Hitler's barbarities, and one whose works on music have been translated into many languages—to take on that part of the ordeal. I finally secured a professor of French, no Italianist being equally competent both in music and in early Italian. We were to meet in Longfellow Hall in the Radcliffe Yard, this building being among the quietest available, and the candidate and four members of the committee assembled at the appointed hour; but our professor of French did not appear. "Well," I said after a twenty-minute wait, during which the candidate was obviously suffering from a case of nerves, "let us begin, and take up the Romance language portion of the examination at the end. Professor Baldensperger, will you be good enough to begin the examination?"

To my astonishment, Professor Baldensperger got up and bowed to me as chairman; and I, thinking perhaps French customs, or at least the customs of comparative literature, differed from the ones I was used to, arose and bowed back to him as profoundly as I could. The distinguished professor of comparative literature asked no questions but launched into a *tirade* worthy of the French stage. He rejoiced that the department had fallen into such capable hands (meaning me, and it hadn't); he expressed with deep emotion his regret at leaving Harvard and his happiness at going home again to his native land. He reviewed the history of comparative literature from its nineteenth-century beginnings, when it was created on the model of comparative anatomy. He regretted that the Americans were such poor masters of foreign tongues, but the English language, he said, was rich, varied, and usable. He thought the peace of the world might depend on foreign languages, since if you cannot communicate, you quarrel. He exhorted the candidate to continue in the ways of scholarly virtue and adjured his colleagues not to desert comparative literature, since, even if its present enrollment was small, it was bound to increase and flourish. Then, bowing to the candidate and to each member of the committee, he sat down.

I waited a moment or two and then said, "Thank you very much, Professor Baldensperger. But have you no questions to put to the candidate concerning, for example, his thesis?"

"Why?" M. Baldensperger replied with a certain bafflement. "It is a good thesis—a very good thesis. It was written under my direction."

Also baffled, I turned to Dr. Leichtentritt, asking him to continue the examination, perhaps touching on the history of music. Dr. Leichtentritt, not to be outdone by M. Baldensperger, arose and bowed as he had done, and I returned the compliment. Dr.

Leichtentritt drew a bundle of notes from his pocket. "The English—I do not speak so well," he said (in less strained circumstances his English was perfectly good), "and therefore, M. Jones, I have taken the liberty of writing out my observations on the dissertation." This he did for a quarter of an hour, and his observations were, I am sure, sound enough, but I was glancing from the clock on the wall to the door through which my French colleague was to come. Dr. Leichtentritt sat down, and again I said, "Thank you, Dr. Leichtentritt. Have you any direct questions you would like to ask the candidate?"

"No," he said politely but firmly. "I do not understand Arabic."

I looked again at the clock—no representative of the French and Italian languages. I turned to Professor Thomson, rubicund, bald-headed, and gruff, whose native burr had not been altered since he left bonnie Scotland. "Mr. Thomson, will you examine the candidate?"

Mr. Thomson cleared his throat, a sound somewhat resembling the bull of Bashan in one of his milder moods. I can imitate his speech only feebly. "I hae noticed, young mon, that in the first two chapters of your excellent study you have translated the Arabic names into English, a custom common enough in England; but in the last three you have transliterated them accord'n to the Garman system. Why is that?"

The candidate looked slightly hurt and greatly bewildered. "But, Professor Thomson," he said, "You will remember that I came to you with this problem some months ago, and after a long discussion we agreed that that was probably the proper thing to do."

"So I did, so I did," rumbled Thomson and thereafter fell silent. We had exhausted the board of examiners present, and there seemed to be nobody left but me, who know nothing about Arabic or musicology. I scrambled around in the back of my mind for some fragment on which to hang a question.

"You must have read a good deal of medieval Latin, I suppose?" I asked the candidate.

"Yes, I did," he answered.

"Did you read any of the *Carmina Burana?*" I asked, referring to the only piece of medieval literature in that language I could think of.

"Yes," he said, "I read all of them."

"What did you think of them?" I asked—a stupid general question which drew an appropriately stupid answer from our student.

"I didn't like 'em," he said briefly.

But Providence is sometimes good, and precisely at this moment the door opened and our savant in Romance languages came in. He had, he said, gone to the wrong building. "It's no matter," I said; "we were just coming to your part of the examination." And for the next forty-five minutes the French professor and the candidate exchanged a wonderful cross fire of question and answer. The allotted time was up, and I asked the candidate to withdraw for a few minutes. He had no sooner shut the door than, after silently looking at each other, all of us save the Frenchman burst into laughter. The candidate passed, and I presided over no more oral examinations in comparative literature.

Robert Frost wandered over most of the United States and lived, at one time or another, in four or five residences as "home." The last one before he died was on Brewster Street in Cambridge, a modest and not wholly attractive two-storey house not far from Theodore and Kay Morrison's or from our home at 14 Francis Avenue, whither he came, usually for dinner, each time leaving me with a feeling of sorrow that I had not hidden a tape recorder somewhere, for, as always, you did not converse with Robert Frost, you listened to him. He respected Bessie for stoutly opposing his conservative political views, and me, I suppose, because on these occasions I said nothing.

A day or two before Christmas Eve, Kay Morrison telephoned to say that Robert had no invitation for that evening, and Bessie at once telephoned him to ask him for dinner. It so happened I had in my course in American literature that year a Professor Pi of Korea University at Seoul, who delighted in Frost's poetry and longed to meet the great man. I thought this as good a time as any, and asked Professor Pi to dinner in order that he might meet his idol. Professor Pi arrived promptly, and I seated him before the fire in the grate and went off to collect Frost in my car, for he could not drive and had no car of his own. I arrived home in about fifteen minutes, an interval during which Professor Pi and Bessie had exchanged various desultory remarks; but when Frost and I came in, Pi fell silent, studying Frost and saying nothing, not even when I introduced the two men. Professor Pi contented himself with a profound bow, and Frost, mildly puzzled, said something inane like "How do you do?" We served drinks, and I brought the poet the sugar, without which no cocktail, whatever its ingredients, was agreeable to him. We went to the table, the Korean saying nothing, and Frost beginning, even during the meal, one of those marvelous soliloquies that are never recorded in any biography. Dinner being ended, the poet and the professor resumed their seats, one by the fire, the other in a settee at right angles to him. I asked Frost some harmless question about his more recent travels, and he was off again, beginning with topography, personalities, and plane service and soon launching into a metaphysical discussion of the nature of poetry.

In the midst of an especially airy flight into philosophy, Professor Pi suddenly interrupted.

"Mr. Frost," he said, "what poets have influenced you most?"

Frost came back from the summits of Parnassus and fixed his eye on the eager Oriental; then, recognizing that Professor Pi had meant no harm, entered upon his usual discourse about having read the bucolic poets in Latin and Greek in his youth. He did not get very far.

"Mr. Frost," interrupted Professor Pi with his own perfect answer, "you have imitated nobody, and nobody can imitate you."

Frost did not even thank Professor Pi, but thereafter he delivered his soliloquy to the Asian scholar, to the intense delight of that gentleman; signed a book of his poems which Professor Pi had hitherto concealed somewhere about his person; and was his delighted slave for the rest of the evening. Frost would have talked till morning, but I, alas! had some sort of academic duty to fulfill, and took him home at midnight, offering Professor Pi a ride to his room. This he modestly declined, preferring to walk and meditate on what was, I assume, one of the most memorable meetings of his life.

Our last glimpse of Robert Frost was a visit to the Peter Bent Brigham Hospital, where he died. Someone—I think the incomparable Kay—had brought from his Brewster Street home as many familiar art objects as they could move. He was physically worn, but his eyes were as full of expression as ever; and as we left, he took Bessie's hands in both of his and said, "We have known each other a long time, haven't we?"

Chapter XX

Harvard
Observed

DISRAELI once observed of the government of England before the various reform bills that that kingdom was ruled like a Venetian oligarchy. He might have made a like observation of Harvard University, at least if he read only the charter and a few subsequent documents. On paper Harvard is a Venetian oligarchy. The president is not merely the president of the college but of ten or twelve other faculties besides; he is president of the Fellows of Harvard College, commonly known as the Corporation, and the president as well of the Board of Overseers, thirty in number, without whose approval no act of the Corporation is valid. Each body has a secretary, who is often one and the same secretary, so that A.B., Secretary of the Corporation, often informs himself, A.B., Secretary of the Overseers, that such-and-such an action has been taken by the Corporation and awaits the approval of the Overseers, which, if it is given (it usually is), requires a second letter sent back to the Corporation. The Corporation is self-perpetuating, and consists of the president, the treasurer, and five other Fellows, and with few exceptions has been for decades made up of Harvard alumni. As the Charter of Harvard College cannot be amended by the legislature, Harvard College is one of the oldest corporations in America.

Members of the Board of Overseers are elected by the alumni, including the holders of honorary degrees. Besides agreeing to the actions of the Corporation (and occasionally disagreeing), the Overseers may recommend to the Corporation actions that should be taken. The Honorable and Reverend Board of Overseers is, as a matter of fact, older than the Corporation, which was originally composed of Fellows who actually taught classes. The Board of Overseers, however, keeps in touch with the actual workings of Harvard as a pedagogical institution through a series of visiting committees, the chairman of each committee being a member of the Board of Overseers and the other members of the committee being notables in their own right in their own fields of learning. Customarily, such a committee gives an annual dinner to the faculty of the department or school which it is appointed to supervise, a dinner which the senior members of a department and sometimes the junior members are requested to attend. If the chairman of the visiting committee is conscientious, he will also keep in touch with the work of the particular department, school, or faculty either by letter or by visitation; and he as well as other members of the committee often spends several days visiting the classes or the laboratories of the department in question.

Not all the parts of Harvard are primarily teaching bodies; the Committee on Harvard University Press, for example, is not composed of scholars as such but of publishers and editors whose valuable contacts are cherished, if not always relished, by the director of Harvard University Press. A visiting committee is commonly only as good as its chairman wants it to be. Some committees, here nameless, might as well not exist, but others are influential; examples of the latter sort are the Committee on Astronomy and, more often than not, the Committee on English. This last, however, sometimes suffers from divided aims: if the chairman is not a scholar and unfamiliar with research work in the humanities, he may seem to dwell upon courses in writing and slight the solid work in the development of language and the history of literature that form the substance of the departmental offerings. The Board of Visitors meets at least eight times a year; and once every third year the chairman of each visiting committee reports in writing, though in intervening years he may merely report orally to the larger body.

The president is the officer through whom requests and recommendations pass among the two governing boards and the several faculties of the university; and in that sense he is, or may be, the most powerful academic personage in the country. But customs arise; implicit power is not necessarily made explicit; and although there have been occasional infractions on what we call academic freedom, from the time when John Leverett was made president in 1707 to the present day, the principle of academic freedom has probably been more solidly maintained at Harvard than at any other university in the United States. A British visitor wrote of Harvard during Leverett's presidency that "no place of Education can well boast a more free air than our little *College may." It is a sentiment that was reechoed under Charles William Eliot, president from 1869 to 1909, in his famous statement that every Harvard professor is master in his own classroom; and it was reaffirmed when, on the resignation of James Bryant Conant, Nathan Marsh Pusey was called to the presidency in 1953 from Lawrence College in Wisconsin, one reason being Mr. Pusey's resistance to the inquisitorial methods of the unlamented Senator Joseph McCarthy of Wisconsin.

Nobody knows what John Harvard looked like, but an idealized statue of him by Daniel Chester French shows him seated and gazing thoughtfully with his bronze eyes at the endless flow of students and sightseers. He suffers little children to climb into his lap and lithe Japanese tourists to stand at his side while the inevitable camera is aimed at him. After his death in 1638, his library—a collection of about 400 volumes, the value of which, at that time, was approximately £800— came to Harvard by the terms of his will; and the Great and General Court of the Massachusetts Bay Colony named the "university in Cambridge" after him. All his books save one were destroyed in the great fire of 1764. This volume is of course piously preserved, and John Harvard's gift has grown to about nine million books, variously distributed over the vast educational empire of the Harvard of today.

At Harvard each professional faculty has its own dean and its own budget, although the president may, if he chooses, preside over the meeting of any professional faculty, as Eliot did when he reorganized the Harvard Medical School. The president commonly presides over the monthly (and special) meetings of the Faculty of Arts and Sciences, sitting with the dean of the Graduate School of Arts and Sciences, the dean of Harvard College, the dean of the whole faculty in arts and sciences, and the secretary of the faculty at an enormous round table brought from the Philippines. This faculty meets on the second floor of University Hall, a Bulfinch masterpiece, in a room rich in portraits and busts of eminent Harvard professors and presidents.

Measured by the age of Oxford, Cambridge, and the University of Paris, from which its curriculum chiefly derives, Harvard is a mere upstart; but in terms of American history it is antique and has, like other traditional institutions, developed customs and a lore of peculiarities all its own. The first head of the school, one Nathaniel Eaton, was, with his wife, discharged for not giving the students enough to eat; and though one of the aims of Harvard was theoretically to carry the blessings of Christianity to the Indians, only one red man, by name Caleb Cheeshahteaumuck, was successful in winning a B.A. degree, in 1665. The institution was first set on its feet, however shakily, by the Reverend Henry Dunster (1609–58/59?). The first printing press in the United

States began work there in 1639 and two years later was moved to the president's house. Unfortunately both for Harvard and for Dunster, Dunster adopted Baptist principles, for which dreadful error he was not only forced to resign the presidency, but was also later indicted by the grand jury for his views and put under bonds. A succession of more orthodox clergymen served as presidents throughout the rest of the seventeenth century, one of them, the Reverend Increase Mather, declining to live in Cambridge. But the Puritan world was not really turned upside down until the election to the presidency of John Leverett, who was not a clergyman but a mere lawyer and public official, who served from 1707/08 to his death in 1724, who infuriated the Mather clan, and who may be fairly said to have inaugurated the policy of intellectual liberalism that Harvard has followed (with some minor exceptions) ever since.

Classes have been held at Harvard continuously since its founding except during the Revolution, when British soldiers briefly occupied the few buildings there were, when, after the British retreat from Concord, Revolutionary forces again briefly occupied the place, and when the Great and General Court met for a few sessions at Harvard while Boston was under siege. Once the British left Boston, the college shortly resumed its sessions.

One of the great glories of eighteenth-century Harvard was in the teaching of natural philosophy, notably by John Winthrop, Hollis Professor of Mathematics for forty years or so, whose varied achievements are chronicled in the *Dictionary of American Biography*, among those of several others also named John Winthrop. Harvard's Winthrop established the first physics laboratory in the future United States, was made a fellow of the Royal Society of London, and was awarded an honorary degree from the University of Edinburgh. He was a founder of the American Academy of Arts and Sciences in Boston and a learned astronomer. Among his other accomplishments was a theory of earthquakes (the region suffered one in 1755), besides innumerable astronomical observations. One of his students was Benjamin Thompson (1753-1814), who, loyal to his king, went to London in 1776, became a colonel of the King's American Dragoons, a count of the Holy Roman Empire (he took the name of Rumford after the town in New Hampshire which later became Concord), was elected an honorary foreign member of the American Academy of Arts and Sciences in 1789, invented a soup for the poor, laid out the "English Garden" in Munich, and left money to Harvard for a professorship, which, "accompanied with proper experiments," was intended to teach "the utility of the physical and mathematical sciences for the improvement of the useful arts" and for social happiness.

But perhaps the true glories of Harvard College as such were in the nineteenth century, when Emerson, Thoreau, Holmes (the doctor, not the legalist), Lowell, Norton, Prescott, Motley, Parkman, Wendell Phillips, Senator Sumner, Longfellow, Agassiz, Benjamin Peirce, and Wyman were either on the faculty or in the graduating classes or both. There were constant student rebellions, the most serious occurring in the presidency of Josiah Quincy (1829-45). His term of office is as characteristic as any other in the pre-Eliot period. Quincy, five times elected mayor of Boston, believed in strong measures to put down discontent, an attitude the students did not like. His effigy was burned in the College Yard, and in 1841 a bomb exploded in the college chapel; explorers of the building after this outrageous performance found written on the wall: "A bone for old Quin to pick." Nevertheless the college made progress under his administration, and he wrote *A History of Harvard University* (1840), long the standard work. There were a score of picturesque characters at Harvard during the years before Eliot's presidency, but none, perhaps, more picturesque than Professor Evangelinus Apostolides Sophocles (1805-83), whose name was largely of his own manufacture. Born in Thessaly near Mt. Pelion, he studied at Cairo and at the almost unapproachable monastery of St. Catherine on Mount Sinai, and afterwards emigrated to Massachusetts. He tried teaching at Amherst and at Hartford, publishing books on Greek grammar, and was appointed tutor at Harvard in 1842. By 1860 he was Professor of Ancient, Byzantine, and Modern Greek, and had exploded most of the current theories about the pronunciation of ancient Greek. The legend was that he kept chickens in his room in the Yard, the fact being that he established a chicken run in what later became the Radcliffe Yard. He was small and short-tempered, except with children, but he was also dignified, courteous, and frugal. To undergraduates he was known as "Old Soph." His bust is in the Faculty Room on the second floor of University Hall. Hasty tourists sometimes mistake it for a bust of Longfellow.

But this is not a history of Harvard University, and I drop down to some of the memorable years I spent there. The chairman of the English department when I arrived was James Buell Munn, affectionately known as Jimmie, the kindest of mortals and immensely well read, but without genuine academic standards. He was accustomed to returning his freshman themes by taxi. The department was run, however, by Dr. Frederick White, a disciplinarian by temperament, who kept Jimmie, the department, the graduate students, and two secretaries in tune. Kittredge was gone, and John Livingston Lowes was failing, to the regret of everyone. Charles Townsend Copeland no longer gave his "readings" in his room in the Yard, but prowled about Harvard aimlessly. Robert Hillyer was Boylston Professor of Rhetoric and Oratory, but taught neither subject, preferring to write his own poetry and supervise the writings of others. All the great names, however, had not vanished: "Fritz" Robinson continued to teach Chaucer with his own driving zest; and Hyder Rollins, in many minds the successor of Kittredge, was the idol of the graduate students. This superb editor of seventeenth-century plays, broadsides, and ballads, this great contributor to the Variorum Shakespeare, this world authority on John Keats, never did quite understand that undergraduates were not embryo Ph.D.'s. But he rejoiced in the admiration of successive waves of graduate students scattered from Greenland's icy mountains to India's coral strand. He was a bachelor and a Texan, a combination familiar to me, so that we got along famously. In order to be as little trouble as possible to the world when dying, he requested to be moved into Jimmie Munn's big house, where he ended his days, and where some time later I was called upon to conduct a memorial service principally out of the sonnets of Shakespeare and Keats. The service being ended, Jimmie said, "Now let's all have tea," and the tea wagon, followed by three puzzled Irish servants, was accordingly wheeled in.

I cannot call the roll of the entire department, but in American literature Kenneth Ballard Murdock had virtually invented the American seventeenth century, became the inimitable master of Leverett House, and was the first master of the Villa I Tatti in Italy, left to Harvard by Bernard Berenson. When you went to a Leverett House dinner, you might sit next to an Anglican bishop or an economic radical, a distinguished novelist or the organizer of a labor union—you never knew, and that was part of the pleasure of being an Associate of the House. Perry Miller carried the theological (cum literary) history of New England from the seventeenth century through the eighteenth century and beyond; and Francis O. Matthiessen, a shy, withdrawn man, devoted himself in the main to the period of American Transcendentalism. He committed suicide, no one knows quite why.

Theodore Morrison was in charge of English A, and, so far as I can make out, made it one of the best freshman writing courses in the country. His wife, universally known as Kay, was Robert Frost's guide, philosopher, friend, secretary, maternal companion, business manager, and man of business, especially after the death of his wife. I know Frost respected and loved her in his curious way, but I have always thought he was too self-centered to take in her endless sacrifices. When the great debate in the Faculty of Arts and Sciences took place over the merits and demerits of something called general education, proponents of the change proposed to move required writing courses out of the English department on the ground that such courses affected all students and not simply those about to major in English—an irrelevant argument, in my judgment. Be that as it may, the over-modest Ted neither defended his own course nor his staff nor the theory of English A; and since no one rose to speak for him, the transfer was made, the results being, I think, not quite all the reformers had anticipated, since a good many years later the college surrounded this inner ring of composition teachers with an outer ring of special satellites, not of the English department, general education, or any other standard part of the college, but of something called "Preceptors in Expository Writing." Of the success of this extracurricular performance I cannot speak, but as I had gone through a similar experience with extracurricular tutors in American history, I have some doubts about the wisdom of the change.

But where did I fit in? For a time I was in charge of English 1, the introductory lecture course in the history of English literature; I also gave a course in recent and contemporary American literature, known as English 170. I offered seminars on various topics, including one on the literary history of Boston which eventuated as *The Many Voices of Boston*, put together by Bessie and me and published for the bicentenary of American independence.

Harvard today has struggled not to succumb to the pressure of numbers that has engulfed so many universities (the University of Michigan, as I write, has 45,000 students!), but it *has* grown in numbers and in the variety of its offerings to the specialists. This in turn inevitably presses on the dining services, the houses, and all the other physical facilities of the institution, and to some degree upon the independence of its spirit. The excellent ideal of President Lowell that each Harvard house be limited in numbers so that the master and the head tutor could know every resident personally, and the amenities, notably in the dining hall, could be preserved, has perforce given way. Three or four students now inhabit a suite originally intended for two, meals are served impersonally in cafeteria style, the coming in of Radcliffe women has not lessened the crowding, and attempts to carry on group seminars overseen by younger and therefore less experienced tutors are not a total success.

One important weakness is the lack of a sense of a hierarchy of values among the various disciplines, and an even greater defect is the diminishing sense of and for history, as "seminar" meetings tend, at the worst, to degenerate into bull sessions and, at the best, cannot present to undergraduates those general views of the historical process that are the purpose and the glory of a well-organized lecture course. The tutor seldom commands either the knowledge or the perspective that the professor has instinctively grasped as fundamental to his discipline. I speak, of course, mainly of the humanities and the social sciences, classing history among the humanities, where, I think, it quintessentially belongs. We are, I trust, in the colleges at any rate, passing the silly stage where "relevance" was the principal test for the inclusion of subject matter. I, for one, insist and shall continue to insist that the creation of a representative republic for all mankind at the end of the eighteenth century is one of the great achievements of that remarkable age; and, no chauvinist, I believe that the aim of higher education is to aid in the formation of an intelligent citizenry who understand at least the rudiments and certainly the responsibility of representative government. The tutor may and, as I think, should see to it that some portion of a program having this for an ideal is carefully studied as an enrichment of the whole, but I very much doubt that a thorough knowledge of the prose of James Joyce, just now an academic favorite, does anything for responsible citizenship, however much it may tickle the mind and contribute to that very "elitism" in the wrong sense that the Joyceans lament. As between Henry James as an exclusive diet and a wider knowledge of lesser novelists and poets who have struggled to depict and understand the American scene, I could spare a large fraction of *The Golden Bowl* and its companion novels for a better understanding of, say, Benét's *John Brown's Body*, thought to be too unintellectual for American students to trouble themselves about. Benét was, at the very least, in love with American names; James, though he pictured some Americans admirably, more and more withdrew into a private universe in which his shadowy characters converse by antennae so fine and fragile, they misunderstand each other with the greatest of ease. I do not think Emerson is Plato, but I think most of the logical positivists are scarcely citizens. Students, even graduate students, need to be reminded more often than they are, that in this age of passion, violence, and unreason, one of the greatest Americans once called the United States the last, best hope of earth.

Others, I know, regard the tutorial system and the small class as great improvements because the student gets more attention, but I submit from this brief examination of the development of Harvard that what I call a profound sense of continuity is the element in the country's oldest institution of higher learning that makes it unique among institutions devoted to the higher learning and has sent forth presidents, governors, senators, clergymen, writers, radicals (think of Jack Reed buried by the walls of the Kremlin), conservatives, politicians, businessmen possessing greatness, social workers, scientists, and scholars of all kinds. There is a stale joke to the effect that you can always tell a Harvard man but you cannot tell him much—something I have never experienced. Harvard is one of the "Ivy Colleges," a term used to conceal both envy and a sneer, but in truth an unintended tribute to some of the oldest and greatest educational institutions of the United States. Harvard has been accused of being a rich man's school; it is not. Harvard has been accused of being exclusive; it is not. Harvard has been accused of knowing only that part of the country that lies east of the Hudson, and not much of that; this is not true. Legends will not die; and if it is possible to point to the elder Senator Henry Cabot Lodge, a Harvard graduate and a man called by Woodrow Wilson "the people's enemy," it is also possible to point to Charles W. Eliot, who, almost single-handed, turned a New England college into a world-famous university. I think, however, that the greatness of Harvard, or rather the essence of the Harvard spirit, is embodied in Eliot's famous command: "Every faculty member is master in his own classroom." And yet this is not it either.

I hold no Harvard degree, except an honorary one, but I remember the sense of release, mounting almost to irony, with which I did my work as a member of the Harvard faculty. I know there are at Harvard, as at every other human institution, jealousies, distrusts, and even hatreds, but I have never experienced in Cambridge that petty infighting that I have seen or experienced at other universities. If intellectual freedom has her home anywhere, it is in the Harvard Yard. There is, of course, much about Harvard that I do not know. I know nothing about the club life at Harvard, or the "finals clubs," or, for that matter, the cold roast Boston, of which somebody always complains. I do not think that Boston is the hub of the universe with Harvard as an auxiliary wheel, and I have found as good friends on Beacon Hill as I have found among the Boston Irish, the Boston Italians, Boston lawyers, Boston physicians and surgeons, and the Boston ministry—and by Boston I mean to include that curious, illogical, and senseless tangle of town, cities, and hamlets that are part or parts of Greater Boston. *Elite* and *elitism* have become, I am sorry to say, nasty words, made so by those enemies of the English language, the social psychologists. To be an elitist can, I suppose, be loosely defined as being a person with a temperamental affinity for some kind of authoritarian government, some regimen in taste, and some dislike for vulgarity. But during the same years that I have watched the decline and fall of a useful term (what were the Medici if they were not the elite of Florence?), I have also listened to a growing cry for leadership. America lacks "leadership," cry the liberal weeklies and some of our more arrogant newspapers. Well, I suggest that you cannot have leadership except as men rise into an exceptional class, and what else is an elite, properly defined, but an exceptional class dedicated to the best of public life and art and thought? I doubt not that Harvard snobbery once existed and exists (I knew snobbery when I saw it at the University of Wisconsin), but take the Harvard "elite" out of the history of America, and tell me, what have you left?

At Harvard, as at other large universities, big lecture courses were usually split into sections, the professor in charge lecturing twice a week, and he with his assistants taking a third day for what may be called the recitation method. This procedure has several advantages. It permits an orderly presentation of material by the professor in charge of the course—something that, in my experience, mere tutoring does not achieve—and allows one, in the "section" meetings, to trace with a considerable degree of accuracy what the students—in these cases mostly undergraduates—have taken in, and, incidentally, to identify the drones. If after these section meetings the whole staff of the course meets together while impressions are fresh in the minds of the assistants, the lecturer can shape his next week's performances more intelligently than he could otherwise do. Moreover, when the hour for the final examination inevitably comes, review sessions are possible in the sections. Two possibilities present themselves for the grading of the final papers, each good in its way but with characteristic weaknesses. The section man can grade the papers from his own class or classes more intelligently because he is familiar with the previous standing of the student; or, contrariwise, he can grade the papers from someone else's section, not allowing quite so wide a margin for human frailty as might the original teacher. When the time came for final grades, it was always my practice to assemble my whole staff and go through the names of the students systematically, giving opportunity for anyone in the instructional group to utter his opinion. The highest grades and the failures were always subject to a second scrutiny by some staff member who had not had the student in his section.

I liked the system. Of course the lecturer is, in a sense, at the mercy of the staff he has chosen; but although some of my section men were rather lacking in talent, this error in selection was counterbalanced by the excellence of the many teaching assistants I had from 1936 to 1962, when I retired. Among these, for example, were men of the caliber of Henry Nash Smith, Mark Schorer, and Albert Guérard. In his book *Virgin Land: The American West as Symbol and Myth* (1950) Henry virtually fulfilled Walter Prescott Webb's hope that some day the West would be written about, not through the eyes of an Eastern-minded historian, but as if the discovery and exploration of America had begun on the Pacific Coast and spread gradually eastward. Henry has been a power in literary scholarship ever since. Mark Schorer, who wrote fiction as well as historical work, put together an enormous book entitled *Sinclair Lewis: An American Life* (1961), after dissecting with extraordinary skill the work of William Blake, a writer about as distant from *Main Street* as one can find. Albert Guérard, the son of the French historian Albert Guérard, has in a sense diffused his remarkable talent as a critic too widely, but he is everywhere respected for the fineness of his perception and his critical skill. These are only three of the assistants I have had at Harvard, but their talent shows what caliber of young men Harvard drew to itself during these decades.

Chapter XXI

Harvard
in Wartime

WHILE I was busy with teaching, learning the rules at Harvard, and picking up lore about its structure and its traditions, Bessie, once she got household matters settled to her satisfaction, took on a more important task in 1939–40. To members of the rising generation World War II, with all its preliminary horrors and continuing brutalities, is a mere fact in history like the Spanish Armada, and unless they are Jewish, they have no real sense of the despair that swept the world from 1914 to 1945. When World War I broke out in 1914, Lord Grey of Fallodon sadly observed that the lamps were being extinguished all over Europe, not to be restored in his lifetime. He was prophetic; the year of his death (1933) was the year Goering and von Papen, Hitler's henchmen, were cordially received by Mussolini. The ultimate terror came when Hitler's armies swept over Europe, from the French coast to the Volga River and from Sicily to Narvik. The Italians, meanwhile, had taken Albania and huge areas in North Africa. The greatest massacre in modern times went relentlessly forward from the thirties until the Russian entry into Berlin and the suicide of Hitler. Some six million Jews (no one knows how many) were tortured, gassed, starved, or burned to death as evidence that the "final solution" of the Jewish problem was going unhesitatingly forward in Germany and Poland.

Some, forewarned, escaped from Europe or were hidden by kindly Christians who risked their lives to protect their fellow men and women. A large percentage of the thousands of Jews who fled Europe for other countries came to the United States. The major Atlantic cities hastily

210

organized rescue committees to meet terrified exiles at the docks and get them clothing, medical care, a place to sleep in safety, and, if possible, a job. One such committee was formed in Cambridge, and Bessie, together with other good-hearted women and men, Jew and Gentile, undertook the difficult task of fitting the exiles into a metropolitan area already crowded. To be sure, some of the wealthier Jews, more foresighted than their fellow countrymen, had managed to come to America with ready cash and commonly found some sort of occupation in business, industry, or the like. A more difficult problem was that of the German-trained doctor, surgeon, lawyer, or other professional, who was helpless in his middle years to continue his profession in the United States; for the lawyer knew nothing about American law practice, the doctor or surgeon or dentist could not be employed by a hospital or set up an office of his own because he could not pass the necessary examinations, required by state laws, given in a language he could perhaps read but not write, so that he either lived on the income of his wife or invented some occupation of his own. The least miserable of this cultivated group were teachers, whom the colleges and universities were glad to welcome as specialists in physics, philosophy, the languages, or a dozen other skills. Of this group Albert Einstein is of course a star of the first magnitude, but American education, both higher and secondary, was immensely enriched by men who brought to classroom and laboratory long years of experience in some foreign university or *Hochschule*.

One of the important steps to be taken was to discover whether the exile had relatives in America and whether these relatives would give them house-room and perhaps a job. This important economic function was part of Bessie's duty, but her real genius showed itself in the management of an unusual non-profit enterprise called The Window Shop, organized to help refugees from Germany and other Nazi-infested countries. She was ably assisted by a charming Viennese, Mary Mohrer, who spoke several languages (her English was flawless) and who could, besides selling, serve as interpreter for those who spoke only German or other foreign tongues. Some of those needing assistance had a few personal possessions to dispose of or skills that could be readily channeled into saleable items for American taste. A deeply concerned committee of Harvard faculty wives (including early in the history of the Shop Elsa Branstrom Ulich, the Swedish wife of Professor Robert Ulich, famous in her own right as the "Angel of Siberia" for her rescue work after the Russian Revolution), had secured at a nominal rent a large unused loft on the second floor of a building not far from the Harvard Cooperative Society. Many of the more privileged newcomers lacked domestic or professional experience, since they had come from homes where servants did everything for them, but others could sew, mend, knit, and even bake delicious continental pastries. When Bessie took charge she set out at once to make a census of the persons and skills available and alert the Cambridge community, especially Harvard wives, to the cause and the services to be offered.

Shortly before Christmas of 1939, when the quarters occupied proved no longer rentable, a benevolent banker, owner of a more ample location on Mount Auburn Street, offered it to the Shop at an absurdly low rent, and here, after major alterations generously supported by the late Mrs. Clement Smith, the establishment enjoyed immediate success from the sale of refugee-made crafts, clothing, and pastries, and eventually added to its operation luncheons and dinners. A devoted group of volunteers assisted, and contributions came from many sympathetic individuals. All proceeds went directly to the refugees themselves or to their special needs, such as courses for required retraining, or to their children.

By 1947 an opportunity to purchase a particularly desirable location on Brattle Street resulted in a third move. This was the historic home of Longfellow's Village Blacksmith, an addition to which had formerly served as a popular Cambridge restaurant. The house, protected as a landmark by the Cambridge Historical Society, could not be drastically altered, but the kitchen was modernized, the rooms were admirably suited for serving lunches and dinners, and the wing, after brilliantly planned architectural changes, became ideal quarters for displaying carefully chosen clothing, gifts, crafts, and, at one inviting counter, delectable European-style pastries obtainable nowhere else in Cambridge. Mary Mohrer, the first and most important employee, eventually became the manager of the Shop and served it for thirty-three years until it was, unfortunately in Bessie's and my view, closed, and its building sold. It was an unhappy loss to Cambridge and the surrounding communities that had greatly valued its unique services and the beautiful objects obtainable throughout its existence, during which it had rehabilitated hundreds of disrupted lives.

Nationally, a new draft law ("selective service" was the preferred term) modeled on that of 1917 went into effect in 1940, was extended in 1941, and, of course, not only with the naval war against Japan but with the 1942 landing in North Africa grew more widespread in its application as we plunged deeper and deeper into the titanic struggle of World War II. Its effect upon colleges and universities was twofold: it interrupted what I may call the normal process of enrollment; and it placed military units in training on the campuses of many a university, Harvard, for example, being turned over to the navy for the education of ensigns, while various secret experiments were carried on in its laboratories. The effectiveness of German aerial warfare became weekly more apparent in the Battle of Britain in 1940, during which a thousand German planes roared from Dover to Scotland. In September alone they killed daily from 300 to 800 persons, mostly civilians, and wounded as many as 3,000 a day. All this had an impact on speeding up the draft in this country. Americans had to fight on two fronts: the Asian and the African-European. In American cities police forces were often reduced in number; yet total blackouts had to be enforced. It was not at all unthinkable that an area such as the Boston-Cambridge one, populous with scientists, engineers, and medical students, might soon be made the target of a vicious German air attack. It was therefore argued that Harvard property, to go no farther, required special protection and that any body of trained men acting as guards might be useful in the case of such a catastrophe.

Members of a "preparedness" group had long been active in explaining that the war, if it came, would by no means spare Harvard. I do not know whether the idea of a Harvard auxiliary police was first born in this committee or whether the Harvard administration turned to the committee for advice. At any rate, the result was the creation of the Harvard Auxiliary Police, with Mason Hammond, the scholar of classics, as chief, and me as assistant chief; and we soon enrolled six companies of volunteers, two companies drilling each weeknight in the big room of the Harvard Memorial Hall. Mason was called away for loftier duties, leaving me with six groups of miscellaneous men, and I suppose a funnier regiment was never seen during any war. We had janitors and professors too old to be drafted or without skills useful to the military; we had students turned down by the draft board for some physical defect, usually mild; we had employees of various Harvard offices and of the buildings and grounds staff; we had ex-soldiers and ex-policemen and employees from shops around Harvard Square. Mason had been compelled to depart without setting up a staff, so that two or three of us went to work to find captains and other officers for the six units we had somehow to manage.

Our first duty was of course to get a company in line, get the names of its members, and see that they took roll call seriously. We then armed them with brooms, sticks, or any other article that would serve as a substitute for a rifle, portioned them off into squads, appointed as corporal the first man in each squad who looked intelligent, and explained to the two companies each night why this effort was necessary. We began with the elements of military drill, and only when some rudiments of order had been instilled in a company or two did I venture to parade through the darkened streets of Cambridge. We were soon armed with truncheons and flashlights, the lenses of which were painted red except for a tiny hole in the middle through which a feeble glimmer of light could be cast on some suspicious object or person, and we learned to march in the dark. Each man wore a white armband, and before we were discharged for honorable service, each of us had also a policeman's whistle and a headgear painted white on the outside and looking like a washbowl. At the signal for a blackout we set forth into the area surrounding the university. Wherever we saw a streak of light showing in window, doorway, or garage, the company commander had to get the thing dimmed down or properly extinguished; and it is a tribute to the good sense of Cantabrigians that they universally obeyed his commands.

I did not feel that this miscellaneous company was in the best of shape for street fighting, should any occur; and as the usual army manual seemed only partially applicable, I was for a time stumped. A professor of chemistry asked to be excused from doing push-ups because of a bad heart, and other "privates," though willing, simply could not stand the prescribed calisthenics, however eager they might be to aid Harvard and the United States. I called a meeting of the company commanders to consider this problem; and after other suggestions had been tried and discarded, they recommended that I appeal to the university's department of physical exercise. I therefore consulted a friend in the department of physical training and tried to explain my problem.

"How many companies are you in charge of?"

"Six," I replied.

"And you say that the normal set of exercises won't do?"

"No," I said, "they won't. These men are of all ages, from the middle teens to sixty or seventy; some of them suffer from diseases that require a certain care in handling, but they are all eager to do what they can."

"And what is the real purpose of these companies?"

"I have no illusion about them as an attack force," said I, "but it is argued that in case of a bomb exploding somewhere in the Harvard neighborhood, the arrival of a body of men who seem to know what they are doing might keep the crowd back, prevent a mob from forming, or in some other way be of assistance to the regular police or the military."

There was a long silence. Finally, my friend asked, "What parts of the body will they chiefly use?"

"Their arms and chests," I responded. "I doubt they will ever get into a real row."

My friend the expert sat silent for a long time, and I as respectfully refrained from speaking. "Ask the buildings and grounds people," he said finally, "to get you enough sawed-off broom handles of equal length. Then get enough tacks to drive one tack in the middle of the broom handles, and from this tack hang, on a string, some small weight, the weights being as nearly equal in ounces as possible. Then, at the word of command, tell your men to hold their arms straight forward without bending their elbows, wind the weight up with their fingers as high as their chins, and then roll it down again at the same rate of speed. Keep them at it until they all do it well."

I thanked him.

"And another thing," he said, "tell each of your policemen to bring to the drill each night a double page out of any newspaper, preferably the latest they can get. Tell each man to open this double sheet, take it by one corner first in one hand and then in the other, and crunch the thing into a ball."

I silently saluted and went away. But I issued the orders he suggested, and the result was one of the funniest sights ever seen in a military training camp. With his truncheon firmly fastened to his belt on one side and his flashlight on the other, and his white washbowl on his head, at the word of command each auxiliary policeman started on what looked like an easy task. Simple it was; easy it was not. After rolling the weight on the tack up and down for a dozen times, one began to feel the strain on the arm and shoulder muscles, and I think very few of our police ever succeeded in squeezing a newspaper into a really compact ball of paper. I know I could not, nor would any of my subordinates admit to any better success.

When we marched full strength through the streets in the darkness, we were sometimes assailed by a stiff shower of pebbles from the kids who came to Harvard Square to see what, if anything, was going on; but as I exhorted my regiment to keep an unbroken line of march, commonly detaching the rear company to chase down the children, the little brats fled, and by and by we ceased to be assailed. Our job was to protect Harvard property and the Harvard neighborhood, and this I think we did pretty well. Our only daylight appearance was on the day the future naval ensigns were commissioned before a great concourse of people in the Harvard stadium. I was instructed to deploy my companies along the proposed line of march, and this we did with at least a minimum of military appearance. I heard some jeering, but for the most part the crowd seemed to respect us.

But I was soon to give up the command of the Harvard Auxiliary Police. Edward Davison, poet, lecturer, organizer of the summer conference for writers at the University of Colorado, and more recently dean of Washington and Jefferson College at "Washpa," Pennsylvania, donned a lieutenant colonel's uniform and, under the direction of the

Provost Marshal General's office, was launched on a unique educational experiment. We already had a great many German POWs in this country, since there was no room for them in England. I do not know what happened to Italian POWs, but German POWs were brought to the United States by the thousands and roughly sorted out. Hopelessly fanatical Nazis were sent to prison camps in the more arid West; but many of the POWs were former Social Democrats, some of whom had fought hard but the larger fraction of whom had surrendered with surprising alacrity to the advancing British and American armies in North Africa, preferably to the American. What to do with them?

Few Americans then or now realize that before hostilities ceased, we were housing almost half a million POWs, scattered over the union and, under guard, performing labors that our diminishing work force (the draft hit the laboring classes very hard) could not do. The POWs were on the whole docile, for how could they escape? They were imprisoned in a vast continent, with two large oceans east and west, and the American air force in training or past training swept the terrain constantly, though civilians did not know it.

After we had cleared most of Italy of the enemy and after Eisenhower had led the magnificent crossing of the English channel, the inflow of prisoners still further increased, and so did tales concerning them. One outfit was sent to the Shenandoah Valley to harvest the apple crop and at a call from a bugle were supposed to return to their trucks and be carried back to their camp for dinner. Unfortunately, two of the POWs, happy in a sense of freedom, climbed higher and higher in a big tree and for some reason did not hear the bugles blow retreat. They picked and picked, then began to notice it was getting darker. Descending from their perches with bags full of excellent fruit, they went to where the trucks should be, and lo! no trucks were there. Hastily concealing their bags of apples, they started down the road to make inquiry, but nobody could tell them where the trucks were going or when they left. The pair trudged on until night overtook them. They slept in a haybarn and continued all the next day to try to surrender to some official person. They were not arrested until they got to somewhere in the neighborhood of Harper's Ferry. Farmers would not believe they were prisoners of war, though their clothing was prisoner grey and each had "P.O.W." clearly stencilled on the back of his shirt.

General Eisenhower had thought it would be useful, once the war should be won and Germany occupied, since Germany would have to be administered for some years as conquered territory, to have reasonably secure support from minor officials who would be repatriated POWs. The general staff held that this was strictly legal because (a) nobody need

216

be retrained in democracy if he were unwilling; and (b) the Geneva articles of war specifically state that, in addition to food, clothing, and care, POWs are entitled to "intellectual diversion." The educational experiment Edward Davison now brought me into was the intellectual diversion. This involved the Provost Marshal General's staff in two separate enterprises: a camp deep in the Adirondacks where the proper sort of POWs could go to school again; and, in the light of the lack of books germane to our purpose, an office where properly qualified writers could put pamphlets together for the use of the Germans. My duty was to write a short history of the United States, a brief topographical description of this country, and an analysis of its forms of government. I wrote these as simply as possible in English, and Henry Ehrmann, German-born professor of political science, translated them as simply as possible into German. As we had no means of knowing how many Germans would consent to be reoriented, I fear there was a considerable overrun of these pamphlets, bound in blue, the English and German texts on facing pages. Our office was in Manhattan, almost at the Battery, and I drew a very competent black typist, universally known as Maggie. I ventured to ask her one day if that was her real name; and after some hesitation, she said her real name was Miss Magnetic Love. Her christening was, I suspect, a practical joke by some wandering hospital intern.

While Ehrmann and I toiled at history, we were joined by the anthropologist and linguist Henry Lee Smith, now in officer's uniform, who had formerly fascinated radio audiences by interviewing anybody who would appear on his program and within five or ten minutes telling the victim what part of the country he was born in. Smith had put together for the benefit of the GIs the simplest possible manual of German, reducing the confusing problem of der, die, and das to a simple d'; and now, assisted by William Moulton, also a witty and distinguished philologist, he reversed the process so that the Germans could learn the elements of English.

Our various tasks completed, we were now transferred to Fort Kearny, a POW camp on an island at the mouth of Narragansett Bay in Rhode Island. Fort Kearny was under the command of a Captain Kunzig of Pennsylvania, whose chief assistant was one Pestalozzi, a name that reeks with pedagogical history. The time of the POWs was entirely at our disposal, so that we decreed that mornings would be spent in learning English and afternoons given over to an hour of American history, an hour of German history, and an hour (pure waste!) on the principles of military government. Ehrmann took charge of our version of German history, notably of the nineteenth century, and I did the

American history and, in a vague way, supervised the learning of English. One important point that Ehrmann and I worked for all it was worth was the fact that the regimes of Bismark and Lincoln fell within the same gamut of time and offered interesting parallels and contrasts in the management of a state. Instruction in English was carried on in groups of eleven, together with an American "informant," who was nothing more than a common or garden variety of the American male—I am tempted to say the commoner the better. It was mildly amusing of a morning to walk around the barracks and hear in deep gutteral voices a greeting " 'Ow are you, Mr. Smeet?" and the response, "I am werry vell, Mr. Schwartz."

I was conspicuous because I was the only person in civilian clothes, though I bore the rank described by one of my students as that of a "stimulated" colonel. Since the only way of escape from Fort Kearny was by sea, and this was constantly watched day and night by airplanes, danger of escape was virtually nil, though I well remember one morning when there was a good deal of agitation over the telephone because a Rhode Island farmer's wife saw a POW on the roadway and was certain he had come to cut her throat. The eloper was the cook for the officer's mess, a funny little Berliner who insisted that everything should be cooked in butter and that the Russians in Berlin had certainly destroyed his café. He appeared one day accompanied by a dog, and a little later, wearing a pair of white gloves. I do not know where he procured this property, and I soon learned that in the POW camp it was better not to ask too many questions.

As the Allied armies advanced through Germany, General Eisenhower was eager to use the graduates of Fort Kearny as soon as possible. Davison, Kunzig, Pestalozzi, and I, after a series of conferences, decided that the termination of our instruction should be marked by a ceremonial that would linger in the memories of our graduates. Davison instructed the officers to wear freshly pressed uniforms for the occasion, and we saw to it that the prisoners' uniforms were exchanged for something a little fresher than what they had been wearing. I went up to Cambridge, got my cap and gown, and picked out the gaudiest of my honorary hoods. This was fine so far as it went, but what should be done about diplomas?

After interminable telephone conversations with Washington, we received permission to print certificates of discharge, which we tried to make as ornate as possible. They contained eulogistic language plagiarized from American diplomas and were individually signed by Davison as commanding officer, Kunzig and Pestalozzi as members of the staff, and Howard Mumford Jones, Professor of English, Cambridge, Mass. U.S.A. These we rolled and tied with red, white, and blue ribbons and arranged in a neat pile on a table borrowed, I think, from the kitchen. The graduating prisoners of war were seated in the front rows of an improvised auditorium, and their unfortunate comrades not yet released sat behind them. Such members of the camp staff who could get away from their duties long enough to do so attended the ceremony, which we made as dignified and formal as we could. My speech was later printed somewhere as "Graduation behind Barbed Wire."

Trouble ensued almost immediately after the ceremony. The democratized POWs were to be sent back to Germany in the U.S.S. *General Tasker H. Bliss*, which was tied up at the army pier in Boston Harbor. Unfortunately, I was the only person at Fort Kearny who knew where the army pier was to be found. I therefore took my seat in the leading military truck, and the other trucks, containing POWs in fresh clothing, followed behind. We had to drive through most of Rhode Island and a large section of eastern Massachusetts, but, unless my memory is faulty, the road signs had all been taken down in order to confuse any invading soldiers from German submarines. I consequently made a good many false turns, and the army trucks behind me, like Alexander Pope's snake, dragged their slow length along.

Eventually, however, we reached the pier. There loomed the *General Tasker H. Bliss*, apparently ready to receive us. But as anybody participating in army business at lower levels knows, something called snafu invariably takes over. The captain of the *Tasker H. Bliss* had never heard of us and refused to have anything to do with us, and neither Captain Kunzig nor Lieutenant Pestalozzi nor written orders from the Provost Marshal General's office in Washington could sway the iron determination of the ship captain not to move this vessel until he had received something official from the branch of the War Department that had charge of army vessels. I was the only person present dressed in civilian clothes and therefore conspicuous.

"Who's he?" snappily demanded the ship's captain.

"That's Dr. Howard Mumford Jones of Harvard University," stoutly replied Captain Kunzig. "And he has been in charge of retraining these Krauts."

I descended from my vehicle, found myself surrounded by amused or irritated army officers, and demanded to see the captain of the marines, who had not hitherto been present. He appeared, and he and I held a long Socratic dialogue while the rest fell silent. As captain of the marines on board the vessel, he began by assuming that these were desperate

Nazis whom it was his duty to transport to Germany, preferably in irons. After a long college lecture on my part, a light broke on his honest face, and he said, "Oh, I see; you want them to have cigarettes."

"Yes," said I, "they should be allowed to keep their cigarettes and also the printed material we have given them. General Eisenhower's orders."

He looked at me suspiciously, but after further conversation he yielded, so that my POWs went back to Europe in relative comfort. Disembarked at some European port I've now forgotten, they were immediately stripped of everything, including the suspicious German-English manuals which we had labored to teach them, and assigned to various POW camps in Normandy or elsewhere.

All was not lost, however. Eisenhower demanded to know where his Social Democrats were, and they were one by one reassembled and assigned various subordinate duties in Germany while my staff and I went happily back to teaching larger schools of POWs on larger islands in Narragansett Bay. The German collapse was swift, however, especially after the suicide of Hitler; and rapidly thereafter our thousands upon thousands of prisoners of war were returned home, vanishing as if they had never been. The educational force of the Provost Marshal General's Office was also dismantled, Teddy Davison returned to his deanship at Washington and Jefferson College (a job he detested), and I went back to Harvard.

Our labors proved not to be entirely fruitless, however. When, sometimes after, I was asked to join Professor Frederick Peters of Reed College, Oregon, in a program of American Studies at Munich, I found that the superintendent of schools (or his German equivalent) in Munich was a former student of mine at Fort Kearny, that the Bavarian radio system was in the charge of another "graduate," and that here and there the influence of our instruction could be traced. Unfortunately for good intentions, the greater fraction of the Germans who sat in our classrooms originated in East Germany, which was then and still is under the control of the Russians, to whom the principles of democracy were those of Lenin, not those of Abraham Lincoln.

Some years later, while I was discharging my regular duties at Harvard, I received an official-looking envelope from Germany and, on opening it, found it was a formal invitation for me to attend a meeting of the alumni of Fort Kearny and to accept some sort of honor. I have always been heartily sorry that other duties prevented me from going to this gathering.

BOOK FIVE

BEYOND THE CLASSROOM

Chapter XXII

Munich

THE WAR CAME to its end amid a confusion that spread over much of the world, my German POWs were shipped home as rapidly as they could be, and the American armies were vastly reduced in strength, even though we had assumed responsibility for our sector in Germany and our part of Berlin. Most of the ex-soldiers wanted to get back to the jobs they had left under pressure from the draft, but others, by the thousands, took advantage of the so-called veteran's bill of rights and entered college at the expense of the federal government. Harvard drew its share of these men. Teaching them was a rewarding experience, since they had two great advantages over the mere high school graduate: they were older in years and richer in experience. My courses in American literature and in British literature of the nineteenth century offered fewer opportunities than did courses in the social sciences or the law school for illuminating reference to the war and its aftermath, but they had the advantage for the most part of not touching on the passions and ferment of the battlefield. It seemed to me that the returned veterans were grateful, though I doubt they would have put it that way, for the enduring calm of the arts, philosophy, and history, but I may have been deceived.

At any rate, the Jones family fell back into accustomed ways. I lectured now and then in other colleges and supervised the usual number of doctoral theses, sat on the usual number of committees, and continued to write books and articles. Bessie continued her usual volunteer work, and my daughter, Eleanor, married to Ray, lived during the winter months at Pelham, New York, and in the summer went to Duck Island, Ray's family's estate near Eaton's Neck. She went on teaching school, first at Rye Neck and later at Scarsdale; and though Ray's job took him away from home all day except for too brief vacations, Eleanor managed to win a good reputation as an English teacher, to be a mother to her two small children, and to deal pleasantly with a numerous clan of her husband's relatives. She also took on courses at New York University, thereby gaining the master's degree necessary for advancement in the school system of the state of New York. But she had the help of a devoted black woman, who became virtually a member of the family.

Life flowed pleasantly on, including in its flow our summers in Peacham, Vermont, where we renovated a little farmhouse we had bought, added on some extra bedrooms, and, "summer people" though we were, got on smoothly with the neighboring farmers. No Vermonter from the neighborhood of St. Johnsbury ever says, I discovered, "Yes," but prefers the cautious "Well, I don't see but what I can." Our summer home was broken into only once during the time we owned it, and the state trooper who telephoned me indicated that the damage was slight, nothing, so far as he could see, having been stolen, and conjectured that hunters, taking refuge from the cold, had probably forced the door for no more baneful purpose than getting out of the cold. I did a good deal of writing during these long summer days, for we were not on a main highway and were under no obligations to join the cocktail-drinking crowd. "Crowd," indeed, is too strong a word: the academicians in or near Peacham did not scorn alcohol, but they drank only temperately.

Returned to Cambridge for the academic year 1949–50, I faced another decision. In Salzburg, Austria, some Americans had ventured to set up what they called "The Salzburg Seminar," courses taught by American professors about the United States and its development from a republic to a democracy. The tuition was low; and Germans, Austrians, Swiss, and others were encouraged to enroll. Meanwhile, in the postwar decade "institutes" of American studies were multiplying in the United States, some of them in graduate schools and some of them for undergraduates. It occurred to a few far-sighted persons that Salzburg had no monopoly on the idea of an American Institute. Bavaria, the principal area under American control, was quiet enough, though five years had not sufficed to erase the scars of war; and the two largest universities, Erlangen (Protestant) and Munich (Roman Catholic), were open and doing the best they could with extremely limited facilities. Since Munich was the most important university in Bavaria, why not start an American Institute there? I do not know how much red tape had to be cut through or unwound, how many offices in Washington had to be consulted, or what was done to sweeten the proposal for the palates of Bavarian teachers; but out of the clouds there emerged the figure of Professor Frederick Peters, as the chief shaper of the courses in things American he wanted to get offered at Munich. He came to see me at Harvard and asked me to join the staff he was putting together. I have forgotten who the American "educator" was who theoretically governed matters in Munich, but the American commissioner was no less a person than James Bryant Conant, whose consent was quickly won. Fred was a persuasive man, and with Bessie's consent to spent the summer in Munich, I said we would take up his offer.

There were two difficulties in reshaping Bavarian universities, one minor and one major. The minor one concerned the American army. When it wanted expert advice on explosives or uniforms or anything else that required professional judgment, it had characteristically enlisted the services of American experts, the great example being the group of scientists who created the atom bomb. Therefore, when the army wanted advice about education—notably, when it was generally thought that Hitlerism had found the school systems of southern Germany a fine seedbed—it turned to schools of education for professional advice; and any school or academy in Bavaria (and elsewhere) had as its principal adviser an American professor of education. Unfortunately, American professors of education commonly knew little or nothing about traditional German universities. They spent their time conferring with Dr. Hundhammer of the Bavarian ministry of education, who had two doctoral degrees and insisted on putting both of them on his calling cards. The second difficulty was simple but troublesome. The war being ended, the Bavarian government naturally wanted its former professors, when they could be found, to take up their old posts in Germany; and since these returned professors despised the Nazis, they wanted to resume the German university programs precisely as they had been before Hitler. The difficulty here was that a German university professor stood so high that ordinary students did not dare to ask him questions, differ from his views, or ask his advice; and Mr. Conant and representatives of the Provost Marshal's office saw with some alarm the beginning of a process that would turn Bavaria back into its old ways. They therefore welcomed the idea of an *Amerika-Institut* taught by American professors in the American way.

All this was during the McCarthy period, and both Peters and I found it difficult to secure passports. I do not know how Fred got his, but I went to Washington to confront Mrs. Shipley, then at the head of the Passport Division, to demand an explanation. I did not see her, the excuse being that she was ill. I met instead a tired young man who was heartily sick of the whole business and who, when I demanded to see what was held against me, got out my record. I had, so the record said, been a member of the American-Soviet Society and I had delivered a pro-Communist speech in a Buffalo high school. I pointed out that Senator Leverett Saltonstall had also been a member of the American-Soviet Society, and I said that I had only once in my life made a speech in Buffalo, about five years earlier, when I had spoken to the Friends of the Buffalo Public Library. (Investigation later revealed that some prankster had put up placards in the Buffalo schools announcing discussions of Communism by such notables as Archibald MacLeish and Howard Mumford Jones.) I dwelt at some length on the absurdity of these charges. The young man said wearily, "Mrs. Shipley is ill. I'm going to quit this damn job next week anyway. I will mail you a passport of some sort so that you can take your trip." He was as good as his word, although the passport was limited in time and forbade me to enter certain countries which I had no intention of entering. Bessie had no such trouble.

And so in the year 1950 Bessie and I went off by plane to Munich and were happily greeted at the airport by Frederick and Helga Peters, each with a bouquet of flowers. As Munich had been thoroughly bombed, they had been fortunate in finding us lodgings in a pension on Kahlbachstrasse, an undamaged, thoroughly German, physically comfortable lodging, the rent for which, like the cost of everything else in Munich, was extraordinarily cheap. We were to have lodgings and breakfast in the European manner and to take our dinners out, usually with the Peterses. Our pension was so extremely well-furnished as to raise doubts in our minds about the honesty of the proprietor and the sources of his beds. Once inside, the occupant would not have been conscious of the ruined city without, except that across the narrow street was an apartment house thoroughly wrecked. On a ground-floor windowsill of that ruin was a spiked helmet which had fallen upside down into the wood, gradually filled with dirt, and grown a single weed as evidence it had ever known life. It stayed there all summer.

The university had but recently reopened; and the Amerika-Institut which Frederick Peters ran was so new that students were a little skittish about taking courses in it, although they were assured that at those dreadful German final examinations, information about America could not be overlooked. For the most part the university buildings had not been severely damaged by bombing, but I thought it characteristic of Bavarian psychology that two great, heavy wooden doors that formerly stood at the entrance were worked on all summer by four or five carpenters as part of the general restoration while classrooms, laboratories, and other essential parts of a modern institution of learning remained unworkable or in ruins. So far as Fred Peters and I were concerned, the most serious handicap under which we suffered was that, the Royal Bavarian Library having been put in crates and taken away to some more distant hiding place during the war, its books were still in their boxes. Our chief library was that of the army PX. Fred taught in German, but my German being imperfect, I taught in English. I was down for two courses—a lecture course on the history of American literature, heavily subscribed for, and a seminar. But what was to be the subject of the seminar? Remembering Mark Twain's love of things German and the German admiration for Mark Twain, I had determined to make him the subject, but I had not dreamed that I would not be able to find at least one set of Mark Twain somewhere in the university. There was none. I made a tour of the many bookstalls in the neighborhood, expecting to find copies of such titles as *Tom Sawyer*, or *Huckleberry Finn*, or *Life on the Mississippi*. To my astonishment these books were as rare as hens' teeth, but every shop had a great number of copies of *A Connecticut Yankee in King Arthur's Court*. I have arrived at no proper explanation of this strange state of affairs, though two possibilities have often occurred to me. One is that other titles by Mark Twain had been bought up, and during the war German universities could secure no books from other countries. A second and more metaphysical explanation is that this marred masterpiece somehow appealed to the Bavarian sense of humor, given the incongruity between the Yankee's American lingo and the speeches Mark Twain puts into the mouths of King Arthur and his court, which pretend to be "early" English. The book ends in the general smashup of the world, as the Yankee's devilish gatling guns mow down the serried ranks of knights in armor. This explanation is probably too fantastic, but it may have something to do with the book's appeal for the Germans.

Like others who taught in German universities then and earlier, I found it difficult to adjust our easygoing ways to the drill-sergeant method of the German classroom. I kept an office hour, but no one, except for one former POW, ever came, it being improper for a mere student to interrupt the august meditation of a professor. When I entered my classroom, everyone rose with Prussian precision and remained standing until the learned professor had seated himself at his desk and had given the young ladies and gentlemen a signal to sit down. In the absence of books, reading assignments were virtually impossible, so that every word which fell from the professor's lips was golden and to be stored in a notebook forever. I did my best to be hail-fellow-well-met with the students because I knew that most of them had had far more interesting experiences than I had had, but not until my departure was I invited by the class to a beer party, toasted, and given a silver stein. Poor devils! I hope they stole it somewhere, since none of them had any superfluous cash; and one young man, who invariably came in a minute late, seemed to have but a single shirt and pair of trousers. On a morning when I managed to corner him, I learned that all the rest of his family had been killed in the war and that his bed at night was a coal bunker.

The head of the English department was Professor Dr. Wolfgang Clemen, author of a text on Shakespearean figures of speech known to the entire learned world. He was my principal friend among the permanent faculty, the other members of which were, I am certain, quite well-intentioned and willing to let bygones be bygones; but nevertheless I was an American Protestant, and they were Bavarian Catholics. Though the United States was obviously doing what it could to restore Bavaria to its former prosperity and Munich to its former splendor, it was natural that my colleagues could not open their hearts to a Yankee. Our occasional evening gatherings were for this reason stiff. But then, in my random observation social gatherings among the German professoriat are always stiff.

Among our favorite restaurants was one called the Halalei. As the Americans, in an excess of precaution, had confiscated every rifle, musket, or revolver in all of Bavaria, the deer had multiplied. But the Americans had overlooked the bow and arrow, and the young Germans went hunting as they did in the days of Otto the Great. Every restaurant served venison as a matter of course. Although money was relatively scarce in Bavaria, innumerable restaurants had reopened, staffed by innumerable waiters, cashiers, cooks, and others, who, the army having been dissolved, had to pick up what work they could. An amusing example was to be found in any restaurant, high-class or cheap, where it usually took four waiters or waitresses to lay a place setting and a small procession to bring the food, however simple, from the kitchen to the table.

Near the university (which, by the way, goes back to 1471) was the Feldherrenhalle, and near the Feldherrenhalle was a charming public garden, a happy place ringed by a succession of *Bierstuben* and *Restaurants*, where it was delightful to sit in an afternoon in the soft summer air, drink the incomparable Munich beer, and meditate on life, death, and eternity. Not far from us was the huge and ugly Haus der

Kunst that Hitler had erected both to display the decadent art of the West and the work of rising young geniuses in the indestructible *Tausendjährige Reich*. Since both the Alte and the Neue Pinakotheken had been destroyed, this ugly new barn was being used for an art gallery, but German artists had been cut off from the living world outside the Reich, so that what was novelty to them was old-hat to us.

Nothing, however, could destroy the beauty of the churches in old Munich, even when they had been damaged by bombing; nothing could destroy the charm of the English garden laid out many decades ago by that Count Rumford who was born in Massachusetts; and nothing could alter the loveliness of certain streets where restoration was going on. Near the Feldherrenhalle, there was a group of private art galleries, which in turn were near the office of the American Express Company; and as I had to make frequent visits to that useful organization, Bessie and I paused frequently to see what they had on display. I thought most of the painting far more interesting than that in Hitler's barn.

One week it rained every day, but we needed money and sallied forth to the American Express Office. I had several times admired an oil painting by Kontny, displayed in a show window, largely imaginative but strongly suggestive of the Bosphorus. I said to Bessie, "I'll go and cash our checks, and you stop in and ask the gallery proprietor at what he values the canvas. If we can afford it, buy it." I went on my errand and she on hers.

"What's the good news?" I asked when we again met.

A look of mischief came into her face. "That man has not had a customer in a week because of the weather. He wanted $400 for the painting, and it's easily worth it, but that's more than we can afford to spend."

"Well?"

"That's what I told him, but he said 'Make me an offer.' I said, 'How about $250?' He paused a moment, then he said, 'You mean crated and sent to America?'" Bessie could not turn down an offering of the gods; I gave him American Express checks for that amount, and in due time this charming picture arrived at 14 Francis Avenue, as fresh and beautiful as ever. It is a seascape that never wearies us.

But I was not always so lucky. On a random walk in Munich's galleries, Bessie and I saw a small-sized version in bronze of Barlach's wonderful *Russian Beggar-Woman*. The dealer was anxious to sell, and Bessie and I were eager to buy. But I had just reckoned up the total sum of American Express checks still in my pocket, and caution unfortunately overcame me. I was not smart enough to make a reasonable offer, which I think the gallery man would have accepted, and we left regretting that we did not have the sculpture. He would have sold it at what for those days was a decent sum, taking my check on an American bank, holding the piece until the check was cashed through the usual channels, and sending me the sculpture when he got the money; but I was stupid, let it go, and missed the opportunity to acquire a priceless work of art, now in a museum.

The Munich Opera House had been destroyed; but we were in Munich in time for the summer festival, when opera was given nightly at the Mozarteum on the Prinzregentenstrasse, an easy walk from our lodgings. Acoustically this theater was perfect; there was no seat in the house from which one could not get a complete view of the stage; and as all the scenery of the old opera had been burned during the bombardment, new staging was required for every production. It was there that we heard and saw a magnificent performance of *Der Rosenkavalier* with a cast including Elisabeth Schwarzkopf in her prime, *Ariadne auf Naxos*, and even *Capriccio*, an opera seldom produced in the United States. It was pleasurable to see more familiar classics restaged and redirected. *Fidelio* I shall never forget, nor shall I forget the Munich production of *Il Trovatore*, which the Germans called *Der Troubadour* because they translate every libretto into German. For example, the male chorus, which is usually lined up behind the footlights like lead soldiers, was scattered in natural groups about the stage; and the lighting of this musical war-horse helped to make it virtually a totally new production. I do not recall all of the works we saw, though I do remember a ridiculous incident when, attending *Die Meistersinger*, which began at four o'clock, Peter Davison and I used the dinner interval to drink altogether too much beer, the result being that Peter had continually to nudge me to stop my snoring.

Fred Peters had somehow picked up an enormous red touring car, in which we had many pleasant jaunts during our time in Munich. Some of the most fascinating of our trips we made to Torwang, a Bavarian peasant village totally untouched by the war. It was just far enough away from Munich to be a comfortable ride southeastward on the *Autobahn*, and it contained a comfortable modern inn, the village and the inn being set in a forest almost primeval except for certain well-marked footpaths. Fred and Helga's little boy, together with his "Oma" (*Bayerisch* for "grandmother"), stayed there with a farmer's family pleasantly smelling of the soil. As Oma spoke only *Bayerisch* and my several attempts to deal with song, comedy, and conversation in that dialect had proved failures, Oma and I contented ourselves with shaking hands and smiling pleasantly. Either by fours or twos we walked in the woods; and I cannot forget discovering in the depths of the forest a memorial cross to Aunt Maria somebody or other, who died unexpectedly at the age of eighty-seven. Our trips, of course, had to be on weekends, and on Sunday mornings the woods would be ever and again traversed by a priest, a crucifer, and a file of worshippers going to church two by two and chanting religious music as they went.

We also visited the various lakes near Munich, and on receiving an invitation to celebrate the Fourth of July with the American consul-general, we went to a pleasant country house he had rented on the banks of the Starnberger See. The house, yellow stucco and brick, was built on the general plan of the Sans Souci of Frederick the Great. A detachment of the American army had been sent to the consul's estate, which was rather extensive, to assist the guests and especially to direct the parking of cars. We parked Fred's enormous vehicle and went through the front entrance, to be confronted by a figure in a coat-of-mail with an American flag stuck in the right side of his armor and another flag which nobody but me recognized on the left side. This second flag was emblazoned with the seal of the State of Mississippi. Once we got past this medieval icon in armor, the consul and his wife (who had all the money because she was a member of the Anheuser-Busch family) received us, the consul with a warm southern smile, his wife with that perfunctory courtesy which attendance at many functions had probably taught her. There were scores of people present.

We were encouraged to explore the house and grounds. We explored the grounds first and discovered at some distance from the house a sweaty Bavarian cook or two frying sausages, it being a well-known fact that fried sausages on the Fourth of July are a truly American dish. There were of course, barrels of beer. From time to time a servant in a top hat and a long-tailed coat circulated among the guests with a box of cigars; and I was tolerably amused to watch a Munich businessman glance furtively over his shoulder before filling his pockets with this rare commodity. Somebody made a speech in German hoping for friendship between the two countries; and when we had exhausted the pleasures of the *Wald*, we went inside. There were innumerable rooms in this chateau, but the most interesting one was a chapel in one wing of the building built out of expensive Bavarian tile and ornamented not only with statues of Christ and the Virgin but with a small regiment of saints, all of the finest Bavarian pottery. I do not think that either the consul or his wife was a Catholic, though perhaps she was devout; and I suppose the chapel had been erected in honor of the church by some former owner of the place. I do not recall bidding farewell to anybody, since, once the last of the guests had arrived, the consul's wife disappeared, and the consul talked business or diplomacy with a small group of Bavarians. Accordingly, we modestly returned to Fred Peters's omnibus and drove back to Munich in the pleasant south German sunset, the Bavarian Alps rising beautifully on our right hand.

At the end of my time of duty at the University of Munich, Bessie and I toured the Scandinavian countries, traveling mainly on that most admirable of transportation systems, the Swedish Liniebus. In Denmark we were driven at midnight by two Danish friends to see the Castle of Elsinore and even to walk its ramparts, but saw neither Hamlet nor his father's ghost. My most vivid memory of Oslo is the amazing collection of nude statuary in the Frogner Park, by the Norse sculptor Vigeland. After Norway we managed to involve ourselves in the most complicated and roundabout railway journey to London ever made by two intelligent persons. From there we flew back home, back to classes at Harvard.

Chapter XXIII

Israel

NOT LONG after the recognition of Israel by the United States, Governor T. R. McKeldin of Maryland, urged on, I think, by rich and cultivated American Jews in Baltimore, issued a call for the creation of an American-Israel Society. The purpose of the organization was to avoid politics and religion, but to do all it could in the way of good will to enrich both countries by cultural exchanges. The founding members were a dozen or fifteen, and the governor addressed his call impartially to Jews and Gentiles alike. The little society opened an office in the old Willard Hotel in Washington, and the governor found an invaluable Irishman by the name of Cassidy to serve as a sort of general manager.

I shall not soon forget the organizational meeting. The governor offered us the hospitality of the fine old Governor's Palace in Annapolis. His wife was opposed to alcoholic beverages in any form, but, forewarned by Cassidy, those of us who knew that the Palace would be dry arrived in Baltimore in time to have a drink or two, and then went by taxi to Annapolis. We met there the unwarned, who had arrived before us. Dinner was long delayed, but I did not learn for a long time why this was so: one of the founding members was an orthodox Jew, who would eat only kosher food, and Mrs. McKeldin had not anticipated this difficulty. After dinner we adjourned to a large parlor and formally organized our society. (The society is now deceased, its place having been taken by a larger and richer organization of almost the same name.) I cannot say that either the governor, whom we elected president, or Cassidy, whom we made secretary-treasurer, was precise and clear

233

about the objects of our society, but that would, they assured us, appear in time.

I remember writing some propaganda pamphlets for our secretary; and by and by, in 1955, he came to me with the proposal that Bessie and I take a trip to Israel at the expense of the society. (I have always secretly suspected that some rich Marylander paid for our trip.) We were to see as much of Israel as we could, talk with as many of the Israelis as we could, inform ourselves of the country's needs, and on our return talk to Americans about what we had seen. Governor McKeldin had, I think, got in touch with the Israeli minister in Washington; and a representative of the Israeli foreign office and a car were to be awaiting us on our arrival in Palestine.

We accepted the mission and flew to Israel that year on one of the planes belonging to El Al Airlines. The plane was crowded, most of its passengers had never been on an airplane before, and during most of the trip the hostesses tried in vain to maintain order. In place of sitting down with their seat belts buckled, our companions not only walked about much of the time but, being conversationally minded, formed little bunches in the single aisle that did not help either safety or comfort. Most of them spoke either Yiddish or Hebrew; and as I know no Hebrew, and my comprehension of Yiddish, that derivation from German, is necessarily limited, I did not find out much about their excitement other than that they were going to the Promised Land. In those primitive times, transatlantic flights paused for refueling at that most desolate of airports, Gander in Newfoundland. We stopped again at London, Paris, and Athens; and we finally reached Lod, or Lydda, which was then the only civil airport in Israel. Most of my fellow voyagers had to await customs, health, and passport inspections and, I think, be frisked for firearms. But since Governor McKeldin had thoughtfully announced the coming of two American emissaries on behalf of the American-Israel Society, we escaped most of these formalities through the intervention of a young officer of the Israeli Department of Foreign Affairs, Zev Suffot, an English Jew. I do not now remember at what ghastly hour the plane arrived; but it was very early in the morning when Suffot escorted us to a waiting automobile, the right-hand front seat of which was occupied by an infantryman with his rifle.

Lydda is at the base of the mountain on which Jerusalem stands, and the bloody and painful process by which the Israeli soldiers in the War of Independence worked their way uphill, the Arabs having of course complete military control of the highway, was plainly evident from the windings and twistings of the road. Moreover, we would ever and again pass a rusted tank, a captured cannon, or some other ghastly relic of a bloody struggle; and as the Arabs still maintained guerrilla fighters who took potshots at passing vehicles, especially those climbing upward, the need of an armed guard became obvious.

At length we saw the walls of Jerusalem, entered the city, and were escorted to a comfortable hotel. The dividing line between that part of Palestine which was then still occupied by the Arabs and that part which the Jews had recaptured in a series of bloody street battles ran through the middle of this ancient city. The results of this division were sometimes very curious. For example, the Wailing Wall, sacred to the Jews, was in the possession of the Arabs, but the Arabs, desirous of maintaining or securing goodwill, saw to it that when the Pope visited Jerusalem, a new and easy road was laid for His Holiness to mount the steep slope. The walls of the old city are for the most part surrounded by a moat; and on a later occasion when a brush fire broke out in the moat, which held no water, I was much amused to see an Israeli fire company and a Jordanian fire company turn out to extinguish the blaze, carefully keeping their backs turned to each other.

Suffot began his duties as guide, philosopher, and friend by arranging for us to pay courtesy visits on the president of the state; on Golda Meir, who was then minister of labor; on other high officials; and on a national public relations official by the name of Cherrick, who, when he discovered that ours was a mixed marriage, though he was voluble enough, viewed us, I thought, with a certain disdain. Although there are no religious restrictions in the little country, and although the Israelis lean over backward in protecting the religious property of Catholics, Greek Catholics, Maronites, innumerable varieties of Protestants, Muslims, and various other sects, and are especially careful not to seem to interfere with the holy places of the Arabs, the state is in fact a religious commonwealth in which race and religion are inextricably interfused. The cabinet includes a Ministry of Religions that is constantly on the watch against any violation of theological tradition; and the state somewhat inconsistently maintains a chief rabbi, who seems to have supreme power over marriage, divorce, and family inheritance. I add parenthetically that his authority, which seems to most Americans rather tyrannical, is being slowly whittled away by the Israeli Supreme Court, a bench of judges that would do honor to any land.

We were also taken to the grounds of the Hebrew University, where I was later to teach. In the division between the new city of the Jews and the old city, then still controlled by the Arabs, the original campus of the Jewish University lay on the Arab side, on an elevation known as Mt. Scopus, where, unfortunately for scholars, the original library also stood. By an ingenious and somewhat Machiavellian arrangement the

Jews were permitted fortnightly to send a single passenger car to the abandoned campus in order to prevent injury or danger to the chemical laboratories and other like parts of a modern institution of learning. Faculty members took turns at these excursions and, after viewing the deserted university buildings with an armed Arab guard, commonly took the opportunity to filch three or four precious books from the library shelves while the guard's attention was directed at something else. Thus, over a period of months they managed to bring back a small but valuable library.

A tract of hitherto unoccupied land was taken over by the tireless Jews west of their part of Jerusalem, this extension being part of the "New City." Here was erected a second set of university buildings, an important element of which was the state library. Pressure of numbers also required the university to rent or commandeer one or two large buildings in the Jewish part of Jerusalem proper. When I came to Israel to teach, in 1964, I found the state library useless for my purposes, since it contained virtually no books in English and very few in any other modern foreign language that had to do with American literature. Under the tireless energy of Professor Adam Mendilow, however, the English department had built up a library of its own, which, with all its gaps, contained such items as the New York edition of the novels and tales of Henry James.

The Hebrew University was on our first visit the only university in the land and was necessarily crowded. There are now universities at Tel Aviv, Beersheba, Ramat–Gan, and Haifa, and associated schools or branches are scattered over an expanded Israel; but to a sympathetic outsider it would seem that their number is greater than the population can support. Then there are also the Technion near Haifa and the world-famous Weizmann Institute, set in its beautiful park and gardens. In 1955 the Hebrew University faculty was principally composed of profesors from the Slavic countries and from Central Europe, men who naturally carried with them their own notion of a university. The institution had two heads: a president and a chancellor, each of whom was biennially chosen by the entire faculty, the president theoretically having charge of the academic side of university life, and the chancellor being a combination of business manager, purchasing agent, and public relations man. The holders of these offices were sometimes reelected, for there is nothing in the tradition of the university which says that they may not serve longer than one term. The enormous administrative machinery which is coming to choke large institutions in America was happily absent from the Hebrew University, an institution that was run by its faculty to a degree that would astonish even Harvard. There was a registrar and a business office, and these then constituted almost the total executive machinery at the university.

Suffot saw to it that we visited the principal sites of Jerusalem and its environs, and I was somewhat amused to discover that the tallest building in the city belongs to the YMCA. We visited the alleged tomb of Abraham, and we approached as near the top of the Mount of Olives as we dared, Jordanian infantrymen visibly peering down at us from higher elevations to decide whether we were worthwhile shooting or not.

Suffot had a government car and a chauffeur, and we proceeded to make a complete tour of Israel, if not from Dan to Beersheba, at least to Beersheba (we did get by airplane to Eilat, where the temperature was 110 degrees). We skirted the edge of the Gaza Strip; we crisscrossed the little state from the Mediterranean to the Sea of Galilee; we visited the old settlement of Safed, once the home of a famous sect of Jewish mystics and frequently attacked because of its commanding military position during the innumerable wars that have swept over Palestine. It still stands and includes some of the narrowest streets and oldest houses in the nation. It has now become something of a center for Israeli painters. We drove as close as we dared to the Golan Heights, the Israeli inhabitants of which slept in underground bunkers for fear of being shelled; we went down the pleasant western shore of the Sea of Galilee, which was already developing summer resorts and doing a good business in fishing, despite occasional shells from the Arabs, and we drove along the Mediterranean coast; we visited Acre, once the chief city of the Latin kingdom of Jerusalem, magnificent in ruin; we drove through endless groves of oranges, dates, and other Mediterranean fruits and vegetables raised for export; and of course we did not neglect the two cities of Tel Aviv and Haifa. Tel Aviv, the Chicago of Israel, has been built from the sand up, since half a century ago there was nothing there, not even a few miserable fishermen's shacks. It is now a very modern city, the chief financial center of Israel. Haifa is also on the Mediterranean coast; and the Israelis had dredged a harbor, constructed piers capable of receiving freight boats, and made it the basis of their own shipping company, the Zim. Joppa, just south of Tel Aviv, was then also being developed into a modern port.

As the YMCA building is the most evident structure in Jerusalem, so the most prominent edifice in Haifa, a city which lies on the seaward side of Mt. Carmel, is the eye-catching golden dome of the Bahai sect, set in a splendid grove of evergreens and a garden arranged in the Persian manner. In the central mausoleum, a sacred spot for believers, lies buried the body of the founder of the sect, whose name was Baha Ullah. When our car arrived at the mausoleum, we found the entrance into the sanctuary locked; but, nothing daunted, Zev Suffot discovered that the secretary was in residence and went to inform that official that two important visitors had only a short time in Haifa and would leave disappointed if they were not admitted to the shrine. The tiny secretary— who was, somewhat to my astonishment, either a Miss Biddle or a Miss Lippincott from Philadelphia—came cheerfully out, greeted us, and unlocked the gate. As we were about to enter in our rude Western way, she said in shocked tones, "Oh, you must know that you take your shoes off!" We therefore followed instructions and one by one entered a chamber of pure marble, hung with the most beautiful Persian silk I have ever seen, stretched like golden cobwebs over the ceiling. The body of the Holy Man is buried in a cenotaph in the center of this remarkable room, and true believers kneel down and kiss it. Most of the floor was covered with exquisite Persian rugs. On the wall facing the door the Bahai creed, which has only ten articles and which is so short and simple that even Lord Chesterfield could have accepted it, is affixed on the one side in Persian lettering and on the other side in English. Here is the English version:

1. The oneness of mankind.
2. Independent investigation of truth.
3. The common foundation of all religions.
4. The essential harmony of science and religion.
5. Equality of men and women.
6. Elimination of prejudice of all kinds.
7. Universal compulsory education.
8. A spiritual solution of the economic problems.
9. A universal auxiliary language.
10. Universal peace upheld by a world government.

Precisely why a man who preached so simple, yet so universal a creed should have been cruelly tormented by the Persians is beyond any explanation I can give.

My final task on my first visit to Israel was to deliver four lectures on the relation of landscape to literature in the history of the United States, the general title being "The Frontier in American Fiction." The first lecture established the thesis of a viable relation between the American land and American literature throughout the history of the republic, and the other three touched upon notable phases of this relation. Thus, the second lecture used James Fenimore Cooper to represent the imaginative impact of a vast new continent in its earlier phases; the third was devoted to Mark Twain or at least to as much of his output as seemed to me to spring from the same symbiosis; and the last was devoted to the novels of Willa Cather, wherever her inspiration seems to spring from the conflict between frontier values and the urbanized life which came in time to overwhelm them. The lectures were printed in paperback form by the Magnes Press of the Hebrew University, but as this was done after my return home, through inadvertency or inexperience the Press forgot to copyright the little book and also failed to assure itself of an American outlet or an American reprint. I am rather sorry that this was the case.

In the second semester of the academic year 1963–64, I again visited Israel, this time as Paley Professor at the Hebrew University. The lectureship I occupied had been set up by William Paley of the Columbia Broadcasting System, and the first Paley Lecturer (who, however, did not really assume the burden of academic work) was Robert Frost. Bessie and I again made the trip by air, finding a vast improvement in the services of El Al, and were greeted at the Israeli airport by Professor Adam Mendilow and his wife, Myriam, two of the most interesting human beings I have ever met. Adam had, at my suggestion, taught at a Harvard Summer Session a year or two earlier and was therefore so familiar with the American academic pattern that he saved me a great many blunders as a temporary member of the Hebrew University faculty.

His wife was a perpetually active woman, whose great interest was getting the beggars off the streets of Jerusalem. As the regular giving of alms is an important part of Jewish tradition, her task was made doubly difficult. Professional begging is virtually an institution in that part of the world. She was also concerned that the elderly have good food and some sort of comfortable home. She founded a movement called "Lifeline for the Old," which began simply enough in an abandoned shop so close to the wall of the old city that the Jordanian sentry, supposed to prevent Israeli intrusion, upon hearing the phonograph which Myriam somehow managed to acquire along with a collection of records, smuggled a message to her please to continue playing the phonograph because sentry duty was a lonesome job.

Rightly convinced that the sense of uselessness was part of the burden of old age, Myriam began simply enough by discovering half a dozen ancient potters and setting them to work in the shop under the walls of Arab Jerusalem. The news got around. By and by she added weaving, bookbinding, and other handicrafts to their repertory. Since she was in no way in competition with the retail stores of Jerusalem, she had no difficulty in selling the products of her shop, especially when both the Israelis and wandering tourists discovered the altruism of her project.

The old people discovered it likewise, and she soon had more applicants than she had space for in the few little rooms she occupied.

By exercising feminine charm, determination, and the ancient Hebrew tradition that he who giveth to the poor lendeth to the Lord, she expanded her quarters, display space, and staff. The first rush of exiled Jews into as much of the Holy City as the Arabs did not then occupy included people of all ages, all kinds of skills, and sometimes of no skill at all. One of her earliest discoveries was that her workers lacked proper food. She therefore begged or bought meats and groceries; ferreted out a couple of elderly cooks, who were delighted to go to work again; and furnished hot lunches for the old who came to work. But she also discovered many bedridden or room-bound old people who were not receiving the right kind of nourishment.

The government of Israel was expending every lira it could lay hands on for the equipment of the armed forces. Partly for this reason and partly as a method of enriching the treasury, the tariff imposed on such things as imported automobiles and phonographs was possibly the highest in the world. A wealthy British family offered to donate an automobile delivery truck which would take hot meals to the bedridden. The problem was to get this gift into Jerusalem. The government was sympathetic but afraid of creating a precedent. Nothing daunted, Myriam besieged the entire cabinet one by one, reproaching them for not having foreseen and taken care of the situation. One by one they yielded, and a fine new delivery truck properly equipped for hot meals came to Haifa duty-free and fulfilled its errand of mercy in the city of King David.

Israel has, when one considers its diminutive size and heterogeneous population, one of the finest medical services on earth. Of course, we visited the great Hadassah Hospital. The original building was then unavailable, since it stood on Mt. Scopus, but the Israelis had built a second installation not far from the university. There are also minor hospitals, one of which I shall never forget. It was built all on one floor. A woman superintendent showed us around. In the course of our tour I began to notice the absence of women nurses, and I inquired if this was accident or policy.

"Nu," said our guide. "I used to have a staff of girls, and every now and then one of them would come to me and ask, 'Miss Helfand, can I have next week off?' 'Why?' I would ask. Then she would hang her head and say, 'I want to get married.' Of course I had to say yes, and she fulfilled her promise to come back to work on the staff. But after some months she would come again. 'Miss Helfand, I shall have to be away for some months.' 'Why?' I would ask. 'Miss Helfand, I am going to have a baby.' Now we have boys. In Israel," said our guide emphatically, "boys do not get pregnant."

The university lent the Mendilows a car to drive us from Lydda to Jerusalem, and I was relieved to see that this time there was no armed infantryman occupying the front seat. Myriam announced that she had arranged for us to occupy the apartment of an American couple who were spending time in the States; and though it was some distance from the university, bus service was regular. We drove to Lovers of Zion Street and stopped in front of an abandoned Arab house on the side of a hill, the third floor of which was to be ours. As a specimen of Arab architecture, the house was rather interesting; but you had to ascend to our quarters by an outside staircase, and when you had got to the top of that, you had to crawl up an inside flight of steps to the third floor. The apartment consisted principally of one enormous room, a small and quite inadequate kitchen, and two or three small bedrooms. It gets cold in Jerusalem during the night, and the central chamber was heated by two kerosene stoves, set in corners as far away from each other as possible. We were assured that the stoves had been inspected and pronounced safe by an engineer brother-in-law of the owner. I doubt they had ever been inspected, for almost the first night we occupied our new quarters, we nearly choked to death from black kerosene smoke filling the room. There was a telephone, but I knew no Hebrew and the operator knew no English; finally, the Yemenite maid awoke and managed to extinguish the wicks. About four o'clock in the morning, we got hold of the engineer brother-in-law. He arrived, discovered that the stoves were thoroughly dirty and the wicks long since past the state of senile decay. He managed to put things to rights, although it was a long time before we slept comfortably. Our comfort was not increased by the discovery that, although the double bed we used had an electric blanket on it, only half the blanket ever got warm.

The apartment was said to be "modern," a term I discovered to mean what I would call Early Greenwich Village. There was not a comfortable chair in the place, the pictures and decorations belonged in a museum of curiosities, and almost all the chinaware was chipped or cracked. Considering that the kerosene had to be taken up a steep eighty steps and that meat and groceries had to make similar ascents, we several times tried to find other accommodations, but Jerusalem is a crowded city, and we spent our entire semester in this esthetic monstrosity. The rest of the building, I later discovered, was an asylum for the blind.

Jerusalem being what it is, most of the restaurants sold nothing but kosher food, although curiously enough, almost under the Knesset, which was then meeting in the city proper, there was a nonkosher meat market where one could buy pork, bacon, and other forbidden articles. The hotels and restaurants were kosher also, but we discovered an alleged Italian restaurant—not, I think, run by an Italian—where you could get not only standard Italian dishes but such luxuries as oysters and clams. Members of the English department were extremely kind, as indeed were the other members of the faculty we met, so that we dined out in a well-appointed home very frequently.

We found Tel Aviv and Haifa as cosmopolitan as New York, but the hotels are compelled to separate their dining rooms (or parts of a large dining room) into two sections: dairy and meat dishes. Once, returning from some expedition late in the afternoon with Herman Wouk and others, Bessie and I were hungry, though it was much too early for dinner. We all went into a hotel. The others ordered something, and I ordered a sandwich and a glass of milk. The waiter disappeared for a long time. Finally sandwiches for all of us arrived, but only after the waiter had had a long altercation in the kitchen with the cook. On another occasion in another hotel Bessie and I were required to sit at separate tables because I had ordered milk and she had ordered something else; and the dietary tradition declares that milk dishes and meat dishes must not be eaten at the same time. I trust the distant God of Israel was satisfied.

My courses at the university were two: a general lecture course in the history of American literature, and a seminar devoted to Mark Twain. Textbooks were hard to come by in a small country halfway around the world, but I did the best I could. The lecture course drew about sixty students, and I faced an educational puzzle. Half the class was composed of American students taking their junior year abroad and the other half of Israeli students whose English was the product of the classroom. I spoke as clearly and carefully as I could, sometimes repeating important information two or three times. As at the University of Munich, so in the Hebrew University in Jerusalem the professor was a minor deity not to be troubled by the intrusion of students even though he announced he would be available in his office at appointed hours. Examinations and what we Americans call term papers presented great difficulty, and in fact there was no genuine final examination in the course because the student expected to be questioned by an appropriate wing of the English department at that distant date when he would come up for a degree.

The seminar had to be held at six in the evening because the temporary quarters of the university provided no extra seminar rooms. It was held in the English library when the last reluctant reader had been driven out by the librarian, theoretically at six. In my experience the seminar is an informal class of advanced students prepared to discuss some topic with the instructor. Here again I faced peculiar difficulties. A few of the students from American universities were of course ready to talk, but the Israeli students felt awkward in using English in view of the fluency of the Americans. After experimenting in vain with devices to bridge this difficulty, I was approached by the Israeli students with a proposition that they could talk with each other, but, given this rare opportunity to sit at the feet of a distinguished visiting professor, they preferred that I do the talking, the consequence being that the seminar turned into a small lecture course. A third peculiarity I never understood. In my pedagogical experience seminar students write reports on some phase of the general topic under review. These reports represent independent research work of their own. Such reports are due on a given date, and in many a seminar I have had the student read his report to his classmates, who are directed to listen to the paper with a critical ear and either write small critiques or in a class discussion call attention to the excellencies or the inadequacies of the writer. In American practice, a seminar grade is based not only on the professor's impression of a student's participation in the whole seminar but also on his paper as amended after it has been discussed. All papers are due on a date fixed well in advance, and are graded while the records of the class and memories of individual students are fresh in the instructor's mind. I consulted Adam Mendilow on practices at the Hebrew University and found to my amazement that I was not supposed to give any grade until the paper had been handed in, that dates for turning in seminar papers were never set, and that the student might postpone his written work, so far as I could make out, to the Day of Judgment.

Since my experiences in Israel I have sometimes been asked to give my impressions of that state. It seems to me any responsible answer must come on two levels. Given an impossible military situation, a doubtful economic one, and a water problem (the desert, which, if it is again to support a population as it did in the days of the Nabataean people, must be made to raise crops), the heroic Jews can only be admired for the tenacity and skill they bring to what seems to me almost an insoluble problem. If this is the Promised Land guaranteed by the Lord, the Lord has dealt very stingily with them.

But the Holy Land is, so the saying goes, the central spot for three great religions and at least one minor one—Bahaism. The city being divided when I was there, I could not enter Old Jerusalem from Israel; and if any satisfaction, any sense of light or of ecstasy, comes when the pious Christian walks the Via Dolorosa, I could not share it. Since I am not a Muslim, it follows even more emphatically that what a follower of

Mohammed may feel when he comes to the Dome of the Rock or some other sacred place is forever hidden from me. I knew that I was walking on that part of the earth where Jesus died, where the Crusaders conquered and then failed, where the Saracens triumphed for a while, where the British failed to carry out a mandate in any generous spirit— and of course there are thousands on the earth who would like to have gone to Jerusalem as we did and roamed Israel from Dan to Elath, from the Dead Sea to the ruins of the castle of Acre. I know I had a historian's curiosity about many and many a spot, but it was never more than that. No faint promise of a Jerusalem the Golden with milk and honey blessed ever sank into my soul. Indeed, I think the land of Israel left profoundly on me the truth of the Book of Ecclesiastes, which barely gets into the Jewish Bible but which is one of the greatest utterances of despair in any literature. Conqueror after conqueror has swept over this plain, these hills; religion after religion has erected its idols or its temples here. The land is strewn with ruins, and the archaeologists at their professional work daily and weekly make new finds. I remember once seeing a well start flowing in the Negev that had been choked since the fall of the Roman Empire. The Crescent and the Cross struggled here for centuries; and the Jews, present occupants of this corridor between the Nile and Mesopotamia, are themselves bitterly divided between the utterly orthodox and the modern, between the Jews of the Orient and the Jews of the Occident. At the present time Jehovah has triumphed over Jesus, though Christians are amply protected by the law. But in Israel even more than in Greece the vision that came to me was of the past and not of the future. The fine modern museum in Israel contains the battered remains of figurines from the chalcolithic period, but it will one day be as much a ruin as the Wailing Wall. Here is displayed Soutine's fine painting *Boy in Blue*, which will seem as odd to our descendants, if the military lets us have any, as do the graven images of Artemis against which the prophets stormed. No vision, no feeling of ecstasy, came to me here. I fear I felt mainly as Koheleth the Preacher felt:

> . . . Man goeth to his long home,
> And the mourners go about the streets;
> Before the silver cord is snapped asunder,
> And the golden bowl is shattered,
> And the pitcher is broken at the fountain,
> And the wheel falleth shattered into the pit;
> And the dust returneth to the earth as it was,
> And the spirit returneth unto God who gave it.
> Vanity of vanities, saith Koheleth;
> All is vanity.

Chapter XXIV

The American
Council of
Learned Societies

The physicists have known sin;
and this is a knowledge which they cannot lose.

—J. Robert Oppenheimer

DURING WORLD WAR II, I served for a few months as dean of the
Graduate School of Arts and Sciences at Harvard; but discovering that
this gaudy title covered a job in which I had responsibility but not
authority, I quit it as soon as I decently could. Unfortunately, I fear,
anything done at Harvard that makes the headlines attracts a certain
amount of attention from the academic world; at least I can find no
other explanation for the fact that I soon found myself engaged in a
number of executive jobs in the scholarly universe. From 1944 to 1951, I
was president of the American Academy of Arts and Sciences, founded in
Boston in 1780 with James Bowdoin its first president and Harlow
Shapley my immediate predecessor. I persuaded the academy to sell its
unused library and to modernize its dusty interior with the money thus
acquired; yet only a few years later, although I thought I had given them
a useful and efficient clubhouse, they moved out of Boston altogether to
a point somewhere in Brookline. (Now they are trying to get back into
Boston or Cambridge.) I was chairman of the Weil Institute, its
headquarters in Cincinnati, an endowment intended to strengthen the
bonds between theology and the humanities. This job ran from 1958 to
1960, and I was gratified that, after I had retired, the Institute asked me

to give the annual lectures, which I did. They were published in 1967 as *Belief and Disbelief in American Literature*. For one year (the constitutional term) I was president of the Modern Language Association of America, one of the few presidents of that organization representing chiefly American letters and one of the still smaller number of its executives to make a serious study of its constitutional structure and devote his presidential address to suggesting changes, most of them carried out, though not always in the spirit in which I had suggested them. But of all these posts, I think the one in which I was most useful was that of chairman of the American Council of Learned Societies (ACLS) from 1955 to 1959.

The American Council of Learned Societies is an organization the constituent members of which are not individuals but various societies in turn composed of scholars devoted to the study of particular branches of learning in the humanities. And here I must pause to comment on these elusive terms, *humanities* and *learned*. Near the end of my period as chairman of the ACLS I put in summary form a definition of the humanities which, it seems to me, states their essential nature.

The humanities are, then, a group of subjects devoted to the study of man as a being other than a biological product and different from a social or sociological entity. They make certain assumptions about human nature and about history. First, they assume that man lives in a dimension lying beyond science and the social sciences. Second, they assume that his profound sense of individuation is one of the most important things about him. Third, they assume that the better traits of humanity, or, if one likes, the enduring elements of human nature, find typical expression in philosophy, in literature, in language, and in the arts, and that history is both the way by which these expressions are preserved and one of the principal modes of interpreting the meaning of these expressions to and in contemporary life. Historically, since they sprang from ancient Greece and Rome, humane studies antecede theology and are not primarily conditioned by theological considerations, but like theology they aim at a better state of being for man. Fourth, the purpose of the humanities is refining and maturing the individual who studies them sympathetically and intelligently, evidence of refinement and maturation being given by increased sympathy with and understanding of philosophy and the arts in past and present time and increased sympathy with and understanding of man not only as he is but as he has been. Humane studies tend to concentrate upon individual development rather more than upon social judgment, and differ from science in this regard also, since science properly seeks to eliminate the personal equation. Incidental to these several aims, humane learning also creates, as it were, methods and disciplines of its own, such as intellectual history. *

* Howard Mumford Jones, *One Great Society: Humane Learning in the United States* (New York: Harcourt, Brace, & Co., 1959), p. 17.

246

As for the term *learned*, in American usage we do not deny that a great physicist is, or may be, a man of great learning, but we commonly use the word to refer to libraries and to scholars who, using these libraries for research purposes, write books. Not all writers, of course, are humanists; and by the terms *humanist* or *learned* we commonly mean a writer who has contributed an important book (or books) in biographical, historical, or critical form. *Humanist* is, by and large, a complimentary term, so that a physical scientist, told that he is no humanist, indignantly maintains that his research has done as much for the comfort and knowledge of mankind as a lexicographer, whom Dr. Johnson once defined as a "harmless drudge."

I think, if I may be allowed another pertinent digression, that the grim and graceless prose that disfigures the pages of learned journals, monographs, scholarly books, and learned lectures is the result of following false gods—the notion that what is scientific or scholarly must be impersonal, and the notion that to announce a scholarly discussion is to renounce personal delight in the making and meaning of discovery. The humanist sometimes worships at this false shrine of objectivity. Great scholars and great scientists are not like this. It was not thus that George Lyman Kittredge or John Livingston Lowes or Karl Viëtor or Jules Jusserand did their writing. If you cut their books, those books will bleed. Such men mastered materials; they did not let materials master them. I suppose the worst professional writing in the world is that of medical men as a group. In their professional journals, it would seem, they perform no experiments; experiments perform themselves and are reported, apparently from a great distance, by telescope. Can one think of *The Origin of Species* or Paul Henry Oehser's *Sons of Science* being written in this manner? But let us get back to the ACLS.

I was a delegate to this body at a period when it had reached its lowest ebb financially and intellectually. But I should explain something of the origins of the Council. It was founded in Washington in 1919 by a small group of scholars with Dana Carleton Munro as chairman. The constituent societies represented in that first year were eight in number, two being the oldest learned societies in the United States, the American Philosophical Society (1743) and the American Academy of Arts and Sciences (1780). In 1920 four more societies were admitted, including the Modern Language Association of America, which was founded in 1883 as a kind of gentlemanly club and has grown into a wholesale organization, the membership of which now runs to about 40,000.

As long as the ACLS was confined to a few harmless meetings of bookish experts, the newspapers left it severely alone or turned a cub reporter loose to bring in a "funny story" about these pedants concerned with cuneiform inscriptions or the paternity of Alexander Hamilton. Even the great national foundations, which had originally contributed to the support of the ACLS, began by and by to withdraw their annual or triennial subventions. If the National Science Foundation could stand on its own feet (but did it?), and the Social Science Research Council could acquire a solid endowment of millions, why couldn't the third great branch of learning do likewise? By 1955 the ACLS had about $100,000 for the current year, out of which to pay its rent, its salaries, its printing bills, and its postage. At the time I knew little about the financial status of this body, when on one gloomy afternoon in Washington, where we delegates had assembled for a meeting of the ACLS, Dean Roger Philip McCutcheon came to see me in the privacy of my hotel room and asked me to take over the helm as chairman of the Board of Directors.

Roger McCutcheon was a man to pay attention to. A Scot by ancestry, he was then dean of the Graduate School at Tulane, a position he had raised from virtually nothing to a place of eminence among both southern and national institutions. He had organized a Southern Conference of Graduate Deans, not omitting the deans of black graduate schools; and though he was a quiet man, you listened to him. I remember once calling with him on the president of Atlanta University at a time when fanatical racists had moved to have the several southern state legislatures designate as the official graduate school for blacks the worst possible Negro college in the state in order that racists might say: "You see! We told you so! You can educate a nigger just so far, but the Almighty has decreed that their brains are inferior and there is nothing the white race can do about it." President Clement of Atlanta University saw the danger in this adroit move, and he and Roger agreed that if you pulled down the standards of graduate school education, black or white, in the long run graduate education in the South would deteriorate.

Roger and I had driven out in a taxi to President Clement's office from our meeting in downtown Atlanta. We had what was, for me at any rate, a long, absorbing, and candid conversation. About one o'clock in the afternoon President Clement suggested lunch, but we had to go back to our meeting, and Roger proposed calling a taxi. President Clement said he would telephone for one if Roger insisted, but that in his experience the last call ever answered by a taxi company was one from Atlanta University. We would get to the Atlanta Biltmore Hotel, where we were domiciled, quicker by public transportation. By and by a streetcar came along, and we boarded it, the only passengers.

In order to prevent racial contamination, blacks in Georgia were then supposed to ride in the rear of such a vehicle and whites in the front. The car stopped more and more often, and more and more blacks got aboard, until Roger and I, the only whites in the vehicle, found ourselves pressed against the body of the motorman. The motorman let us off at the hotel, and the car went on its way to the black business district of Atlanta. Roger and I looked at each other, shook ourselves slightly, said nothing, and went to our meeting. I thought I detected a special note of suppressed indignation in Roger's luncheon address. At any rate, the wretched legislation proposed by white segregationists was not passed by any southern state.

The ACLS, to return to my account, was composed of representatives of member societies, and the expenses of the annual meeting were at that time supposed to be borne by a fee exacted from each member of each society and sent to the ACLS treasury by the treasurer of the member society. But such a treasurer had no means of collecting the fee from his organization's membership, and the central office of the ACLS had no way of compelling him to do so. A huge organization like the Modern Language Association could, I suppose, have supported the ACLS out of its treasury, whereas a tiny organization like the American Numismatic Society did not contribute enough to pay for postage. The ACLS had no control over the admission of members to constituent societies nor of the dues they should pay. Thus, the Mediaeval Academy of America was "hard to get into," whereas, whatever the rules, almost any adult could become a member of the American Historical Association.

We were thus dealing with an association of societies, each society having, through delegation, one vote. Unfortunately, delegates were not necessarily chosen for their political sagacity or for their diplomatic skill; and the only continuing officer in any society was likely to be the secretary, who had to brief his representatives about what was going on. The practical way to meet this issue was to form, so to speak, an inner ring of participants and an outer ring of secretaries. The inner ring sat at a long table and voted, and the outer ring—secretaries and "stateless" people who had no vote—had valuable information which the delegates or the president or the chairman of the meeting felt free to tap when needed. These parliamentary absurdities finally resulted in the creation of two societies, one of the delegates proper, who legally constituted the Council, and the other the Council of Secretaries, who sometimes sat with the ACLS proper and sometimes met apart. There was still a third ring, composed of the staff of the central office, who frequently were acquainted with some problems before the ACLS and sat with that body unless formally requested to withdraw. Business meetings commonly lasted two days. They were conducted with dispatch because the chairman of the ACLS was a permanent officer until he resigned, and he had therefore acquired experience in running so amorphous an organization. None of these elements could be spared, yet the presence of all at an annual meeting cost a good deal of money, since the ACLS paid all travel expenses for each individual and since the high point of a session included an expensive dinner with a noted speaker.

After Roger McCutcheon had asked me to take over as chairman of the board, I consulted Mortimer Graves, the permanent head of the organization, I consulted Rensselaer Lee of Princeton, I consulted Whitney J. Oates, the treasurer (known as Mike Oates), I consulted those members of the permanent staff who seemed to have their heads screwed on their shoulders, I consulted other bodies with permanent officers in Washington, I consulted everybody and anybody who seemed to me to have useful information. I consulted the representatives of the foundations, and I reached four conclusions:

1. The foundations had, for whatever reason, lost confidence in Mortimer Graves.
2. The headquarters of the ACLS would have to be moved out of Washington to New York.
3. The organization would have year after year to present to the nation a public program, or else stand idly by as an antiquarian curiosity.
4. The Council needed to have a solid financial structure.

Mortimer Graves was a fine scholar in the tradition of philology, an admirable citizen, and a modest man. One of his difficulties was that, like the poet Gray, he never spoke out. He had general organizing ability up to a point, and to him, more than to anyone else, we owe the shape of the ACLS. He had also a certain prophetic insight: long before the country anticipated danger in the Far East, he had insisted over considerable opposition that the ACLS set to work to prepare elementary manuals in Tagalog, Thai, and other dialects and languages used in Southeast Asia. To these the army gratefully turned after Pearl Harbor. He was a gentleman and a scholar. Why, then, had the heads of all the principal foundations that had earlier backed the ACLS later ceased to have confidence either in him or in the organization? I do not really know the answer, but my guess is that he was overly modest. He did not make noise enough in the raucous chorus of Washington, and he lacked that genius for personal influence only too evident among lobbyists in the national capital. At any rate, one by one the big foundations in New York refused to give money towards the support of the humanities.

The ACLS was housed on the second floor of an ancient brick building not far from the Capitol. This might well have been built by the

Pecksniff firm when *Martin Chuzzlewit* was a new book. The offices were at the end of a long flight of stairs almost unlighted, down which an imaginative person might have expected Little Dorrit to descend, and he would not have been surprised if, when he reached the top landing and opened the door, he had seen Tom Pinch mending a quill pen. Mortimer alone had an office to himself; his staff—also gathered, as it seemed to me at first, out of Dickens—seated themselves where they could. There was neither sufficient shelf space nor closet room for the records. The largest room on our floor of the building was taken up by a long deal table where the Council held its meetings. There were a few modern touches, like a telephone or two and some typewriters, but when one opened the door of the ACLS for the first time, he stepped back a hundred years. The lower floor was given over to the offices of a dentist or a doctor, I forget which; but at any rate he announced his intention of purchasing the whole building, a fact which compelled us to move, whether we wanted to or not.

This looked like the end of the line for the American Council of Learned Societies. There was about enough money in the treasury to pay the salaries of the staff for the next three months, and I could not see any prospect of income beyond that time.

Fortunately, darkness preceded dawn. Frederick Burkhardt, president of Bennington College, had taken all he could stand of that "progressive institution" and had resigned as president. As he was, fortunately for us, still a delegate to the ACLS, Mike Oates, Rens Lee, and I, with a few others, huddled together in secret session with Burkhardt like members of a Venetian Council of Four. We persuaded Burkhardt to take over Graves's job as the permanent head of the Council, changing his title to that of "president," while I kept that of "chairman." This we did in order that Fred might not lose any diplomatic dignity. He accepted—an act of courage for which I admire him to this day—and we four insurgents set about reinvigorating the organization without changing its outward form.

As chairman I summoned, that evening or the next, most of the Council to a virtually secret dinner in a Chinese restaurant somewhere in Washington, explaining later to those who had not received the invitation in time that we had had difficulty in locating their addresses. That dinner lasted until past midnight. We had four immediate problems. The first, of course, was the invention of the office of president, which, as chairman of the Board of Directors, I had little difficulty in achieving. The second, more difficult, question was tactfully retiring Mortimer Graves. The third was moving the Council out of Washington; and the fourth was the eternal problem of money.

After a long discussion, we hypocrites decided that Mortimer Graves had given the best of his life to the service of the Council, and as he was getting older, he should not be called upon to bear this burden any longer. By way of expressing our gratitude for his services, we gave him a year's leave on pay and resolved to make the next annual dinner one in his honor. When I went to see Mortimer next day, as I was bound in duty to do, he took it like the gentleman he was and congratulated us on securing the services of Fred Burkhardt.

The next item aroused a storm of contention. The ACLS had always been in Washington. Why should it move now? We insurgents pointed out that, like it or not, we would have to move in three months, that the offices of all the great foundations with few exception were in New York, and that it was far more efficacious to make an appointment with the head of a foundation by telephone and go to see him than it was to write long letters or to talk endlessly over long-distance telephone. Happily, I found unexpected support from associates who were sick of the old brick building and longed for the business atmosphere of New York. My two real reasons for pressing this move I did not at the time make public. The first was that Washington is a city in which conversation takes the place of action and a problem is supposed to have been solved when it has only been talked about. My second reason was what I called the three-martinis-for-lunch fallacy. No problem could even be talked about except at lunch, no lunch could be held unless three martinis had been drunk, and no business could be done on a Washington afternoon, since luncheons commonly began at one and ended at four. My office experiences in New York had been transient, but I had learned that there was a smaller consumption of martinis, a more direct discussion of problems, a quality of decision-making, and a general air of business alertness such as I could never discover in Washington. Members of the staff with homes in Washington naturally protested about being uprooted and growled about higher costs of living. Nevertheless, where were we to go in Washington? When this point was made, I announced to two startled associates—Fred Burkhardt and Mike Oates—that they and I would constitute a committee to investigate possibilities in Manhattan. I had picked them after considerable thought, but I had said nothing. I was never more fortunate in my choices. President Burkhardt had been intimately associated with those parts of Manhattan which had to do with school and college finances; and Mike Oates had a brother who was high up in investment circles and, worshipping Mike as a scholar, gave Mike the best of down-to-earth business advice. There remained the ultimate question of funds, but my hunch was that, once the ACLS showed signs of life, money would be found.

Fred proved to be a whiz when it came to negotiating with that thick-skinned class, New York City realtors; and as I watched him in action, I learned something about when a president has to be hard-boiled and when he can afford to be lenient. In those years the United Nations building had at last been finished on land ceded by the federal government and the city government, which gave it in perpetuity to an independent political unit, freeing it from all local police and traffic regulations. However the land was laid out, it was to interfere as little as possible with the normal flow of New York traffic. The United Nations had its own police force, its own postal department, its own set of laws, and its own guides. In 1950 the land was first occupied; in 1952 the first General Assembly was held on its own land. The United Nations occupies all the territory along the East River from Forty-second Street to Forty-ninth; and of course since the first building went up other structures have been erected. The Rockefellers gave $8,500,000 to acquire the land on the shore of the East River, an area formerly known as Turtle Bay and notorious for its breweries, slaughterhouses, and cheap tenements. The swiftness with which these blotches on the riverbank disappeared, to be replaced by a nest of modern buildings, a park, sculpture, and other improvements, is a tribute alike to city officials and to Wallace K. Harrison, the supervising architect.

Indeed, the effect upon the whole area was almost magical. Ancient brick structures came tumbling down as new and modern buildings fronting both the East River and the United Nations Plaza took their places. In one of these, a building at the foot of East Forty-sixth Street that housed such international organizations as the Carnegie Endowment for International Peace, Fred found the space and the quality of rooms we needed. We moved into our brand-new quarters without quite knowing how to pay the rent. I shall not forget the feeling of pride with which the ACLS Council met for the first time around a modern table in a bright room with modern fenestration, not to speak of the cloakrooms, the conference rooms, the library, the telephones, modern electric lighting, and the thousand and one conveniences the business executive takes for granted. We left one representative temporarily in Washington, and some of the old staff declined to move; but the rest followed us, and Burkhardt shortly filled any vacancies with a corps of assistants whom he knew where to find and how to keep.

Who was to pay for all this? We were running a magnificent bluff. We visited various foundation heads, some of whom seemed startled to learn of our new address, but none of whom seemed inclined to grant us a large sum of money, or, if they were so inclined, did so only for a limited project and a limited time. Mike Oates and I did most of the soliciting, since Burkhardt had to return to Vermont to tie off the odds and ends of his presidential term. Mike Oates's face tended to redden under question or opposition, but he controlled himself magnificently. I do not know what I looked like. Hard-boiled foundation heads, more used to beggary than not, were inclined to ask perpetually the same questions: Why are you continually coming to us? The National Science people don't. Why don't you get an endowment like the Social Science Research Council? Why are we expected to pass on your projects, and how long are they going to last?

I think I did most of the replying, but I do not mean that Mike was silent. He pointed out that the National Science people could always fall back on the federal government if they had to; and he and I together pointed out that although some of the foundation secretaries swore that they never gave any money for endowment, the millions which formed the security of the Social Science Research Council was a gift from one of the foundations long ago. "Perhaps so," said the official to whom we were then talking. I retorted: "The humanities have been here a long time. They were here before the social sciences were born. They were here long before anybody had dreamed up a National Science Council. They are probably the oldest intellectual invention of man. They will be here when you and I are dead, whether you give us any money or not. This is a basic fact of civilization. You can either help us or not, but the responsibility will be yours.

"Your policy of not granting the ACLS money sufficient for an endowment simply means that we must come to you or some other foundation, hat in hand, to beg for a sum sufficient to carry out a needed project. In fact, it gives you complete intellectual control over what we do, since you alone supply the money. If you and your friends wish to occupy the seats of a bench of dictators, there is nothing we can do about it. It is possible, of course, that we can pick up a few thousand here and there, but in comparison with what you have just pointed to as the solid foundation of the Social Science Research Council, we shall look like mere weaklings. We have already furnished you with a list of national projects that need doing, and Mr. Oates and I can go back to the office and double the list if this is what you want. We are the experts in the branches of humane learning—something the country greatly needs—and I submit that you are not."

Neither Mike nor I knew that the man in front of us had been newly appointed to the Ford Foundation, and he had not yet learned that the essential art of a foundation official is to say no gracefully if he can, firmly if he must. He was W. McNeil Lowry, and I think he was deeply impressed and somewhat moved by my oration. At any rate, the meeting broke up, he shook our hands warmly, and he assured us we would hear from him tomorrow or the next day. I do not know what conferences were held among members of the higher staff of the Ford Foundation, nor what intercourse they had with the Carnegie people, but within a very few days as chairman of the ACLS I received a letter from the Ford Foundation granting us several million dollars for an endowment and additional millions for several projects that seemed to us and to them essential. Carnegie also came across. Since that time the ACLS annual budget has increased to almost four million, and the dozen or so societies which sent delegates to the Council in my time have reached the number of forty or more.

There was a second source of funds to which we might appeal if a change of administration in Washington or some other cause reduced or erased the annual grants from the great foundations. This was the business world, and I had not been long in my seat as chairman of the ACLS before I discovered that even highly placed executives were not *au courant* with the humanities. Mike told me, as I remember, that even his brother—a corporation president and obviously proud of Mike's great repute as treasurer of the ACLS—did not seem to know what is meant by scholarly research or what good it does in a busy world. The Council of the society and I discussed this problem at several meetings; and it was finally voted that the ACLS set up a commission, with Mike Oates and me as members, to produce a document that in simple terms would explain to a generous-minded but puzzled organization chief what the ACLS was all about and what it intended to do.

The Council decided wisely that if the job were worth doing at all, it must be done well; and they therefore granted the commission, or—what is the same thing—secured from other sources, enough money to finance the project for two years. Some of the members died before the report was completed, and one, I regret to state, withdrew. But when our book came out, it seemed evident to me, as it did, I think, to a wide audience, that the commission was so constituted as to touch on all aspects of the problem. From the business world we secured the help of Arthur A. Houghton, Jr., of Corning Glass, and of Louis M. Rabinowitz, once dubbed "the zipper king of America" but chosen because he was a bibliophile who respected learning. Harvie Branscomb of Vanderbilt, an experienced executive, represented the interests of theology, religion, and the humanities; Lawrence H. Chamberlain of Columbia University and William C. De Vane of Yale were appointed because they could see the humanities from the point of view of the whole college curriculum.

Charles W. Hendel came aboard as a philosopher, and Pendleton Herring, then chairman of the Social Science Research Council, took time off from his daily duties to see where the humanities and the social sciences clashed and where they met. Robert Oppenheimer spoke out for the scientists. Roger H. Sessions represented the fine arts, in his case, of course, music; the philosophic Francis Henry Taylor, quondam director of the Metropolitan Museum in New York, helped us to see the blending of history and the creative artist. And there was Robert Ulich, formerly of the Harvard Graduate School of Education, German-trained, who was less a pedagogue than a European philosopher.

Except for the summers, the commission met monthly for dinner at the Harvard Club of New York City during most of 1955 and 1956, beginning its deliberations before dinner and continuing them afterwards. Before his death Francis Henry Taylor arranged in the spring of 1956 a remarkable three-day session of the commission, the whole board of directors of the ACLS, and several invited scholars and museum directors at the Worcester Art Museum. Having had some experience with meetings of this sort, I am led to say that I have never been to a large meeting on a general subject that stuck as closely to its theme as did this three-day session. At the conclusion of our many meetings, I was authorized as chairman to write the report, which was published as *One Great Society* in 1959, the preface making clear that I was not speaking for myself but for the consensus of the commission and of those whom individual commissioners had consulted.

The report begins by putting eleven questions it had gathered from businessmen, government officials, and other sorts of citizens, the first one being "What are the humanities?" and the last, "I feel I have a responsibility as a business leader and a citizen to apply time and energy, and support the things that are worth while. Are you suggesting things that will take my time, energy, support? If so, why should they have priority over my present interests that help keep the community running?" These questions were answered, at least in part, by a book of 241 pages, written as simply and directly as possible and approved as a whole by the members of the commission. One part of the study was devoted to showing, one by one, what the societies constituting the ACLS were trying to do, and the last section, to the question "How can the layman help?"

Let me add as a modest appendix to this brief discussion that I put the book together, chapter by chapter, while I was a Fellow at the Center for Advanced Study in the Behavioral Sciences near Stanford University from August, 1957, through January, 1958; and I circulated the text, chapter by chapter, among the nearly fifty Fellows at that admirable institution. I cannot better express the purpose of these years than by quoting from the last part of the preface of the book:

A philologist cannot hope to compete with an atomic physicist for acclaim or for support, nor does this report make any such assumption. It does assume, however, that there is a limit of neglect below which a great nation cannot afford to sink its support of humane learning. This book is intended to help restore balance, not in the sense of taking his money away from the scientist or his key position in government or business from the social scientist, but in the sense of indicating that, wonderful as science is and influential as are the social sciences, they are not the whole of culture. Thoughtful scientists and social scientists never argue that they are. But that portion of the public which is essentially concerned about the drift of American values is not perhaps as fully informed about the theory and practice of humane learning as it would like to be; and it is to such citizens that this volume is directed.

I have written and published a good many books, but I think I have been responsible for none more directly aimed at American values than is *One Great Society*. "There is," wrote Wordsworth, "One great society alone on earth: / The noble Living and the noble Dead."

BOOK SIX

RETIREMENT: FORMING A PHILOSOPHY

Chapter XXV

Nearing
Pier 85

BY NOW the reader may have begun to wonder whether I spent any time in the classrooms of Harvard at all. Let him be reassured. My leaves of absence for the various jobs I have discussed were regularly granted, and most of the time in the fifties and sixties until I was retired I regularly met classes, sat in on examinations, supervised doctoral dissertations, and attended both committee and faculty meetings.

One of the most memorable courses I taught at Harvard was also one of the last I taught there. I called it "Neglected Masterpieces," and it drew a small group of bewildered but interested students. I had attended so many oral examinations that I began making lists of books the students knew by title only, and I thought it might be instructive to examine these books with the same care that an English department lavishes upon Wordsworth. My reading list is too long to quote, but it ran from Rossetti's *The House of Life*, intellectually one of the most difficult performances in the nineteenth century, to Owen Meredith's *Lucile*, which once used to lie on the table of every family with some pretensions to culture. I am not sure that even now I understand every sonnet in *The House of Life*, whereas *Lucile* is easy reading, a novel in verse of the most sentimental kind. I do not see, however, that it is worse than some of the standard titles in the usual curriculum, and it contains at least one unforgettable stanza:

> We may live without poetry, music and art;
> We may live without conscience, and live without heart;
> We may live without friends; we may live without books;
> But civilized man cannot live without cooks.

Is not sentimentalism entitled to its masterpieces? Another book title that sometimes came up in these examinations was Sheridan Le Fanu's incomparable *Uncle Silas* (1864). Le Fanu is gradually coming into his own, owing in part to the incessant labors of that specialist in Gothicism, Devendra P. Varma of Dalhousie University in Canada, who has brought out a complete edition of this writer. If *Uncle Silas* is not available to the reader, let him try *The House by the Churchyard*, which is also masterly in its kind. I did not, I now remember with regret, include Wilkie Collins's *Armadale* in my list. I found that most students could tell me about *The Moonstone* and *The Woman in White*, but the mention of *Armadale* always drew a blank. That book has, I tend to think, the most complicated plot ever put together; and I am sorry I did not have an opportunity to compare the villainous Miss Gwilt in *Armadale* with the devilish governess in *Uncle Silas*, Mme. de la Rougierre. That I had struck pay dirt, so to speak, is evident from the fact that scarce a year passes but somebody writes in for a copy of the list.

Two years before I retired I was given the new and honorable chair of Abbott Lawrence Lowell Professor of the Humanities. I think I was the first member of the regular faculty to occupy this seat, though it had been briefly given the previous year to Edmund Wilson, the critic. Wilson, however, had made no effort to undertake the full duties of a professorship, and—tell it not in Gath, publish it not in the streets of Askelon—the students and the faculty found him disappointing as a teacher. On the occasion of my appointment in 1960 I delivered a full-dress lecture on the meaning of the humanities, and more especially on the need for them, but as I have already discussed both the need and the theory in *One Great Society*, I shall not repeat myself. Some years after my retirement—in 1973 to be exact—the national society of the Phi Beta Kappa honored me with the award of a prize and a medal for my labors in the cause of humanism.

Under the ordinary rules I should have been retired in my sixty-fifth year, in 1957, but the president, the dean, and the two governing boards have the power to waive the regulation if they see fit, and I was kept in service until I was seventy. The combined problems of retirement and tenure have of recent years been very much in the public eye, one reason being that we have lengthened the life expectancy in America, and another reason being that however much *réclame* a professor may bring to an institution, that institution cannot survive unless it is continually fed with fresh young talent. The problem is delicate, and I can only say with Robert Browning that it is an awkward thing to play with souls. There is also, for better or worse, a sort of rule-of-thumb philosophy at work: mathematicians and scientists are said to burn out earlier than do humanists and historians. Unfortunately, like so many other rules of thumb, there are always enough exceptions to shake one's faith in the rule. Dear old Alfred North Whitehead, who joined the Harvard faculty in his sixties and served as a faculty member through his mid-seventies, seemed as alert and alive as the most promising of young Ph.D.'s; and a distinguished biologist did his best research work, or so I am told, when he retired from both his administrative and his academic posts. And what shall one say of Henry Wadsworth Longfellow, once a full professor at Harvard, who is, I know, no longer fashionable (he has been victimized by anthologists) but who produced some of his finest poems in the last decades of his life? For the fiftieth reunion of the class of 1825 he wrote "Morituri Salutamus," and I find it difficult to shake off the powerful impression this poem made on me when first I read it, and which it makes on me still:

> The scholar and the world! The endless strife,
> The discord in the harmonies of life!
> The love of learning, the sequestered nooks,
> And all the sweet serenity of books;
> The market-place, the eager love of gain,
> Whose aim is vanity, and whose end is pain!
> .   .   .   .
> What then? Shall we sit idly down and say
> The night hath come; it is no longer day?
> The night hath not yet come; we are not quite
> Cut off from labor by the failing light;
> Something remains for us to do or dare;
> Even the oldest tree some fruit may bear.

Longfellow had noted earlier in the poem the cases of Goethe; Chaucer; Theophrastus, who began his "Characters of Men" at eighty; Sophocles; Simonides; and Cato, who learned Greek at eighty. An astonishing performance, this poem, for an old man of sixty-eight, equalled in our own time only by the unquenchable creativity of Robert Frost!

This is not the place to discuss Longfellow or Frost, and it is a platitude hoary with age that men are the worst judges in their own cases. But what is an autobiography but a man's final judgment on himself? My own feeling is that the last two decades of my life have been the most productive and the most thoughtful in their dedication to the task of fusing humanism and history.

Retired as a professor emeritus, I was recalled to active service briefly to revive that highly respectable periodical the *Harvard Library Bulletin*, which, after a year of preparation, came to life again with volume 15 in January, 1967. A short foreword by Merle Fainsod, then the director of the Harvard University Libraries, states the intent of this quarterly: "It is published in the belief that one of the great libraries of the world cannot meet in full the responsibilities inherent in its position unless it has a regular publication which will make known to the Harvard community and to the scholarly world in general its collections, its experience, and its ideas." Merle, alas, is no longer among the living, but he was quoting Keyes D. Metcalf, that internationally known librarian who in a sense founded the *Bulletin* and who, as I write, is very much alive. It is melancholy to remember that the first two numbers of the revived journal had to contain a memorial of William Alexander Jackson, bibliophile and teacher, who headed the Houghton Library, but who died in 1964. This article (in two parts) was written by his friend and successor at the Houghton, William H. Bond. My place on the *Bulletin* is now filled by Edwin E. Williams, who served with me as associate editor. As Harvard now has something like nine million books, besides untold quantities of archives and manuscripts, I think that, barring total catastrophe, the *Bulletin* is destined for a long life.

I say "barring total catastrophe" advisedly, for my final philosophy has become a somber one. Putting aside *ad hoc* articles, edited works, and the necessary busywork of my profession, I have produced eleven books between 1962 and the date of this one. Obviously they are not all of equal weight. Of *Belief and Disbelief in American Literature* I have already spoken. *History and the Contemporary* and *Violence and Reason* are collections of essays, the first put together as one of the requirements of the post I occupied as a visiting professor at my alma mater, the University of Wisconsin; the second was compiled with the kindly assistance of Thomas J. Wilson when he left the directorship of Harvard University Press for commercial publishing, only to die prematurely. The gap he left in the lives of those who knew him can never be filled. The nature of *A Guide to American Literature and Its Backgrounds* is evident from its title; it would not have been useful had I not had as my colleague for successive editions of the little volume the man to whom this autobiography is dedicated. *The Many Voices of Boston* Bessie and I got out together; it is an anthology intended to destroy the legend that only the Puritan, the Brahmin, and the Irish created the Athens of America.

Jeffersonianism and the American Novel had so queer a history I think it must be told. The University of California at Berkeley has an annual lectureship devoted to some phase of Jefferson's interests. The chair has been filled by such eminent scholars as Dumas Malone, Jefferson's biographer. I felt honored when I was asked to become the Jefferson lecturer in the sixties and set about finding a topic within my competence as a literary scholar. I selected "Jeffersonianism and the American Novel" for the lectures I proposed to give.

When I sifted through the enormous body of Jefferson's printed words, I discovered that he took contradictory views of the novel. Like many other eighteenth-century worthies, he thought most novels were trash and warned young people against wasting time on them. But again, like some others of the period, he also said a novel can touch the heart, awaken right emotions, lead the soul to virtue, especially domestic virtue, and make a wiser citizen out of the reader. This part of Jefferson's views led me to think that what Jefferson wanted out of novel-reading was a lesson in civic morality, rationalism, and the duties of domesticity. This test being peculiarly Jeffersonian, notably in its emphasis on reason, I applied it to American novelists from the beginning to the present day. Thus the novels of Cooper, whether one agrees with his political view or not, do teach civic duty. So likewise do the novels of Howells and, more weakly, those of James. It seems to me impossible, however, that a responsible representative republic can rest on the shoulders of the characters in Faulkner's fiction—for example, the entire Snopes tribe or, for that matter, almost all of his creations save one or two. I said this, adding that this was not a total valuation of Faulkner. Indeed, modern fiction, colored by the uncritical adoption of Freudian and post-Freudian psychology, would undoubtedly have made Jefferson unhappy; and I plainly said this, though declaring not once but several times that this was not the whole story of twentieth-century American novel-writing. Other scholars have remarked the rise of the antihero as the central character in American fiction.

Under the terms of the Jefferson lectureship, the lecturer, after delivering his addresses, receives one half his fee, the other half being paid when he turns in a manuscript to the University of California Press. My custom, when I am to give an important set of lectures, is to write them out so that, with very few revisions, they can go at once to the publisher. This I did at Berkeley and received the total fee in one check. Many weeks went by, and I heard nothing from either the president of the university or the director of the University of California Press.

Manuscripts are not accepted by the director of the Press until they have been approved by the editors or syndics (or whatever their title may be) representing all of the many campuses of the University of California. Apparently nobody informed this committee of the circumstances in which my lectures were given, nor, I should guess, did they know Jefferson. At any rate, they reported I was badly informed about the development of American letters and my manuscript was therefore not worth publishing. It was returned to me by the Press. I was at the time a Fellow at the Center for Advanced Study in the Behavioral Sciences near Stanford; and after consulting with a number of my colleagues there, I wrote to the president of the University of California, saying that I had carried out my part of the bargain. Why did he permit the University of California Press to get out from under its obligation? The answer I received was curiously evasive, not only in my opinion but in the opinion of my colleagues at the Center. Accordingly, I withdrew the manuscript and went through it carefully, erasing any reference to California or to the Jefferson lectureship; and through the kindness of Lawrence Cremin, then a Fellow at the Center, the book was published by the Teachers College Press of Columbia University, which seemed not only glad to get it but raised no question of my competence as a cultural historian.

But now let me concentrate on my general view of history and humanism. The reader may recall that *America and French Culture* (1927) was applauded because it seemed to give a better background, a richer setting for American literature down to about 1850. I think I may truthfully say that this book was an unconscious prelude to what I shall refer to as my trilogy: *O Strange New World* (1964), *Revolution and Romanticism* (1974), and *The Age of Energy* (1971). I put these titles in what I may call their historical order, not in the order of their publication. At points they overlap because they were not written schematically, nor was the order and pattern of any volume necessarily neat and logical like a legal brief; the only word I can think of that will illuminate their structure is *symphonic*. By this I mean that in each volume I seized upon three or four major themes and studied their development in American history as closely as I could. The trilogy is therefore not a consecutive history either of American culture or of American literature, but the intent of the whole is to analyze what was happening in the mainland colonies and the United States, not alone in the light of what seems important to us today but also in the light of our relations with the Old World. *O Strange New World*, for example, pays great attention to Latin America in the fifteenth and sixteenth centuries, and I regret that I could not find the space, even if I had the knowledge, to continue studying the relations and parallels between the two New World continents. It sometimes seems to me that every new presidential administration in the United States resolves on friendlier relations with Latin America, but even in the twentieth century most American universities pay insufficient attention to Latin American culture, or no attention at all. One of our difficulties is that history is in most institutions political and social. Viewed unfavorably, the history of Latin America seems to be a monotonous succession of revolutions, dictatorships, rebellions, and mismanagement. If, however, historians of American culture would take their eyes off Latin American rulers and turn their attention to Latin American thinkers and philosophers, we should have, in my opinion, a far juster understanding of the culture (or cultures) south of us. Leading American thinkers in South America believe, or at least some of them believe, that their destiny is to become the "cosmic race," by which phrase they mean, as I understand it, that their intermingling of races—Indian, Negro, European, Asiatic, and so on—promises more happiness for mankind than does our enigmatic interpretation of doctrines of liberty, equality, and fraternity. If this is unacceptable to the reader, let him at least remember that the institutions of this country are North European (Germanic, Teutonic) in their distant origins, Protestant in spirit, and focused on London, whereas the countries of Latin America are Mediterranean and Amerindian in their beginnings, Roman Catholic in their value systems, and look to Paris as the great focal point of the Latin mind and of Latin values. Undoubtedly there are exceptions to these rough generalizations, but they at least go beyond the "banana republic" attitude of too many North Americans. There is a "dark legend" of Spanish cruelty in that part of the world; it is a much exaggerated legend, and when all the cards are down, it would be difficult to show that the treatment of the Indians by Spanish and Portuguese conquerors was worse than the treatment of these same people by the various governments that have ruled the United States-to-be.

O Strange New World has its inception in the historical truth that Britain came late into the colonial era and found Latin American culture already old in most of the New World west of the Mississippi and of course in French Canada. The theme of the book is the ambivalent nature of European experiences on continents as strange to them as life on Mars, if there is any, would seem to us. As part of this complex story, I tried in this volume to give both sides of the medal—the emotional glow with which news of the discovery of riches in the New World was received, and, on the other hand, the fright and horror that alternated with the golden glory. I then went on to discuss how far the Renaissance culture of Europe, whether of the south or of the north, influenced voyages of discovery, the ownership of land, the finding, or the disappointment in not finding, of gold, silver, and jewels all over the Americas. In both North and South America the formulas of discovery, invasion, conquest, and settlement began by being military; but because the church universal was and is a unit, or likes to think so, the endless ecclesiastical squabbles that distinguish and disgrace the seventeenth and eighteenth centuries in the future United States were not shaping forces in the development of all New World civilizations. I then went back and confined myself for a while to the British Isles in an effort to discuss why this great seafaring people had been so loath to cross the Atlantic; and I suppose for most readers the new note here was my comparison, historically justified, of the wild Irish and the wild Indians. I then went on to trace as well as I could the leading ethical values and political ideals of the British colonies, contrasting these from time to time with the principles regnant in Spanish or Portuguese America. Perhaps the most interesting chapter in the last third of the book, "Roman Virtue," points out the paradox that, though the American republic was never part of the Roman Empire, classical concepts in art and government have played their important roles in the earlier history of the United States. I traced the history of this fashion through the World's Columbian Exposition of 1893.

Turning next to the American Revolution, I made the point that the United States in its beginning was a republic that contradicted the good sense of all European rulers by being too large to govern; and I simultaneously dwelt upon the fears of Europe (perhaps not altogether unjustified) that this upstart nation would corrupt ancient values. But the Americans were afraid that the values of Europe would corrupt the United States, and this fear led Washington to warn the country against entangling alliances; Jefferson to advise young travelers visiting the courts of Europe to look at them as if they were going to a zoo; and Monroe to sanction the Monroe Doctrine (convenient to the British Foreign Ministry), which boldly announced what was even more brashly stated later in American history by Secretary of State Olney during the Venezuelan crisis, when he bluntly declared in 1895 that the policy of the United States was paramount over the entire New World. Secretary Olney and other members of the cabinet managed to avoid a war with Germany over the Venezuelan debt question; but we conveniently forget that, despite Washington, Jefferson, and Monroe, this country has been constantly or intermittently involved in the affairs of Europe from the undeclared naval war on France in the administration of John Adams, through various attempts to reform or occupy Caribbean lands or the Hawaiian Islands, to our second and fantastic war with Great Britain and our refusal to recognize as valid an imperial system in Mexico, instigated and for a short time upheld by Louis Napoleon of France. In the twentieth century, of course, we have been as mixed up with Europe as any true European power could be.

The final chapter of O Strange New World has to do with the effects on our history of wildness in the uninhabited forests, the savage rivers, the great lakes, the great plains, and the lofty mountains east and west which have created so diversified a climate for the American republic. For this volume I received the Pulitzer Prize and the Emerson award of the Phi Beta Kappa Society.

Since the 1960s were the centenary of the American Civil War, I thought of doing a book on this vast conflict and its causes, but so many excellent volumes by other historians were issued, I decided to forego the opportunity. There is therefore an awkward gap in time between the era covered by *O Strange New World* and the period I have discussed in *The Age of Energy*.

On rereading *The Age of Energy* I find it a better organized book than *O Strange New World* but one which is unfortunately written in denser prose. The impulse to write the volume came from my increasing distaste for the uncritical opinion of many historians, an opinion summed up in that vicious standard phrase "the Gilded Age." This phrase implies both a moral condemnation of whatever is narrated before the reader has had time to form his own value judgments, and a fixed opinion that nothing good could come out of so superficial and coarse a culture. Scoundrelism in finance, public life, and politics is supposed to be matched or produced by "the Gilded Age," a phrase that stops all critical investigation and damns beyond salvation, except in the case of a few protestors, the immense American library produced by the period. Historians have also apparently forgotten, if they ever knew it, the wise injunction of Edmund Burke that he did not know how to indict a whole people. It seemed to me, therefore, that the Gilded Age and the Genteel Tradition alike required a new analysis.

I warned the reader at the beginning of my study that I was not going to moralize upon either the actions or the personages prominent in these decades. I myself doubt that the distribution of good and evil in the era differs greatly from the distribution of good and evil in any other half century. Seeking out some title that would express the actual central characteristics of the five decades between our Civil War and World War I, I arrived at the phrase "the Age of Energy." In a sense my idea is self-evident, though I again warned the reader that even though I gave him the technological definition of energy in engineering and physics, I was going to use the term loosely—the energy of style, the energy of personality, and energy in politics, in religion, in science, in the industrial world, and in the economic life of the nation—in short, wherever I should find it. I came to feel that the age of energy moved relentlessly to a climax in the two presidencies of Theodore Roosevelt.

As for the Gilded Age, I threw overboard a whole library of stale and superficial generalizations uttered by the "authorities" on this period, many of whom, I am impolite enough to think, have never studied the context or the accomplishments of the period. They seem to forget the Emersonian injunction that every scripture should be read in the light of the same spirit which gave it forth. Possibly the most important "fact" inevitably inducing the esthetic theories we associate with the Gilded Age was American weariness with romanticism in all its phases and the feeling that, however fine romantic masterpieces might be, artists, thinkers, and writers were more often than not deficient in technique. Accordingly, a rising generation determined to master technique, or, if one prefers, return to the ancient tradition of form as quintessential to art. As Dante Gabriel Rossetti once noted, poetry is the product of brainpower. This search for a way out of the fragmentation of romanticism, particularly in the United States, inevitably meant a return to the study of Europe, which I applaud. By praising these artists for their European orientation, I do not in the least denigrate American achievements (at least I hope I do not), but I do emphasize that American modernism in the post-Civil War period and European modernism in the same decade were very much alike. In fact, I was prepared to, and do, affirm that Europe, instead of extending to the Alleghenies, where Emerson cut it off, now extends to the Pacific Coast and the islands of the sea or wherever a powerful new American-European influence has been felt since 1865. Great new ideas, especially in the sciences, in these years seem in the main to have originated in the Old World; but when they were translated to North America, they were often redefined, modified in utilitarian fashion, and put to use on a far larger scale than was possible in the country of their origin. Thus, although the railway is principally a cosmopolitan invention in which British engineering genius had a great part to play, by 1900 the American railway system was the finest in the world. (Alas, where is that system now? Replaced by airliners flying at incredible heights and unbelievable speeds and producing from time to time disasters far worse than anything the railroads experienced in their short period of perfection.) Reviewers were more puzzled than enlightened by my emphasis upon this return to the Old World for basic ideas, a return that grew constantly in bulk and importance not alone in the areas of art and literature but in the practical worlds of agriculture, industry, and commerce.

But if reviewers were cautious in their appraisals of *The Age of Energy*, they were often baffled by both the structure and the contents of *Revolution and Romanticism*. One newspaper reviewer said quaintly, "Mr. Jones has read too many books." Newspaper editors in some cases sent my volume to a specialist on the American Revolution or the French Revolution, since that dread noun appeared in the title and since, on leafing through the pages, they found that my discussion had something to do with revolution, they were not sure what. The resulting reviews naturally saw no point to my intense study of the meaning of classicism, neoclassicism, the preromantics, the proclaimers of sensibility as a mode of life, and the earlier achievements of romanticism. Other book editors sent the volume to specialists in literary history or its equivalent, and these gentry were puzzled to read chapters on the American Revolution and the French Revolution in a book that spent a great deal of time on forgotten authors or at least authors unread by Americans, such as the influential German philosopher Hamann. Since I could not count on any general knowledge of such notable creations as Goethe's *Faust*, Hugo's *Hernani*, Wordsworth's *The Prelude*, or even Byron's *Manfred*—masterpieces which now seem to be confined to college classrooms and are not always discovered even there—I found it necessary to detail the plots of works like these, to analyze at some length the contents and purpose of the great romantic achievements in words, just as I had found it necessary to differentiate between the austere classicism of the Age of Louis XIV, the neoclassicism of much of the eighteenth century, and (to confound confusion) the romantic classicism evident in poets like Keats and de Vigny, in sculptors such as Canova or Thorwaldsen, and in many musical compositions, and, to conclude this list of difficulties, to differentiate between romantic classicism and the romantic return to the worship of throne and altar that was part of the passionate reaction against the French Revolution and the Napoleonic Empire.

I had to deal with the Western world in one of the most intricate chapters of its history, one that runs from the death of Louis XIV to the display of Gautier's red waistcoat at the riot produced by that shattering experience, the first production of Hugo's *Hernani* in 1830. Possibly my intent would have been clearer if I had quoted as an epigraph the statement by Hugo that the revolution of 1830 was a revolution stopped half way. I doubt that contemporary readers would catch the force of the allusion.

But all this, although I think it true enough, does not get at the heart of the problem I was trying to solve. Let me put it this way. Between 1763 and 1861 there were two gigantic upheavals in the Western world, the one in the sphere of politics, the other in the world of esthetics. The first was a tremendous political revolution, the end of which seems to me not yet in sight; the other was a great esthetic and philosophic revolution which may or may not be dead, depending upon one's view of recent literature, contemporary paintings, modern architecture, and what passes nowadays for sculpture. During the period the book discusses, three potent forces struggled both against and with each other. One was the idea of republican man evident in both revolutions but more particularly in the American rebellion; one was the rights of the people, supposed to lie at the heart of the French Revolution, yet unable throughout the nineteenth century to produce a stable government in France; and the third was the infinite variety of the romantic rebellion in art, thought, and conduct. These are interwoven as giant vines interweave trees in a tropical forest. Not all romantics were revolutionaries and not all revolutionaries were romantics, though history would be much simpler if this were true. In general, the American Revolution, whatever its dates, lies within the boundaries of eighteenth-century values and is touched only slightly by romantic doctrine, though a case can be made for the effect of eighteenth-century sensibility upon some of the participants. But the French revolutionaries began their rebellion the same year the new government of the United States took over under the Federal Constitution (a thoroughly eighteenth-century document); the leading personalities in France seemed, to me at least, for the most part romantic personalities, their conduct and their style, particularly in oratory, anticipating the rhetoric of the German romantic schools, the French romantic schools, and the French romantic rebels of 1829–30. Principal characters in the French Revolution, especially after 1793, could have been invented by Byron. Doubtless we shall never comprehend the romantic movement in its entirety, though it altered the sensibility, the style, and the philosophy, not to speak of the political theory, of the whole Western world. Fortunately, however, the doctrine which formerly held that romanticism was a mere puzzling emotional release—a favorite theory of the late Irving Babbitt—has now given way to a deeper understanding of a movement which reshaped human life and values. My study does not touch upon the curious relation between romantic humanism and modern technology, but that relation nevertheless exists. It exists, just as our enthusiasm for scientific exploration leads us to spend billions trying to get to the moon or Mars, presumably to take care of the surplus population of our world.

In its origins American literature was of local interest, a merely provincial affair. Just before and during the American Revolution—indeed, beyond the age of Jackson—its proponents regarded themselves as unique. Prose writers of the American Revolution, after the republic seemed well established, continued to regard themselves not merely as unique souls but as prophets leading Western man to a sort of popular utopia. This was the continuing theme of the dull poets we know as the Connecticut Wits, and it was even strong enough to color the utterances of a man like Emerson when he said that American youth had listened too long to the courtly muses of Europe. As evolutionary theory crept from geology to anthropology and from anthropology to social history, including the history of the arts, the British were perhaps justified in regarding the American muse as given to braggadocio; yet American writers, when the country began to have an assured place in the world were, with certain exceptions such as Walt Whitman, quite content to rejoin the Old World and to become a province in the literary empire of Europe. We, though we will not admit it, rejoined the Atlantic Community.

If the United States is not merely to survive but also make its way amid this immense confusion, it must begin by understanding itself. The nation now contains but will not face a cultural dilemma. The republic was built on certain philosophic principles evident in the writings of the founding fathers. These principles were common assumptions among progressive eighteenth-century thinkers, who studied Locke, Montesquieu, and the ancients, who accepted the faculty psychology of their time, and who assumed as a matter of course that man is sufficiently rational to choose his rulers wisely. Their vision was that of a happy agrarian republic.

By the generation of Emerson the basic interpretation of human nature was shifting from rationality to intuition, from geometry to dynamism, from mind to soul; and when one reads Emerson's attacks on Boston's financial center, State Street, together with those of Hawthorne, Melville, and others, one realizes that a split was developing—the split noted in 1915 by Van Wyck Brooks when he said that one-half of America was descended from Benjamin Franklin the businessman and the other half from Jonathan Edwards the idealist.

But the soul disappeared in 1890 when, in his *Principles of Psychology*, William James banished it as a concept useless to the scientific psychologist. In the twentieth century the agrarian republic has also vanished into what Henry Miller calls our air-conditioned nightmare and what kindlier commentators describe as the triumph of our technological skills. There are other changes. One is the decline of the church as a guide of life. A second is the increasing importance of higher education as a surrogate for religion. A third is the virtual disappearance of the radical left and the emergence of the radical right. A fourth is the uncritical acceptance of a shallow doctrine of human nature as fundamentally irrational. This theory is now the stock-in-trade of the arts, and, unfortunately, of many humanists, and is flatly contradicted by the dazzling success of rationality in other fields. Poets and novelists, filled with zeal for irrationalism, inconsistently continue to go to the dentist, the doctor, and the surgeon for physiological repair on scientific principles discovered by rational research.

The profound disharmony between the theory of human nature as inevitably irrational and art as subliminal self-expression and the triumphs of the intellect in a mensurational civilization is the principal cultural problem of our time. René Dubos observes that our civilization has become intoxicated with its technological proficiency. But you do not correct the alleged inhumanity of a mensurational culture by celebrating the superiority of a nonrational art. No one desires to control the artist. But the humanist has the legitimate function of seeing the arts in terms of their general cultural responsibility and not merely in terms of themselves. Is not this the highest responsibility of scholarship? The duty of scholarship is to bring philosophy to the interpretation of the arts, not merely to derive its modes of interpretation from current practitioners of art and of criticism.

Whatever fashions may crowd the hour, the nobility of art and of scholarship must be what the sculptor Ernst Barlach meant when he said: "What man can suffer and must suffer, the grandeur and the need of man: to that I am committed." The emphasis is clear. It is not on the easy way of suffering but on the difficult way of grandeur.

Epilogue

I WRITE these concluding pages about two weeks before my eighty-fifth birthday, which, if I live to see it, will occur on April 16, 1977. I have lived fifteen years beyond the Biblical allotment and two years longer than did that wisest of Europeans, Goethe. I have tried to teach myself stoicism and control, and I watch with a certain sardonic amusement the decline, miscarriage, or fall of most of the things I have struggled for. Science and technology take over more and more space and require more skill in business, in education, in science, in politics, and in domestic law. We pride ourselves on being a peace-loving country; yet— omitting the conflicts between the English colonies and the French, the Spaniards, the Dutch, the British and the Indians before 1776—during the two hundred years elapsing between the Declaration of Independence and 1976, we have fought at least one war every eighteen years. I do not count as war the occupation of Vera Cruz that precluded the Mexican War, our several invasions of Haiti and Nicaragua, the Boxer Rebellion, or Pershing's futile pursuit of Pancho Villa into Mexico. I also omit most Indian warfare, although there was nothing lovely about the battle of Fallen Timbers or the massacre of Custer and his cavalrymen on the Little Big Horn. If these, and various other military and naval engagements, were included, I think our belligerency would rise to a war every ten or twelve years. War was solemnly outlawed by international agreement in 1927. Since then we have participated in World War II and in a bloody civil war in Korea, where we still keep troops; our armed forces are still protecting West Germany from the Soviets; and we lost a useless conflict in Vietnam. I find it difficult to equate our love of peace with the untold billions we have spent on "national defense" and on our "allies."

The American Constitution has been regarded by our own people and by many foreign visitors as a sacrosanct document, a miracle of wisdom not to be tampered with. Revered it may be; unalterable it is not. Within five years of its adoption it had been amended eleven times. A "woman's liberation" amendment has, as I write, been ratified by most of the states, though not yet by two-thirds of them, and may result in another amendment; but putting that aside, we have altered the Constitution approximately once every twenty-five years since its adoption. Moreover, the Supreme Court, as some wise historian has remarked, sits as a perpetual constitutional convention shifting the meaning of this or that passage in the original document or its amendments. Originally, voting was confined to adult males eligible to cast a ballot for the larger of the two houses of each state legislature, and in all the states the right to vote was at first confined to male citizens twenty-one years or older and possessed of sufficient wealth, land, income, or status to assure the courts they were genuine citizens of a stable community. We have swept this away by the "one man, one vote" argument. Originally the two senators from each state were chosen by the legislature of that commonwealth, which was assumed to possess sovereignty; now they are elected by popular vote. Whether popular election has made the senate a wiser body is an open question; and the cost for a senatorial election in Delaware—which in the 1970s had a population of about 573,000 living in an area of 2,057 square miles—is one thing, that for the population of California—which in the same period was approximately twenty million people living in an area of 158,693 square miles—is something else. This is scarcely popular equality.

The Founding Fathers thought of election to the presidency as a sort of sifting process that would separate the wheat from the chaff. The people elected the lower house of a legislature and sometimes, though not always, the upper house or senate of the commonwealth, able men, it was presumed, the "wise and good." The people were also every four years to elect their best men to an electoral college equal in number to the total of senators and congressmen from that state; and the electoral college, meeting in the state capitol, was to look over the whole field and pick the two wisest men they could find, a presidential candidate from one state, a vice-presidential candidate from another. The votes of this body, which then dissolved, were sent to Washington. These ballots, including the names of those who failed to win, were then sent in a sealed package to the president of the Senate, who, at a joint meeting of the Senate and the House of Representatives, opened the boxes and announced the vote of the several states. All the votes were then counted, and the person receiving the majority was to be president. The person receiving the next highest number was to be vice-president, though he could not come from the same state as the president. Elaborate provisions were made to solve the puzzle of a tie vote. Most living Americans regard the "electoral college" as obsolete and want to get rid of it, since it might again happen, as it has a few times in our past, that a candidate receiving a majority of the popular votes would lose to a candidate receiving a majority of the electoral college. The intent, however, was Jeffersonian. It was an attempt to sift out the best men for these two great offices. The Constitution makes no provision for a party system, parties being regarded as "factions" by the Founding Fathers. We in our wisdom think the popular majority should prevail, the electoral college be abolished, and the most popular candidate proceed to the White House. Unfortunately, charm, popularity, platform presence on radio or television, a skillful public relations staff, and a melodious voice are no necessary indications of either political experience or diplomatic skill; and James Bryce long ago observed that the American system was a mechanism for choosing mediocrity over talent. We no longer refer to ourselves as a representative republic, but as a "democracy," a word that horrified the majority of the members of the Constitutional Convention, who apparently anticipated Byron in thinking that democratic France would get drunk with blood, to vomit crime.

We are a free country, we believe in God (who does not appear in the Constitution except as part of a date), and we assumed that constitutional governments like ours would spread by a sort of political osmosis. According to Freedom House, however, less than 20 percent of the people on the earth live in freedom—a word, to be sure, never quite defined, but a necessary value nevertheless. The report cautiously puts certain countries—for example, El Salvador—in the category of the half-free, but most of the population of the earth lives under despotism, tyranny, dictatorship, or a one-party system. Within our own nation, we have fifty state constitutions, a Federal Constitution, and thousands upon thousands of statute laws; and "Liberty under the Law" is a favorite slogan. I do not know how to estimate the amount of criminality elsewhere; I know only that our daily papers and our news weeklies are filled with exposures of graft and corruption, and accounts of crimes of violence—murder, rape, mugging, robbery—and that neither our parks nor our streets nor our automobiles are safe.

We hold that lawful government rests upon the consent of the governed, but our expansion as a nation has not been brought about by this maxim. We bought Louisiana, but we did not consult the Louisianians as to whether they wanted us for their overlords or no; we conquered half of Mexico on a similar lack of principle; we bullied Spain into giving us Florida in return for cash, just as we bought Alaska from Russia without asking the Eskimos to vote; and we may sing until we are blue in the face about

> Columbia, the gem of the ocean,
> The home of the brave and the free,
> The shrine of each patriot's devotion
> All the world offers homage to thee.

But all the world does no such thing. Our modern poets do not sing about Columbia as Longfellow, or Lowell, or Whittier, or even Whitman sang; they prefer to go along with Robinson Jeffers and celebrate the ghastly light of his poem "Shine, Perishing Republic," which begins:

> While this America settles in the mold of its vulgarity, heavily thickening to empire . . .

In a world in which science has impartially equipped a good many nations with bombs and weapons, any one of which might destroy a country, a continent, or the world, singing about America the beautiful seems singularly fatuous.

I am weary of the doctrine that research is a beautiful end in itself. The people who first split the atom were brilliant scientists and very bad philosophers, and a good many of them quickly formed a society of atomic physicists to plead for the abolition of what they had done. I am weary of business for the sake of business, of hearing about secret bank accounts in Switzerland, of international cartels that think bribery is an elegant and elusive weapon in diplomacy, and of a world in which mediocre men called diplomats promise one thing in order to conceal the fact that the country they represent is doing quite something else. I am weary, too, of a world in which Christian theology elevates mediocrity to the pulpit and tries to equate the folklore of Moses with the findings of anthropologists, biologists, and those who specialize in fossils and prehistory and discover that *Homo sapiens* and his hominoid predecessors appeared on the earth millions of years before 4004 B.C. This nation is in theory a representative republic in which the wise and good should be chosen to rule. But the nation that has substituted instant pleasure for the pursuit of happiness is scarcely what Lincoln thought of as the last, best hope of earth.

All this, doubtless, sounds splenetic. Perhaps it is. But deeper than the sociology of crime and the vulgarity of our amusements is the paradox we will not face, namely, that we are descended from two contradictory traditions: the tradition of human nature according to eighteenth-century philosophy, and the tradition, younger but in the long run more powerful, of irrational man.

The men who drew up the two fundamental documents on which this government rests—the Declaration of Independence and the Federal Constitution—were representatives of a dominant strain in eighteenth-century thought, that of John Locke, later supported in large degree by the so-called Scottish or Common-Sense School of Philosophy. Their central doctrine, which they did not invent but which can be traced back at least to Aristotle, held that some supernal power had dowered every human being in greater or less degree with a faculty which is called reason, though some have less of it than others—children, for example, and some whom our namby-pamby modern idiom calls the underprivileged. But on the whole all the peoples of the earth, whether they live in civilized Paris or on the utmost islands of the sea, had as a quintessential part of their birthright this mysterious but important faculty. Even a Fiji Islander knew that two and two make four. And if they invented a theory of the state that could do without the divine right of kings and the privileges of a hereditary aristocracy, the foundation of their commonwealth was for them the axiomatic truth that reason is mighty and will in the end prevail. The governing and the governed can agree that the reasonable demands of each group can be thoughtfully considered and if possible met; hence, our elections every two or four years in which reasonable dissatisfaction can be expressed or a rational approbation take the form of a majority vote. One element in a rational society was some form of status—the possession of wealth, or of land, or of a fixed status in a social group, or a profession—in fact, almost anything which indicated that the person involved was reliable, stable, trustworthy, gaining the confidence of other men and returning that confidence to his fellows. Contrary to the misrepresentations of some "philosophers," reasonable men did not lack emotions nor ignore the existence of a passionate drive in their lives and in lives around them; on the contrary, the emotions (sensibility, the passions) were a laudable part of human nature but one which, in most circumstances, was subordinate to the faculty of reason. As the faculty of reason was universalized, the voice of the people became, on occasions, the voice of God—that God who had created the earth for the support and happiness of men. Evil there was in the world—evil and criminality, injustice and selfishness, in short, all that the Christian meant by sin—but as ancient restrictions were lessened, ancient habitual abuses corrected, obsolete habits and institutions thrown aside, the sunlight of reason would illumine the dark corners of man's heart just as the sun illumined the earth at sunrise. Any man could be a philosopher who would grasp this simple truth and act on it; hence it was that government of the people, by the people, and for the people was possible. "Modern" psychologists and philosophers—men of the stature of David Hume, William James, and Sigmund Freud— have been poking holes in this theory ever since it was invented, but it is a noble creed nonetheless.

The political expression of the working of the faculty of reason was the vote. Each voter was supposed to have status in a stable community, and as soon as he proved to officials in charge of the balloting that he was such an American, he cast his vote secretly, in writing, for whatsoever candidate seemed in his judgment a proper official. Nobody else need know how he voted, unless he chose himself to make it public.

And here, precisely, in political life was the weakness of the theory. All men were equal and should participate in choosing their government; but were all men alike? The rich man and the poor man were, in this instance, placed on an equal plane, but did that necessarily make for happiness? Where was the line to be drawn defining the right of government to forbid this or that pastime, this or that occupation, this or that mode of life? Did all this necessarily make for fraternity? Groups of voters might get together before an election and agree to support such-and-such a man for office and to throw out his rival—"factions" Washington warned the country against—but did this necessarily make for liberty? We have been struggling with the problem since the creation of the representative republic we now mistakenly classify as a democracy.

Romantic man, however, implied not equality but uniqueness. As J.-J. Rousseau put it in his *Confessions:* I am like no one in the whole world. My desires, my passions, my capacities, my experience, the romantic individualist says, are my own and cannot be shared with anyone else. Freedom means, does it not, the right to be one's self? Lining up in a queue of voters does not express me. I do not worry about the form of government I live under, provided it lets me alone. If I want to work, I shall work. If I want to stop work and meditate, I shall not labor until the need for labor overcomes me once more. They tell me that the right to vote is an absolute right and that it is a right I share with other men. But I do not wish to share my personality with other men. I prefer to go out in the woods and live alone with Thoreau, to think my own thoughts like Emerson, to jump overboard and drown as did Hart Crane, to cook my own meals in the wilderness with Daniel Boone or Davy Crockett, to run away from your boasted government with its iron rules into the wilderness with the woman of my choice like Chateaubriand's Atala, to share my wealth, if I have any, with those I trust and those who trust me and no others, like the Brook Farm community or the modern commune. The heart has its reasons which the legislature knows nothing of.

They tell me that, being a man, I am above the animals, but the anthropologists, the sociologists, the biologists do not say so. The animals are neither Christian nor pagan, neither Hebraic nor Mohammedan, neither sun-worshippers nor creations of the devil. In fact, they have no religion; they are simply glad to be alive, as I am. As for your institutions, political, moral, religious, social, or whatever else you wish to call them, I shall make only such use of them as suits my purposes; and if you look at the records of men like me who lived on the earth as you do, persons real or imaginary such as Chateaubriand, René, Byron, Shelley, Kleist, Don Juan, Ruy Blas, Rimbaud, Van Gogh, Mary Wollstonecraft, Cleopatra, the Empress Catherine—persons who lived to the full as long as they could—do you not envy them? What if they broke the laws and were punished? Did they not obey their inner impulses, which are of nature as much as is your Declaration of Independence?

You throw Hooker and John Locke at me, John Adams and George Washington; has not one of your greatest poets written:

> There is a pleasure in the pathless woods,
> There is a rapture on the lonely shore,
> There is society, where none intrudes,
> By the deep sea, and music in its roar:
> I love not man the less, but Nature more,
> From these our interviews, in which I steal
> From all I may be, or have been before,
> To mingle with the Universe, and feel
> What I can ne'er express—yet cannot all conceal.

Such—in extreme form, if you will—was romantic individualism. But we learn from extremes. And before we dismiss Byron's lines above as "mere poetry," let us remember our parks, our beaches, our mountain trails, our camps, our hikes, and ask whether these elements in American culture do not represent what is left to us amid the roar of machines and automobiles—in sum, what is left of romantic man? Why do our environmentalists struggle to cling to the last acre of swamp, the last bit of wildness, the last trout stream or waterfall they discover, if not to get away from the herd that has voted a new sewage plant or a new president, a new tariff or a new governor, into their brief existences?

Rational human nature and romantic human nature are the thesis and antithesis of life and of man, but I do not know where to find the healing synthesis of a Hegelian triad. How shall Euclid and Freud meet together? How shall Descartes and Jung ever agree? How get Hobbes and Shelley into one tent? Our political system in America points one way; our popular psychology, our philosophy so far as we have any, our poetry, our drama, and our fiction point in precisely the opposite direction. I am not wise enough to analyze, much less solve, the tensions in contemporary culture, the contradictions in modern man, which are enough to make the stars throw down their spears and water heaven with their tears. Why fly through outer space to find another planet we can desecrate? Why not fly through outer space to demonstrate the immense superiority of human skill over what is commonly called nature? I do not know, and I shall not live long enough to find out. Yet, like William Faulker, I decline to accept the end of man, and in the last paragraphs of the last book I wrote in what I have called my trilogy, I said in part:

Man is more than the sum of his blunders. The state has been with us longer than the youth commune, and is likely to be with us for a long time to come. The grave central problem of our day is not the destruction of the state or of institutions or of ordinary forms of decorum by casual violence; the great central problem of the Western world is how to adjust the civic processes descending from the American and French revolutions to the romantic theory that every human being is an inviolable end in himself. I do not find this answer on the shores of Walden Pond. The answer is to be found, if it ever is to be found, in the nature of man, that rare and curious species who is at home neither in the animal world nor in the spiritual universe of our ancestors. I think the answer, if there be one . . . is in [a] sense of an indestructible center of all human individuality . . . the enduring gift of romanticism to modern times. . . . There cannot be citizenship unless there is man, and the rights of man is a phrase essentially without meaning unless one believes, as the romantics did, that each human being is more than the totality of his own history.

INDEX

Index

Index

Index

Index

Index

DESIGNED BY IRA NEWMAN
COMPOSED BY FOX VALLEY TYPESETTING, MENASHA, WISCONSIN
MANUFACTURED BY CUSHING MALLOY, INC., ANN ARBOR, MICHIGAN
TEXT IS SET IN CALEDONIA, DISPLAY LINES IN
COMSTOCK AND CALEDONIA

Library of Congress Cataloging in Publication Data
Jones, Howard Mumford, 1892-
Howard Mumford Jones: an autobiography.
Includes index.
1. Jones, Howard Mumford, 1892- — Biography.
2. Authors, American — 20th century — Biography.
3. Educators — United States — Biography.
PS3519.0425Z465   809 [B]   78-65013
ISBN 0-299-07770-5